P9-DNP-910

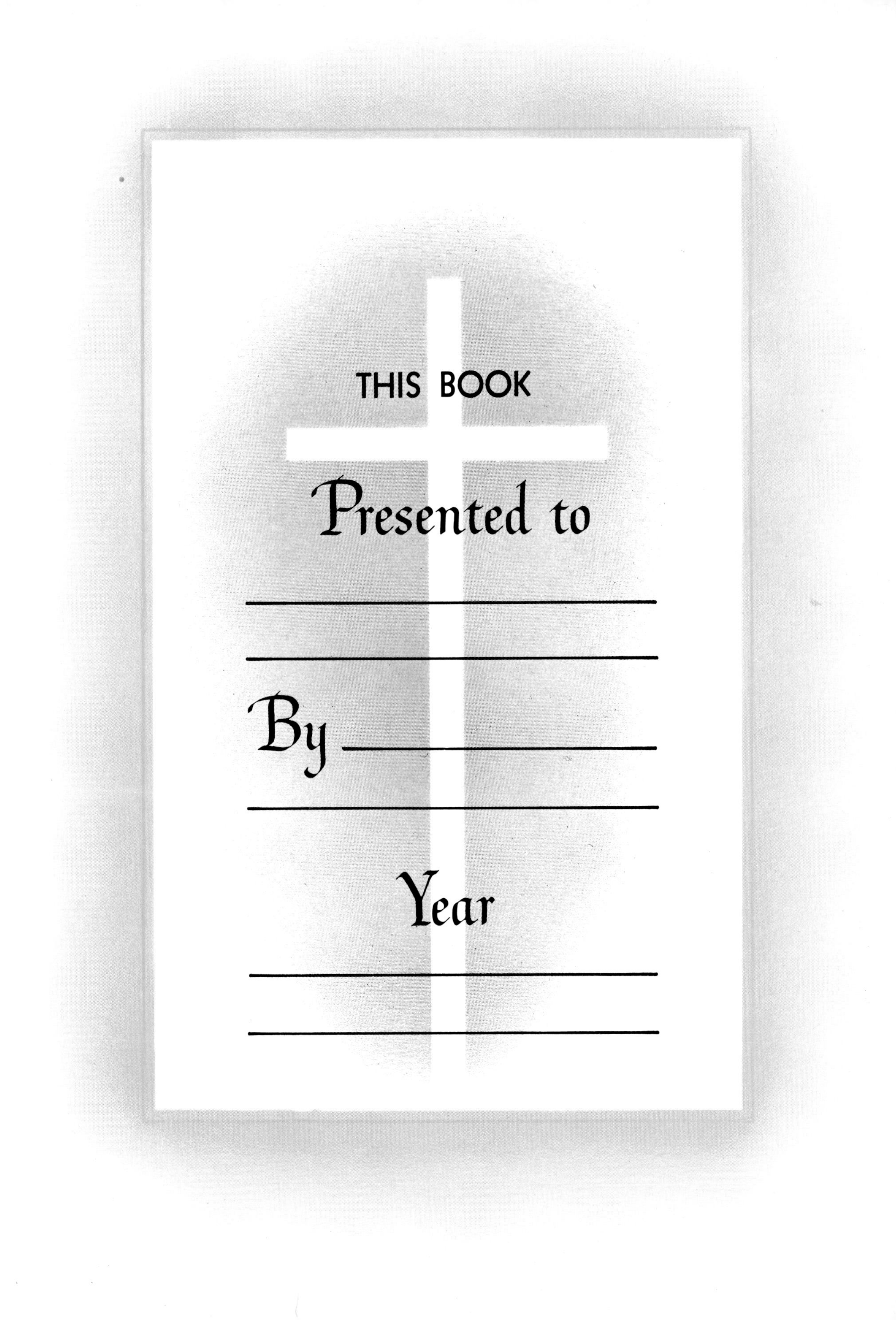
THIS BOOK
Presented to
By
Year

Jesus Blesses Little Children

Beautiful Bible Stories

By Patricia Summerlin Martin

THE SOUTHWESTERN COMPANY
NASHVILLE, TENNESSEE

PRINTED ON RECYCLED PAPER

Copyright © 1964 by
The Southwestern Company, Nashville, Tennessee

Library of Congress Catalog Card No. 64-18238

Text Illustrations by Camera Clix, Inc.,
and Three Lions, Inc.
R.R.D. 1-76

FOREWORD

WHY do you plan to read these Bible stories to your children? Why do you feel that it is important that they learn and remember them? Is it because they contain valuable moral lessons? Because they are exciting and adventurous? Or because they are a part of our literary heritage? To be sure, they are all of these things, but so are fables, fairy tales, and many novels. The important difference is that these stories are a part of God's Word. Our Father deemed them valuable enough to preserve them through centuries in order that we might learn of Him and His divine nature and of the way we can embrace a part of that nature in our acceptance of Jesus Christ. This knowledge complicates the task of one who attempts to retell Bible stories and at the same time ennobles his work.

With this in mind, I set about to relate in this book the most familiar Bible stories, maintaining some continuity between each one in order to present the grand picture of God's plan for His people in this world. The outcome was one hundred two stories—from Adam, through Abraham, Moses, the kings, and the prophets to Jesus Christ and His followers. The facts have been taken directly from the Biblical narrative, with no attempt to introduce a particular denominational creed or doctrine. To attract the child's interest, I have improvised and invented conversations between characters; but in cases where they are recorded, even these are from the Scriptures themselves.

I have attempted to retain the dignity of the message and, at the same time, make it interesting and understandable to children. The book is designed for the elementary school child, for the older child to read for himself and for the parent or teacher to read to the younger ones.

You may easily adapt these stories to your teaching and make effective use of the memory verses in your classroom or in devotionals at home. The questions at the end of each story will give you a review of the facts you should remember about that particular character or event or some lesson the story contained.

My appreciation is extended to the publishers who have insisted upon the beautiful paintings to accompany every story and the sturdy, attractive binding that will allow the book to remain a permanent part of your religious library.

May the stories in this book point your child to Jesus and instill in him a love for God and a thankfulness to Him for the gift of His Son.

PATRICIA SUMMERLIN MARTIN

CONTENTS

COLOR ILLUSTRATIONS

Old Testament

COLOR ILLUSTRATIONS

New Testament

The Beginning of Things

In the beginning God created the heaven and the earth.
Gen. 1:1

FROM the very beginning, there has been a God. Even before there was a world, or the sky, or animals, or people, God was living, for He was the One who made them all.

Because there was darkness everywhere, God first created, or made, the light. As its brightness shone through the dark, He was pleased and knew that it was good. He called this light Day. But God knew that darkness was needed also, so He allowed some of it to stay and called it Night. These God created on the same day, the *first* day of creation.

On the *second* day, God created the air that is all around us. When we look up as far as we can see, the air seems to be blue, and we call this air that God made the sky or Heaven.

Next, God gathered together the waters to form oceans, rivers, and lakes and separated them from the dry land. On the dry land, He caused the grass and trees and plants to grow and make it green and lovely. As the *third* day ended, our earth was beginning to look like it does to us now.

The sun and moon were created on the *fourth* day to brighten the day and the night. Even the twinkling star lights were set in place by God's hand on this day.

The Creation

The *fifth* day God brought forth living things to fill the water and the air—fish for the seas and birds for the heavens. Then on the *sixth* day, more living things were made by Him—every sort of animal that lives on the earth, every kind you can imagine.

As this sixth and last day of the creation was ending, God made a man. The Bible says that He made this man "in his image," or somewhat like Himself. This means that the man was to be higher than the animals and to rule over them. God placed this man in the wonderful world that He had made.

For six days God had worked to finish His creation. On the *seventh* day He looked at all He had made—the day with the sun and the night with the moon, the seas filled with fish and the air with birds, the earth covered with plants and animals of every sort, and a man in His own image—and God knew that it was good. He blessed this day and rested from His work.

Questions:

1. How long has God lived? 2. What did God call the light He made on the first day of creation? The darkness? 3. What did God do with the water that covered the earth? 4. Name three shining lights God put in the sky on the fourth day. 5. Name some living things God placed: first, in the water; second, in the air; and last, on the dry ground. 6. What was the last and greatest thing God created? 7. What did God do after His work was finished?

The First People

But of the tree of the knowledge of good and evil, thou shalt not eat of it: for in the day that thou eatest thereof thou shalt surely die.
Gen. 2:17

ON the sixth day of the creation, God made a man "from the dust of the ground." He called this man Adam. Now Adam was different from the rest of the things God had created because he was made in God's own image. This meant that Adam was somewhat like God Himself—not nearly so good and great and powerful, but more so than any of the other things God had made. Because of this, Adam was higher than the animals and able to rule over them. God even let Adam name all the different kinds of animals and birds that he found in his new earth home.

Perhaps as Adam searched for the animals, naming them, he noticed that all the creatures that lived around him had others of their own kind to be with. This made him feel alone and lonesome. We know that God did see that Adam needed a helper, so one day He caused Adam to fall into a deep sleep. While Adam was asleep, God took one of his ribs and from it made a woman to be with Adam. When Adam woke up, he was very happy to find the woman. He called her Eve.

In a place called Eden, God made an especially beautiful garden to be a home for Adam and Eve. Friendly animals of every sort lived in its woods and fields, and birds sang

Adam and Eve Driven from the Garden of Eden

lovely songs from the tops of the trees. Four rivers flowed through the garden and caused many different kinds of plants to grow. The most unusual of these plants were two very special trees that stood in the middle of the garden—the Tree of Life and the Tree of Knowledge of Good and Evil.

It was Adam's job to take care of this garden; and in return, he and Eve were free to live there and to eat of the luscious fruits and vegetables that were growing there. God gave them only one rule to follow: they were not to eat from the Tree of Knowledge.

What a happy life this couple had! All that they knew was good. God had given them only one rule to follow. As yet there was no sickness nor wrong nor sadness in the world.

Even as far back as the time of Adam and Eve, the devil was working against God and the good that God wanted man to do. Satan tried to figure out a plan that would make Adam and Eve do wrong. One day he appeared in their garden home disguised as a serpent and tried to persuade them to eat from the tree that God had forbidden.

"Did God tell you not to eat of any certain tree in the garden?" he cunningly asked.

Eve answered, "We can eat from every tree here except the Tree of Knowledge, and God has told us not to touch its fruit or we will die."

"Oh, you will not die," said the devil, trying to fool them. "Actually, it will make you as wise as God is and you will be able to understand things as He does."

Foolish Eve believed what the serpent told her and she took some of the fruit from the tree and ate it. Then she gave some to Adam and he ate it, also. Immediately they knew they had done wrong and began trying to hide from God.

Of course, Adam and Eve were not able to hide from God, for He always knows about everything we do. It made Him very angry to think that Adam and Eve had disobeyed the one rule that He had given them. He was disappointed that they had believed the devil instead of Him. He was so upset that He sent them away from the garden. He told them that they would have to work very hard, that they would have trouble and sickness, and that one day they would die. If only this first couple had chosen to do right instead of wrong, these terrible things might not have ever come into the world.

Even though God had to punish Adam and Eve, He still loved his creation, and He promised then that someday He would save mankind. We know that He did this when He sent His Son, Jesus Christ, into the world. Through Him, God can forgive men for the wrong they have done.

Questions:

1. In what way was Adam different from everything else God had made? 2. How did God make Adam's partner? 3. What was her name? 4. Tell about the Garden of Eden. 5. Which tree were Adam and Eve not to eat from? 6. How did the devil fool Eve? 7. How did God punish Adam and Eve?

Two Offerings

And the Lord had respect unto Abel and to his offering;
but unto Cain and to his offering he had not respect.
Gen. 4:4-5

AFTER Adam and Eve had disobeyed and eaten of the forbidden fruit, God sent them away from the Garden of Eden forever. He even sent angels to guard the Tree of Life and to keep them from returning to their first home. Surely Adam and Eve were not as happy away from their home, but one day something wonderful did happen to them —they had a little baby boy. They named him Cain; and later when they had another little boy, they called him Abel. These first babies must have looked beautiful to their mother and father, just as new babies do to us today.

As they were growing up, Cain and Abel were interested in different things. Cain liked to farm and watch things growing in the ground. Abel liked best to be around the animals and to look after the sheep his father kept.

In these early times, people did not worship God by going to church. Instead, they brought something that they had for the Lord and burned it. The offering was called a *sacrifice,* and usually it was burned on a rock or some stones called an *altar.*

One day Cain and Abel brought sacrifices to the Lord. Cain brought some of the fruits and vegetables that he had grown in his garden. Abel brought some of the finest sheep

Cain and Abel

from his flocks. We do not understand exactly why, but God was not pleased with the offering that Cain made, while He thought that Abel's was good. This made Cain very angry, and the Bible tells us that it even showed on his face how displeased he was.

God spoke to Cain and asked him not to look so angry. He told Cain that He would give him another chance to do right and that he could be as pleasing as Abel was. But Cain kept brooding about the way that God had not accepted his offering instead of trying to change and do right. Not only was he angry with God, but he began to blame his brother as well. One day when they were out in a field together, Cain got so upset about it that he killed Abel.

Of course the Lord knew about this terrible thing that Cain had done, but just to test Cain, He asked him where Abel was. Cain puffed up in anger and tried to cover his sin by asking, "Am I my brother's keeper?"

God told Cain that He had known about the murder all along, and because Cain had failed to do right, He was going to punish him by sending him away from his home. But God put a special mark on Cain so that the strangers whom he met as he wandered about would not harm him. God always loves us even when we do wrong, but He has to punish us to help us remember to obey.

Questions:

1. How did God make sure that Adam and Eve would not return to the Garden? 2. Who were the first two babies born in the world? 3. Were these brothers alike or different?

4. What did Cain bring for his sacrifice? What did Abel have? 5. Did God give Cain more than one chance to obey? 6. What terrible thing did Cain finally do? 7. How did God punish him?

Noah Builds a Boat

And Noah did according unto all that the Lord commanded him.
Gen. 7:5

ADAM and Eve had other children besides Cain and Abel, and then they had grandchildren. Before many years passed, there were many people on the earth. Although some of the people, like Abel, tried to obey God, many did not listen to Him. These wicked people got worse and worse, and more of the good people began following their example. As time went on, nearly all the world was evil. When God looked at men, He was sorry He had ever made them; and He decided to destroy these bad people with a great flood of water.

The Lord knew, however, that there was one good man living in those days. His name was Noah. Although everyone around him was doing wrong, Noah would have nothing to do with them. He remembered God and taught his three boys—Shem, Ham, and Japheth—to obey God. The Lord wanted to save Noah, so He told him to build a great ship called an ark. He told Noah the kind of wood to use and the size to make the boat. It was to have a great door and three decks. There were to be rooms inside for people, pens for animals, and storerooms of food for all.

For many years, maybe a hundred, Noah worked on the ark, believing that God was going to send the flood some day. While he worked, he tried to tell those that made fun

Noah Building the Ark

of him that God was going to destroy them unless they quit doing wrong. But no one believed Noah and no one changed. They only laughed at Noah's funny boat sitting on dry land.

Finally the ark was finished. God told Noah to go into the ark and to take with him his wife, his sons, and his sons' wives. He also sent Noah a pair of every kind of animal and bird on the earth to put into the ark. Noah even included seven of the animals that were good for food. When they were all inside, God shut them in. For seven days they waited in suspense, and then it began to rain. It rained as it had never rained before—as though the windows of the sky had opened. The oceans began to rise over the land, and all the rivers and lakes overflowed their banks. Soon all the land was covered, and the people had to run to the mountains for safety; but as the waters rose higher and higher, finally even the mountaintops went out of sight. Everybody had drowned. The only thing that could be seen was the ark, as it floated on waters that had no shore. Inside, Noah and those with him were safe while God Himself watched them and kept them from harm.

For forty days and forty nights it rained without stopping, and then God caused it to stop. The water, however, stayed on the earth for many days until He made winds to blow over it and help it dry. Gradually, the water got lower until the ark quit floating and rested on one of the high mountains of Ararat. Then other mountaintops began to appear. One day Noah sent out a raven to see if there was any dry ground. Now the raven can fly for a long time without resting and it can eat dead things, so it never came back. Later Noah sent out a dove, but the dove likes to rest in the trees and eat their seeds, and he came back when he found no trees. After a week, Noah let the dove fly out again. This time it returned with a tree branch in its beak. Noah knew that the waters had gone down enough for the trees to put on leaves again. When he let the dove go after another week, it never returned. Noah knew then that the time of the flood, which had lasted a whole year, was over. He opened the door of the ark and out poured the eight people and all the animals that God had saved.

What a beautiful sight the fresh, green earth must have been to them after being closed up so long! How grateful they must have been to God for keeping them safe! The first thing they wanted to do was to thank God, so Noah made an altar and burned an animal sacrifice on it as Abel had done.

God was pleased with Noah and his sons, and He made a promise to them that He would never again destroy the earth with such a flood. Until the end of the world, He would keep on sending days and nights, spring, summer, fall, and winter. As a sign of His promise, He set the rainbow in the clouds. It is formed when the sunlight shines on the raindrops in the air, and it reminded them of God's pledge. This same promise belongs to us today, and we can remember it and thank God every time we see a rainbow in the sky.

Questions:

1. Did the people on the earth grow better or worse? 2. Whom did God want to save? 3. What strange thing did God have Noah make? 4. What went into the ark? 5. How long did it rain? 6. How did Noah tell when it was safe to leave the ark? 7. How did Noah thank God for keeping him safe? 8. What promise did God make to Noah?

A Tower to the Sky

And they said, Go to, let us build us a city and
a tower, whose top may reach unto heaven.
Gen. 11:4

NOAH and his sons had a fresh, new world in which to begin life again. This family was the only one on the earth, as Adam's family once had been. They made new homes; and after a while, Shem, Ham, and Japheth—Noah's sons—each had a big family of his own. Their children grew up and had children of their own, and again there were many people on the earth. Before the flood, everyone had lived near each other, but now they began to scatter and build their homes in different places. God wanted them to move so that one day people would use all parts of the earth for their homes. That way, a family like Noah's, who wanted to do right, could move away from the wicked people they were living near and either go off by themselves or move near other godly familes.

Some of the people moved south from Mount Ararat, where the ark had landed, and lived on a plain in the land of Shinar. This land had the materials for making bricks, and from these bricks the men were able to make strong houses and walls. When they saw that their city was going to be a strong one, they began to feel very important and said to one another, "Let us build a great tower that will

The Tower of Babel

reach up to the sky. Then we will not be scattered about the earth and separated from one another."

They set about with energy to build the tower. Some made bricks, some made mortar to hold the bricks together, and others laid them one story above the other. As the tower rose higher and higher, the people felt more and more important and pleased with themselves.

When God saw the city and tower that the men were building, He was not pleased. He knew that the men were beginning to think less of Him and more of their own importance. Some day they might quit thinking of Him altogether and worship the things they were able to make. Besides that, it was not God's plan that all men live close together as they had before the flood. He knew that once more the wicked could lead the good away from Him, and all the world would become wicked again.

In order to stop the building of the tower, God caused them to speak different languages. Up until this time, everyone had spoken the same language, so that everyone could understand what everyone else said. Now, however, those of one family could not understand what their neighbors of another family were saying. Those working in the city could not understand what people had come to sell or buy. Most important, those building the tower could not understand their fellow workers well enough to work together. They left the tower without finishing it, and it stayed forever that way. As God had planned, gradually families began moving away to other places, where they could be with those whom they could understand.

Afterward, the city where the tower was built was named Babel, which means "confusion." Surely everyone had been confused, or mixed up, by the many languages. Much later on, it was known as Babylon and was a great city in that part of the world. We shall hear of Babylon again as we learn of God's people.

Questions:

1. Why did God want people to move away from one place? 2. What did the people in the land of Shinar decide to build? 3. Why was God displeased with the tower? 4. Why was the tower never finished? 5. Name the place where the unfinished tower stood.

A Man Who Would Not Change

The Lord gave, and the Lord hath taken away; blessed be the name of the Lord.
Job 1:21

LONG ago, in the Old Testament times, there lived in the land of Uz a man named Job. Now Job was the richest man in that part of the world. Besides having great herds of cattle and sheep and camels, he had a fine, large family—seven grown sons and three daughters.

Job was very rich, but he was also very good. He worshiped God with sacrifices and prayed every day. Not only did he pray for himself, but Job also prayed for his children. "It may be that one of my sons has done wrong and has not asked God to forgive him yet," Job thought.

Now the Lord noticed all that Job did and was pleased with him. One day the Lord mentioned Job to Satan. "Have you noticed my servant, Job?" he asked. "There is no one on earth as good as he, so careful to turn away from evil and do right."

"It is true that Job serves you," Satan replied, "but it is not hard for him to do, because you have blessed him so. Now if something bad were to happen to him, he would probably turn away from you."

Job and His Friends

"Try him and see," the Lord said. "Do anything you wish to anything he has, only do not hurt him."

Before long, Job began having a lot of trouble. One day a servant came running to him and said: "Master, we were out plowing with the oxen a while ago when the Sabeans came and took them. All of the other servants were killed in the fight—I am the only one who escaped!"

The servant had hardly finished telling his bad news when another ran up, looking very excited.

"Lightning from the sky just struck all the sheep and the servants who were watching them," he cried. "I am the only one still alive!"

Then another came to Job with bad news: "The Chaldeans made a raid upon our camels. They took the animals and killed the servants who were with them."

If this were not enough, another servant came in with the worst report of all. "Job," he said, "your children were all having dinner together at your oldest son's house when a great wind blew the house down and killed them all."

Poor Job! In one day he had lost his children, his servants, his flocks and herds—everything he owned. Job tore his clothes and fell upon the ground, but he did not say anything against God. "The Lord gave them all to me," he said, "so they were His to take away. I still bless His name."

Satan hardly knew what to think of the way Job acted. He complained to the Lord: "Job has not turned away from you yet because he himself has not been hurt. If something were to happen to him, he would curse you, I know."

"You may try to find out," the Lord replied, "only do not take his life."

So Satan caused terrible boils to break out on Job's skin. These sores covered him from the top of his head to the bottom of his feet. It hurt him to stand up or sit down or lie down. Any way he turned, he seemed to press against one of the sore places. Job was so sick and hurt so badly that even his wife thought it would be better for him to die.

Three of Job's friends came to see him while he was sick. They tried to tell him that God was sending him these troubles because he had done some wrong. They told Job that God was punishing him.

But Job knew that he had tried to do right and that the Lord was with him. He would not agree with his friends or say anything against the Lord.

Finally Satan saw that there was no use trying to turn Job away from God. He had proved that he really was a good and faithful man. After this, Satan let Job alone. God blessed him and gave him twice as much as he ever had before. Once again he had seven sons and three daughters to make his life happy, and his pastures and fields were covered with healthy animals. He lived to be a very old man and served God all of his days.

Questions:

1. What did Job have that made him rich? 2. Why did Job pray for his children? 3. Did Satan think he could make Job turn away from God? 4. What troubles did he send to Job? 5. Did Job curse God? 6. Then what did Satan cause to happen to Job? 7. What did Job's friends tell him?

Lot Makes a Choice

And Abram said unto Lot, Let there be no strife, I pray thee, between me and thee, and between my herdmen and thy herdmen; for we be brethren.
Gen. 13:8

SOME of the people who moved from Babel after God confused the languages built a city not too far away to the north. These people called their city Ur, the name of the moon god idol they worshiped. One good man in the city worshiped the true God, just as Noah had done once upon a time. God did not want this man's family to grow up in such a wicked place, so He appeared to the man, whose name was Abram. He told Abram to leave Ur and follow Him to a land far away. In this new land, Abram's family would grow in number and become a great nation. One day the new land would be theirs. God even promised that all the families of the world would be blessed because of Abram's son and his family.

Abram did not understand all that God said to him. Already he was getting old, and he did not have even one child. How could the world be blessed through his family when he had none? He could not understand that the great blessing to the world that God was speaking of was Jesus Christ. Many, many years later Christ was born into the very family of which Abram had been a father. This way Abram's family gave all the world a blessing by giving them a Savior.

Abraham's Journey to Canaan

Although Abram did not understand all that God told him, he obeyed through *faith.* This means that he obeyed God and believed what God said even though he could not yet see the new land or his large family or the blessings to come. He just knew that God would keep His promise.

Abram had no children, but he actually did have a family to move with him to the new land. He had his wife, Sarai, his old father, Terah, and Lot, the son of Abram's brother who had died. Lot had come to live with his uncle Abram since he had no father. Besides these, there were many servants who tended Abram's flocks. All of them packed their belongings and left Ur with Abram. As they journeyed along, they would watch for streams of water. When they found one, they would pitch their tent homes and let the animals enjoy the water for a while. At one place called Haran, they stayed for a long time. Perhaps Terah was too old and tired to go any farther because we know that he died there. Abram was very sad, but he gathered the rest of his family together and they began to travel slowly once more toward the strange land of which God had spoken.

After a long journey, Abram reached the land of the Canaanites, or Canaan. It was near a great sea and had sloping hills and grass, perfect for cattle and sheep grazing. The Canaanites had built some cities in their land, but Abram continued to live on the open fields in his tent. As he was setting up his tent near an oak tree, God appeared to him again and told him that this was the land that would be his. Believing and trusting in God, Abram built an altar there and worshiped.

Except for a little time that he spent in Egypt when food for the cattle was scarce, Abram continued to live in Canaan. The number of his cattle and sheep grew and he gained much silver and gold, as well. He became a very rich man. By this time, Lot had grown up; and he owned many flocks and herds, too. Between them there were more tents and sheep and cattle than one spot of land could hold.

Because they were so crowded, it was natural that both Abram's and Lot's servants would try to get the best land and most water for his own master's cattle. These herdsmen began quarreling and arguing over the grazing lands until news of it reached Abram.

When Abram heard about the trouble, he understood right away what a problem the men were having. There *were* too many animals to feed on the land at that place. He went to Lot and said, "There should be no quarreling between you and me, or between our herdsmen, because we are of the same family. Is there not enough room around here for all of us to live at peace? Let us separate. Whichever direction you choose to settle in, I will go the other way."

As Abram spoke, Lot looked out at the land stretched before him. On one side he saw the green valley through which the Jordan River flowed. "That is the land I must have for my own," he thought selfishly to himself. Actually, all the land had been promised to Abram by God, but Abram was kind enough and so willing to agree that he gave Lot his first choice.

Lot gathered his servants and flocks together and moved toward the Jordan Valley, confident that he could grow richer and more successful there. But before Abram turned the other direction, where the land was not quite so good, God spoke to him: "Look from the place where you are standing toward every direction. East, west, north, and south—all this land is going to be yours some day. And it will belong to your children, as well."

Again, Abram had to believe God by faith because he still had no children. But he did trust God, and when he came to a place called Hebron and pitched his tents under the oak trees there, he worshiped God with a sacrifice.

Questions:

1. Tell about the city that was Abram's first home. 2. Who moved with Abram? 3. What was the name of the land God promised to Abram? 4. Why did Lot's and Abram's servants quarrel? 5. How did Abram solve the argument? 6. Did Lot make an unselfish choice?

A Runaway Slave

Behold, my covenant is with thee, and
thou shalt be a father of many nations.
Gen. 17:4

ABRAM and his family stayed in Canaan once they had gotten there, except for a time that they spent in Egypt to escape a famine, a period when the land did not grow enough food for the cattle. When they returned, they brought with them an Egyptian girl named Hagar to be Sarai's maid. When years passed and still Abram and Sarai had no children, Sarai suggested to Abram that Hagar have a child and it could be the child God had spoken of in His promise. It could be the one to whom Abram could give the land and the blessings God had given him.

After Sarai had made these plans, however, Hagar did something to make her very angry. Sarai was sorry that she had wanted Hagar to be the mother of the promised child, and she punished her severely. Hagar ran away toward the desert, toward her home in Egypt, but she got so tired that she finally stopped to rest by a fountain. Here an angel of the Lord found her and said: "Hagar, where are you going?"

"I am running away from Sarai, my mistress, because I do not want to serve her any longer," replied Hagar.

"Go back to Sarai and obey her," the angel said. "God will be with you and will help you. You will have a son who will grow to be a strong man."

Hagar and Ishmael

Hagar returned to the house of her mistress and she did have a son. Abram named him "Ishmael," which means "God hears." But even though Abram loved Ishmael, he was not the son God had promised. One day Abram and Sarai had a baby boy of their own. This was the one whom God promised to bless and to make of him a great nation. His name was Isaac. Ishmael was older than Isaac, but he often played with the baby. Sarai did not like the older boy playing with her son, and she asked Abram to send him and his mother away.

Now Abram felt sorry for Hagar and Ishmael, but God told him not to worry about them, because He was going to begin a nation with the boy Ishmael, too. So Abram sent Hagar and Ishmael off with some food and water for their trip. They traveled toward Egypt again, but on the journey they used up all the food and water. In the hot sun and burning sand, they could go no farther. Hagar laid poor Ishmael down in the shade of a tiny bush because she said, "I cannot bear to see my boy suffer and die."

God heard Hagar in the desert a second time, and again He sent an angel to her. The angel told her that God would take care of her and Ishmael. Surely enough, when the angel disappeared, Hagar saw a spring of water bubbling out of the dry ground near her. She filled their empty water bottles and gave Ishmael a drink.

Hagar and Ishmael never returned to Egypt, but made their home in the wilderness, away from other people. Ishmael grew up there to be a strong outdoor man, very skillful with the bow and arrow. His children, like him, grew up in the desert and became a strong, wandering nation called the Ishmaelites.

Questions:

1. When did Hagar come to live with Abram and Sarai? 2. Why did Sarai want Hagar to have a child? 3. Why did Hagar run away the first time? 4. Was Hagar's child the one God had promised to Abram? Who was? 5. What promise did God make about Hagar's son? 6. Why did Ishmael grow sick in the desert? 7. How was he saved?

A Wicked City

And the Lord said, If I find in Sodom fifty righteous within the city, then I will spare all the place for their sakes.
Gen. 18:26

WHEN Abram gave Lot his choice of the land for his flocks, Lot thought that he had done well to choose the land near the Jordan. Here the fields were greener and the waters were plentiful. But beyond the fields and the river lay two great cities, Sodom and Gomorrah, and the people of these cities were very wicked indeed. As Lot's cattle ate the grasses of one field and he moved them on to another, he found himself moving closer and closer to Sodom, until finally he was living right among the evil people of the city.

Lot tried to do better than the other people of Sodom, but it was hard to keep from getting into trouble. Once when some foreign kings captured the king of Sodom, Lot was taken as a prisoner right along with the others in the city. His uncle Abram had to gather together some men and come and rescue him. You might think that this would have taught Lot a lesson, but it did not seem to. He went right back to Sodom to live.

While Lot was living in Sodom, Abram continued to live in his tent home under the oak trees at Hebron. Away from wicked people, it was easier for him to obey God and to worship Him with sacrifices upon an altar. One day when

Lot and His Daughters

Abram was sitting at the door of his tent about noon, three strange men suddenly appeared before him.

Now Abram had never seen these men before and did not know who they were, but he hurried to do what he could for them. He bowed low before them and asked them to stay a while with him. He offered them water to wash themselves and a place to rest, and he told Sarai to prepare some food. After they had cleaned up and rested, he served the strangers a wonderful meal of meat and cheese and tender cakes that Sarai had made.

After they had eaten, one of the men began to speak to Abram about the blessings God had promised him. You see, this stranger was the Lord Himself! He told Abram that his promised son was going to be born soon. But He had some sad news for Abram, too. He was on His way to Sodom and Gomorrah to see just how wicked and sinful the cities were. If it was true that they were as bad as they had been said to be, He was going to have to punish them.

Abram grew worried about his nephew Lot. "Are you going to destroy the good right along with the bad?" he asked. "Would you save the city if there were fifty good people in it?"

The Lord agreed to save the city if fifty good people could be found there. But Abram must have known there were not that many people in Sodom who were trying to do right, so he made another bargain with the Lord. "I know I am not worthy to suggest it, but if fifty could not be found, would you save it for forty-five?" Again the Lord agreed.

"Suppose there were just forty? Thirty? Twenty? Ten?"

At last the Lord agreed to save the city if only ten good people could be found there.

Now the two men that had visited Abram along with the Lord had gone ahead to Sodom. Lot was sitting in an important place at the gate of the city when he saw the men approaching. Like Abram, he bowed before the unusual strangers and asked that they stay in his home that night.

"No," the men replied. "We will sleep out here in the street."

But Lot was afraid for them to stay outside where the wicked people of the city could find them. At last he persuaded them to come home with him.

After they had eaten supper and were getting ready for bed, there came a banging at the door and the sounds of a crowd in the street. Someone outside called to Lot, "Where are the strangers that came to you today? Send them out here to us." It was the wicked men of Sodom, and they had come to hurt the men from God.

Lot stepped outside the door and closed it behind him. He begged the men not to harm his guests. But the men pushed Lot aside and began trying to break the door down.

Suddenly the visitors opened the door and drew Lot inside. Then they caused the wicked men of the city to become blind so that they wandered away, not knowing where they were going.

Then the men told Lot that the Lord was going to destroy Sodom. They told Lot to gather his family together and leave at once. All night Lot begged his sons-in-law, who were soon to marry his daughters, to leave with him. But they just laughed and made fun of him.

Toward morning, the angels told Lot to leave behind the sons-in-law, but at least to take his wife and daughters away. Still Lot lingered in the city, until finally the men had to lead him outside the city gates. There they urged Lot: "Run for your life! Do not stop or even look back!"

As Lot and his family hurried to a nearby city, the Lord rained fire out of heaven and destroyed Sodom and Gomorrah. But Lot's wife could not resist, and she turned and looked back. When she did, she turned into a pillar of salt.

Questions:

1. Where did Lot finally go to live? 2. Who came to visit Abram? 3. What message did they bring? 4. For how many good people did the Lord agree to save Sodom? 5. Could they be found? 6. Were the people of Sodom friendly to the strangers? 7. How did God destroy the city? 8. Who was saved?

Abraham's Greatest Test

And Abraham said, My son, God will provide himself a lamb for a burnt offering.
Gen. 22:8

FOR a long time Abram did not understand God's promise to him that his family would be great and number as the stars in the sky. It was hard for him to believe because he did not have a child. He thought that perhaps Ishmael could be the son God promised, but when God sent Ishmael and his mother away, He showed Abram that Ishmael was not the one. God wanted Sarai, Abram's wife, to be the child's mother, not an Egyptian servant girl.

God repeated his promise to Abram several times. Sometimes this promise is called the "old covenant" because it was given to Abram. The "new covenant" or promise is the one given in Christ. One time when God was speaking to Abram, he told him He was going to change his name to Abraham, which means "the father of many nations." He changed Sarai's name to Sarah, which means "a princess."

When Abraham was ninety-nine years old and Sarah was nearly that old, God visited them and told them that the time had come for their son to come. Sarah laughed when she heard that she was going to have a baby because she thought she was too old. But sure enough, God sent them a little baby boy, and they named him Isaac. Isaac made everyone very happy. Abraham and Sarah were very

The Sacrifice of Isaac

proud of him and they gave a great dinner to show him to their friends when he was still a little boy barely walking about. They took good care of him and he grew to be a fine boy, obedient to his parents.

One day God gave Abraham a very hard thing to do. He wanted to see if Abraham really believed in Him and loved Him more than anything else in the world, even his son. He asked him to take Isaac and offer him like a sacrifice on an altar.

Of course, this made Abraham very sad. He loved his boy very much. God had made Abraham the promise that Isaac would be the ancestor, or father, of a great nation of people and that they would someday own the land of Canaan. How could God keep this promise if Isaac were killed? Abraham wondered about this, but he prepared to obey God.

The next morning Abraham and Isaac set off for Mount Moriah to worship God. They took with them two servant men, their donkeys, and wood for the offering. For two days and nights they traveled. On the third day, they saw the mountain in the distance. Abraham and Isaac alighted from their donkeys. Abraham said to the servants, "You keep our donkeys here while Isaac and I go up on the mountain and worship. When we have finished, we will come back." He then gave Isaac the wood they had brought for the offering and he took the pitcher with fire in it.

Isaac looked about and asked, "My father! Here you have the fire and I have the wood for our offering. Where is the animal to sacrifice?"

"God Himself will provide a lamb for the offering, my son," Abraham replied.

Together they started up the mountain. When they reached the place of worship, they set up stones for an altar and lay the wood upon it. Then perhaps Isaac realized that he was the offering God was providing. The Bible tells us that he allowed his father to bind him and lay him across the wood. Sadly and slowly, Abraham raised his knife to kill his only son, the promised one for whom he had waited so many years. Surely the thoughts of all the promises of God crossed his mind at that moment.

But as he lowered the hand that was clutching the knife, an angel of the Lord called out to him, "Abraham! Abraham!"

With relief, Abraham dropped the knife and answered, "Here I am."

"There is no need for you to kill your son, Abraham. God knows now that you trust Him and love Him more than anything—even your own son." This was the message that the angel brought.

Abraham then raised his eyes and as he did, he spied a ram with its horns caught in a thicket. It was the offering God had provided. He untied Isaac, and they worshiped God together with the sacrifice that He had given them.

Abraham named the place on Mount Moriah where he and Isaac had built this altar, "The Lord will provide." Surely it was a place that they never forgot, for it was here Abraham had passed the greatest test that God ever gave him.

Questions:

1. To what did God change Abram's name? Sarai's? 2. Who was the real son God had promised to Abraham? 3. What hard thing did God ask Abraham to do? 4. Where did they go to offer the sacrifice? 5. Who stopped Abraham from offering Isaac? 6. What did he offer instead? 7. What did God find out about Abraham?

A Birthright for a Bowl of Stew

And the boys grew: and Esau was a cunning hunter, a man of the field; and Jacob was a plain man, dwelling in tents.
Gen. 25:27

AFTER Abraham had lived to be an old man and had seen his son Isaac grow up and marry a fine and beautiful wife, he died. From the years long before when God had called him to leave his home in Ur, he had followed God's every command. He had even been ready to sacrifice his own son, Isaac, when the Lord asked him to do that. God had blessed Abraham for his goodness, even though some of His promises did not come true until many more years had passed. Abraham had become the first of God's specially chosen people, chosen to learn His ways. Into this same family one day God planned to have His own Son be born. Until then, He planned to watch over and lead His people, the children of Abraham, and to give them the land of Canaan for their home.

Now Isaac and his wife Rebekah were like Abraham and Sarah—they, too, were married a long time before they had any children. Like Abraham, Isaac wondered how God was going to make theirs a great and wonderful family when they had no children. Rebekah wanted a baby very badly, and Isaac prayed to God that He would give her one.

John H. Eggers Publications and The New York Public Library

Jacob and Esau

God heard Isaac's prayer and He answered it by giving them not one son, but two—twin boys. Now some twins are just alike, but these were very different. The first one to be born was a red little boy, covered with soft hair. They named him Esau, which means "hairy." The second baby was smooth-skinned and pink, and they called him Jacob.

Before the babies were born, God had told Rebekah a strange thing about them. He had said: "These children are to be two different nations. One people will be stronger than the other; and the older shall serve the younger." As the twins grew up, it certainly appeared that Esau was the stronger. He was a rugged boy who loved to hunt and stay outdoors. Jacob was not weak, but he was quieter and more gentle.

It was too bad that the boys were against each other from the beginning. Esau, with his red face and thick hair, was Isaac's favorite. After a day of hunting, Esau would bring Isaac some of the deer meat he had gotten and tell him of the adventures of the hunt. Isaac loved to eat the meat and listen to Esau. He was proud of his strong son, and he loved Esau best. Jacob, however, was his mother's favorite. Rebekah could see that Jacob was the stronger in goodness.

After the boys were grown, Esau continued his life of hunting. Jacob was the family shepherd and farmer. One day, probably as he was in the field with the sheep or working with the crops, Jacob stopped to build a fire and cook himself a little pot of stew. As he was stirring it, Esau came in, tired and hungry from an unlucky hunt.

When he saw the stew Jacob was cooking, he asked Jacob for some of it. Perhaps there was only enough for one and Jacob argued with him about it. Finally, Esau grew very tired and said, "I would give anything I owned for something to eat!"

"Even your birthright?" asked Jacob.

"What good would a birthright be to me if I died of hunger?" answered Esau.

"Promise the birthright shall be mine, and the stew will be yours," said Jacob.

So Esau promised and eagerly grabbed the mess of pottage, as stew was sometimes called. Just that easily, Esau gave up the greatest thing he owned. You see, the birthright usually belonged to the oldest son; and it meant that when the father died, he would be the head of the family and own all that the father had owned. It also meant that he would be the leader of the family, the wisest one, the closest to God. For just a little food to make him happy at the moment, Esau traded these blessings.

Actually, this foolish trade had a place in God's plans although neither Esau nor Jacob nor their parents realized it. God was letting this happen to make true his promise to Rebekah that "the older shall serve the younger." Esau, the older, had given up the birthright to Jacob, who was the younger.

Questions:

1. What did God plan to do for Abraham's family? 2. How many children did Abraham's son, Isaac, have? 3. How were

the twins different? 4. What did the boys do after they were grown? 5. What did Esau exchange for some stew? 6. What does having a "birthright" mean?

Jacob and Rebekah Play a Trick

And Isaac answered and said unto Esau, Behold, I have made him thy lord, and all his brethren have I given to him for servants.
Gen. 27:37

THE day came when Isaac had grown very old. He had to stay in bed most of the time, and he could hardly see. He knew that he would not live much longer. He called Esau to him and asked, "Take your bow and arrows and go hunt for me. Bring me a deer and cook it the way that I love so well. Perhaps it will make me feel better. We can talk—you can tell me about your hunt, and then I will give you the blessing that is your birthright."

Now Rebekah heard Isaac talking with Esau; and as Esau hurried out to obey his father's wish, she called to Jacob. Perhaps she knew that Jacob had bargained with Esau for the birthright and saw that this was the time to claim it. Together they planned to play a trick on Isaac. They would send Jacob in, pretending to be Esau, and get Isaac to give him the birthright.

Jacob was timid about trying to fool his father and said, "What if he should discover who I am and become angry at me?"

"Let his anger be on me," answered Rebekah. "Now go, and let us hurry to carry out my plan."

Isaac Blesses Jacob

So Jacob fetched two little goats from his father's flock, as his mother told him. They killed the goats and skinned them. With the meat Rebekah prepared a stew, seasoning it and cooking it as she would deer meat. She knew that Isaac, as old and sick as he was, would probably not be able to tell the difference. Then she took the skin of the goats and wound it around Jacob's hands and the part of his neck that showed. She wanted Isaac to think that he was touching Esau's hairy skin.

At last Rebekah brought out one of Esau's robes for Jacob to wear. She wanted even the smell of the clothes to lead Isaac to think that this was his favorite, older son. Giving Jacob the stew and some bread, she told him to go to his father. Jacob was frightened, but he took it and went to the old man's room.

"Father?" said Jacob.

"Here I am," said Isaac. "Who are you, my son?" He could scarcely see, and Jacob probably spoke softly so his voice would not be recognized.

"I am Esau, your oldest son," lied Jacob. "I have done just as you asked me, Father. Try to sit up and eat some of the deer I have brought. Then give me your blessing."

Poor Isaac could not see, but he was not easily fooled. Questions came to his mind. He asked, "How did you find a deer so quickly?"

"God was with me, and I came upon him very soon," said Jacob.

Still Isaac was not satisfied. He asked Jacob to come near in order that he might feel him. As he felt the goats' hair that Jacob had on his neck and hands, he was further puzzled. Again he asked if this was really Esau. Then he had Jacob come near so that he could smell of his clothes. As he smelled the outdoor odor that still clung to Esau's robes, he felt satisfied and prepared to give his blessing.

Solemnly he placed his hands on Jacob and said, "God give you the best in heaven and on earth and plenty to eat and drink. Let people serve you and nations honor you. Let your brothers bow down to you. Let him that curses you be cursed and blessed be he that blesses you."

So Jacob received the blessing.

No sooner had Jacob left Isaac, than Esau came in from the hunt. He hurried to make the deer stew his father was so fond of and brought it to him.

"Who is it now?" asked Isaac.

"Esau, your oldest son." This voice could not be mistaken. The smell of the woods and the freshly killed deer still came from Esau's skin and clothes.

Immediately Isaac realized that he had been fooled. Perhaps anger rose within him, but he knew that it was too late. He knew that God could bring good even out of lies. He could make things work for the best in his plans. He remembered that even before the twins were born, God had told Rebekah that the younger would rule.

Esau would not listen to such talk. He begged for the blessing, but Isaac could give it only once. He had already made Jacob a ruler over Esau.

Even a great, strong man like Esau cried over his lost birthright. He asked, "Have you no blessing for me, Father?"

Isaac gave Esau what blessing he could, but it was not the same one he gave Jacob. Esau was furious and left full of anger for the brother that had taken his birthright and blessing.

Questions:

1. What did Isaac ask Esau to do? 2. What did Rebekah and Jacob plan while Esau was gone? 3. Why did Isaac think that Jacob was really Esau? 4. How did he bless Jacob? 5. What did Esau do when he found out?

Jacob's Wonderful Dream

And he dreamed, and behold a ladder set up on the earth, and the top of it reached to heaven: and behold the angels of God ascending and descending on it.
Gen. 28:12

WHEN Esau discovered that Jacob had claimed the blessing that really belonged to him, he became so angry that he wanted to kill his brother. He planned to wait until their father died. Then when Jacob took over his father's possessions, Esau would kill him and have the land and cattle for his own.

But Rebekah still protected her favorite, Jacob; and she sent for him when she heard of Esau's evil plans. She warned Jacob to leave at once.

"Go to my brother Laban, who lives at Haran. Stay and visit with him a while, and then perhaps Esau will forget his anger. When he does, I will send for you to come back to us, for I cannot bear to lose both you and your father."

Rebekah did not tell old Isaac about the quarrel between their sons. Instead she told him that Jacob was going to seek a good wife from among their own people. Both Isaac and Rebekah were disappointed in the foreign women that Esau took for his wives, and Isaac agreed that Jacob should find a woman that worshiped the true God. Like most fathers, he forgave Jacob for fooling him about the birthright, and he gave him his parting blessing.

John H. Eggers Publications and The New York Public Library

Jacob's Dream

Bidding his mother and father goodbye, Jacob set out on the long journey alone. As he traveled slowly on his way, he thought of the trouble that he had brought upon himself. He was afraid that his own brother would kill him, and he did not know if he would ever feel safe to return home. He wondered if he would ever see his old father again. What good was the stolen birthright now that he might never be able to go back and take his father's place?

Jacob was sorry that Esau hated him and that he might never own his father's lands and flocks; but more than that, he was afraid that God was not pleased with him. He knew that he had lied, cheated, and stolen something which was not his. Perhaps he prayed to God for forgiveness as he trudged along his lonely path. Whatever his thoughts, we know that God was listening to them.

As the sun went down, Jacob probably felt lonelier than ever. He was very tired, however, and looked for a good place to stop for the night. Finding a smooth stone on which to rest his head, he lay down to sleep.

While he slept, God sent him a wonderful dream. He saw a ladder that reached all the way from earth to heaven. On the ladder were beautiful angels, climbing up and down—from heaven, to earth, and back to their heavenly home. God Himself stood at the top of the ladder and spoke to Jacob: "I am the God of your grandfather Abraham and of your father Isaac. This land where you are lying, I will give to you and to your children. Your family will be great, with as many people as there are specks of dust on the earth; and through your family, all the peoples of the earth will be blessed. Now, I am with you and will be with you wherever you go, and I will bring you back to this land some day. I will never leave you until I make this promise come true."

We have heard these wonderful words before. God had spoken them to Abraham and to Isaac, and these very words had kept them close to God throughout their lives. Now they had been repeated to Jacob. How good he must have felt when he awoke! No longer was he alone. "Surely the Lord is in this place and I did not know it," he whispered to himself. "Why, this is the house of God, the gate of heaven!" he said as he looked about.

Taking the stone that had been his pillow, he set it up as a marker to God, the God of Abraham, of Isaac, and now of Jacob. He named the place Bethel, which means "the house of God," and he made a promise to God that he would give back to Him part of all that God gave him.

After the wonderful dream, Jacob must have felt much better as he continued on his journey. With God traveling with him, the tiresome trip seemed easy.

Questions:

1. Why was Esau waiting to kill Jacob? 2. Where did Rebekah send Jacob? 3. What happened to him on his journey? 4. What did Jacob see in the dream? 5. What did God promise to Jacob? 6. To whom had God given this same promise? 7. How did Jacob mark the place where he had had the wonderful dream?

Jacob and His Uncle Laban

And Jacob served seven years for Rachel; and they seemed unto him but a few days, for the love he had to her.
Gen. 29:20

FOR days and days after his wonderful dream, Jacob traveled, running away from his brother Esau, who was so angry with Jacob that he wanted to kill him. Finally, the day came when he saw some men in the distance, standing near a well with their sheep. Jacob thought to himself, "Perhaps I am near the place for which I am looking. I will ask these men just exactly where we are." So he called out, "What place are you from?"

"From Haran," came the answer.

"Do you know a man from Haran named Laban?" asked Jacob. You see, Laban was Jacob's uncle whom he was coming to visit.

"Yes, we know him," they replied. "Look, here comes his daughter Rachel with his sheep."

Surely enough, his cousin was walking toward them, leading her father's sheep, for she tended to them. This was the time of day that she brought them to drink at the well. Jacob hurried to meet her and rolled away the stone that covered the well. He offered to water her sheep for her, and he told her that he was her kinsman, the son of her father's sister, Rebekah.

Jacob and Rachel

Rebekah was a name that Rachel had heard all her life. She knew that this was her aunt who had gone long ago to the land of Canaan to become the wife of Abraham's son, Isaac. It had been years since they had heard from Rebekah, and now here was her own son! The cousins greeted each other warmly, and then Rachel ran in a great hurry to tell her father that Jacob had come.

Laban was glad to have news of his sister Rebekah and he ran out to meet Jacob. He brought him to his house and listened for a long time to the tales Jacob had to tell of the land of Canaan, his home. All during the evening, however, Jacob could not keep from looking back to the lovely shepherdess, Rachel. He thought she was the kindest and most beautiful girl he had ever seen.

Jacob had worked as a shepherd at home, so he began helping Laban with his flocks. After a month of this, Laban offered to pay him for his work. "What will you have me pay you?" he asked Jacob.

Jacob knew right away what he wanted Laban to give him. "I will work seven years for you if you will give me your daughter Rachel to be my wife," he said.

"You are the kind of husband I would choose for my daughter," said Laban, agreeing to Jacob's request. You see, in those days it was not unusual for the bridegroom to give some kind of payment like this; so the bargain did not seem as strange to them as it seems to us.

For seven years Jacob worked to win his lovely Rachel, but he loved her so much that it seemed to him only a few days. When the seven years were over, Jacob came to

Laban and asked for his bride. Laban arranged for a great wedding feast; and in the evening, he brought in the bride. She was beautifully dressed according to the custom then —every bit of her was covered with a heavy veil through the whole ceremony. It was not until everything was over and the veil taken away that Jacob discovered that he had not married Rachel at all! Instead, Laban had brought in Leah, Rachel's older sister, and *she* had become Jacob's wife.

Leah was not as beautiful as her younger sister, and Jacob did not love her as he did Rachel. Once he had fooled his old father, but now someone had played a trick on *him,* and he realized how it felt to be cheated. He complained to Laban that he had been unfair. Laban explained that in their country the older daughter was supposed to marry first. But he was willing to make another agreement with Jacob. "If you will work for me another seven years, I will give you Rachel for your wife, also," he said. In those days, we know that God allowed men to have more than one wife.

Because Jacob loved Rachel so, he worked another seven years for her father. When those years were over, Jacob wanted to return again to Canaan, but Laban persuaded him to enter into a third bargain. Laban agreed to give Jacob part of his flocks and herds if Jacob would serve him another six years. This way Jacob was able to take care of his growing family.

During these last six years, the Lord blessed Jacob. His herds grew great in number; he acquired a number of servants; and his wives gave him a large family. But troubles began to develop between Jacob and Laban. Laban looked at Jacob's blessings and was jealous. He changed Jacob's wages ten times, and the two began quarreling over their property.

Then the Lord appeared to Jacob and told him that he had been with Laban long enough. The time had come for him to return to Canaan. God promised to guide him on the journey home.

When God appeared to Jacob, Laban was away shearing his sheep, so Jacob called his two wives to him, gathered up the rest of his family and his flocks, and left Haran without letting him know. When Laban came home and found that they had gone, three days had already passed. How upset he became! He took several men with him and rode after them; but before he reached them, the Lord appeared to him, also. He warned Laban not to harm his son-in-law.

Laban was not so angry with Jacob after this warning. When he found him, the two were able to settle their troubles. "The Lord watch over us while we are apart," said Laban; and he kissed his daughters and grandchildren a warm goodbye. Then he turned back toward his home in Haran; and Jacob's family continued once again their journey to the land of Canaan.

Questions:

1. Whom did Jacob meet at a well? 2. How long did Jacob agree to work in order to have Rachel for his bride? 3. Whom

did Laban give him to marry after the seven years? 4. How did he finally get to marry Rachel? 5. Why did Jacob decide to leave Haran? 6. What did Laban do when he found out? 7. Did they leave each other on friendly terms?

A Fight with an Angel

And he said, Thy name shall be called no more Jacob, but Israel.
Gen. 32:28

TWENTY years had passed since Jacob ran away from his home and from his brother Esau. He had left as a lonely young man; and now he was returning with two wives, eleven sons and a daughter, many servants, and large flocks and herds. Still he wondered if his brother was angry with him. Had he been forgiven? Was it safe to return?

God sent angels to strengthen Jacob on his trip, but still he decided to send some messengers ahead to announce to Esau that he was coming. The messengers found Esau living in a land southeast of Canaan and returned to Jacob with the message that Esau was coming to meet him. He was bringing with him four hundred men.

This message frightened Jacob. He thought that Esau was coming to kill him. He divided his family and possessions into two groups with the hope that if one was destroyed, the other would be able to escape. Earnestly he prayed that God would spare them, especially for the sake of the mothers and young children. Finally, he chose from his flocks and herds hundreds of animals to send ahead in droves as a present to Esau. The servants leading each drove of animals were to tell Esau when they met him that these were gifts to him from Jacob.

Jacob Wrestling with the Angel

Having sent these rich gifts, Jacob moved his family across a brook in the night; but he stayed on the other side of the bank to pray. As he prayed there in the dark, a strange man came and took hold of him and began to wrestle. All night the two fought; neither of them was able to get the better of the other. Finally as the dawn was breaking, Jacob realized that this was an angel of the Lord that he held.

"Let me go, for day is breaking," said the angel.

Jacob answered, "I will not let you go until you bless me."

"What is your name?" the angel asked.

"Jacob."

"From now on, your name will not be Jacob, but Israel, because you have wrestled with God," was the angel's reply. Israel means "a prince of God."

The strange contest left Jacob crippled in the hip, but he was no longer afraid to meet his brother. He rose to see Esau coming in the distance, and he went forward to meet him. When he reached him, he bowed before him in a very humble way seven times. There was no mistake about the way Esau felt now. He rushed to put his arms around Jacob, to kiss him, and to cry tears of joy.

Afterward Esau had questions about the company of women and children with Jacob. Jacob explained how God had blessed him greatly while he was in Haran and given him this fine family. Esau also inquired about the droves of animals that had met him. When he heard that they were gifts for him, he refused to take them, saying that he had great herds himself. Finally Jacob insisted that he take them, and he accepted.

Esau begged Jacob to return to his home with him, but Jacob wished to continue on toward Canaan. Esau left, and Jacob took his family to Shechem. Later God commanded that he go to Bethel, where he had seen the wonderful dream. God repeated His promise to him again there, and He also called Jacob by his new name, Israel.

From Bethel, Israel returned to his old home where his father Isaac was still living. On the way, a sad thing happened. His wife Rachel died when a little boy named Benjamin was born to her.

Poor old Isaac was glad to see his son return, but he did not live much longer. Together, his twin sons, Jacob and Esau, buried their father in the same cave where their mother, Rebekah, and their grandparents, Abraham and Sarah, lay. Many years of fighting for Jacob and Esau finally ended in love.

Questions:

1. Why was Jacob afraid to go home? 2. What did Jacob do so that Esau would forget his anger? 3. Who came to Jacob during the night? 4. What did he and Jacob do? 5. What did the angel tell Jacob? 6. Whom in the Bible do we call "Israelites"? 7. Was Esau still angry at Jacob?

Joseph, the Dreamer

Now Israel loved Joseph more than all his children, because he was the son of his old age: and he made him a coat of many colors.
Gen. 37:3

JACOB, whose new name was Israel, had a fine, large family of twelve sons; but there was one son he loved better than the others. This was Joseph, the oldest son of Rachel, the wife he had really chosen and cared for the most. Rachel died when her second little boy, Benjamin, was born; and Jacob then gave all his attention to Joseph. He gave Joseph a beautiful coat of many colors, and when Joseph wore it, everyone knew that he was the favorite son of a rich father.

Now all of Joseph's brothers except Benjamin were older than he was, and they disliked having their father pay so much attention to their younger brother. When Jacob gave Joseph the beautiful coat, they began to hate the boy. They never spoke kindly to Joseph. Finally, what made them most angry were the dreams that Joseph had.

In one dream, he and his brothers were in a field binding sheaves of grain. Joseph's sheaf stood upright, while those of the brothers bowed down to it. In the other dream he saw the sun, moon, and eleven stars bowing down to him. When Joseph told the boys of these dreams they became furious. "Do you think you are going to rule over us?" they asked angrily.

Joseph's Brothers with the Coat

Jacob himself wondered about his son's dreams. He wondered if the sun and moon in the dreams stood for Joseph's mother and father and the eleven stars for his brothers. Was it right for a father and mother to bow down to their son? He thought over the meaning of these things.

One day when Joseph was seventeen, Jacob called him to do an errand for him: "Your brothers have taken our flocks up to Shechem to find grass, and they have been gone quite a while now. I would like for you to take a few days and go up there to see how they are doing. You can bring news of them back to me."

It was a long trip for Joseph, and he had trouble finding his brothers, but at last he saw them with their great flocks in the distance. Meanwhile, Joseph's brothers had spotted him, for his bright coat was easy to recognize even far away.

"Here comes the dreamer," said one brother, making fun.

"I have heard enough from him," said another. "Let us get rid of him and then see what comes of his wonderful dreams."

"We can kill him and throw him into a pit."

"People will think that a wild animal got him." The others began to agree.

But Reuben, the oldest son, felt a little more kindly toward Joseph. "Let us not kill him; after all, he is our own brother. We can just put him down in this pit and leave him." In his heart Reuben planned to come back later and rescue Joseph.

So Joseph's own brothers grabbed him roughly, took his beautiful coat from him, and threw him down into an empty pit. Down in the darkness and dampness of the pit, Joseph cried to them to help him; but with no concern for him, the cruel men sat down and ate their lunch. While they were eating, they looked up to see someone else coming across the plain—not just a lonely traveler, but a whole caravan of merchants, traveling to Egypt with spices to sell.

"Here is a way to be rid of our brother and make some money, too," said Judah, one of the brothers. "Let us sell him to these Ishmaelite merchants." The others were willing, so they drew Joseph out of the pit and traded him to the merchants for twenty pieces of silver. As they divided the money among themselves, Joseph was carried away toward Egypt in the caravan of strangers. He looked back toward his brothers and his homeland, thinking that he would never see them again.

The brothers hoped that this was the last of Joseph. As far as they were concerned, the dreamer was gone forever! Reuben, however, had been gone when Joseph was sold. He was the one who had persuaded the others not to kill Joseph earlier. When he came back, hoping to rescue Joseph from the pit, he was dismayed to find him gone. Crying out, he turned to his brothers and asked how he could face their father. When they admitted to having sold Joseph, they made up a story to tell Jacob. Killing a goat from the flock, they dipped Joseph's coat in its blood.

When Jacob saw Joseph's coat, torn and rust-colored from blood, he thought that his son had been killed by some wild animal. He mourned for many days and could not be comforted. "I will go to my grave broken-hearted over my son," he wept. The brothers turned their eyes so their father could not see how guilty they looked, but they never told him the truth about Joseph.

God, however, knew just where Joseph was. It was He who had sent Joseph his strange dreams, and now He was planning to use Joseph's troubles to make these very dreams come true.

Questions:

1. How many children did Jacob have? 2. Who was his favorite? 3. Why did the other brothers hate Joseph? 4. What did they do to Joseph when he came looking for them? 5. Who wanted to save him? 6. What did the brothers tell their father about Joseph?

From Slave to Ruler

And Pharaoh said unto Joseph, Forasmuch as God hath shewed thee all this, there is none so discreet and wise as thou art.
Gen. 41:39

AFTER a long, slow trip with the camel caravan of Ishmaelites, to whom he had been sold by his brothers, Joseph finally arrived in the strange land of Egypt. As he looked about, he saw that the people looked different from his own; they spoke a language he did not understand. He was taken to a crowded market place and thrust upon a stand to be sold as a slave. Shoppers stopped to look him over, feel his muscle, and measure his strength. Surely he felt strange and alone. Finally, Potiphar, a captain of the guard and a friend of the Egyptian king, bought Joseph and took him to his home.

In this strange land and in a new home, doing the lowly work of a household slave, Joseph never forgot about the God that his father, Jacob, had served and taught him to love. The thought that God was with him made Joseph happy; and he worked busily, doing all his jobs well. Soon Potiphar noticed what a fine bargain he had gotten when he bought Joseph. He began to give more important jobs to him and soon Joseph was the manager of all Potiphar's house and his business.

Now Potiphar's wife was a wicked woman and she tried to get Joseph to do something wrong. He would not agree, knowing that Potiphar trusted him and more important,

Joseph Interprets Prisoners' Dreams

God was watching over him. Finally, when Potiphar's wife saw that he could not be persuaded, she decided to get even with him. When Potiphar came home, she told him lies about Joseph, lies that made Potiphar so angry that he had Joseph thrown in prison.

It seems unfair that Joseph was made to suffer so badly a second time for the evil of others, but this was God's way of causing something good to happen that would bring Joseph honor.

Bound in chains in an Egyptian jail, Joseph did not pout and feel sorry for himself, but he made friends with the others in the prison, even the jail-keeper himself. Soon the jail-keeper came to trust him as Potiphar once did, and he put Joseph in charge of all the other prisoners.

One day two new prisoners were given to Joseph to watch. Both came from the palace of the king, and the king had them thrown in prison for doing something that made him angry. One had been his chief butler; and the other, the chief baker. After they had been in the ward for a while, Joseph woke one morning to find both of them looking sad. Each had had a dream that left him worried.

"Tell me your dreams," said Joseph. "Perhaps my God will help us understand them."

"I dreamed I made wine from a vine that had three branches, and I gave the wine to Pharaoh, the king, in his cup," said the butler.

"This means that in three days you will be pardoned and placed back in Pharaoh's service. When you are set free, please remember me, for I have done nothing that they should put me in this prison."

The butler was happy and promised that he would.

Encouraged by the meaning of the butler's dream, the baker told his to Joseph: "In my dream there were three baskets of food for Pharaoh on my head. Birds came and ate out of the baskets."

"Your dream means that in three days you will be hanged and the birds will eat your flesh," Joseph said sadly.

Within three days all that Joseph had said did come true, but in his happiness at being back in Pharaoh's service, the butler forgot all about Joseph. For two more years Joseph waited in prison.

Then Pharaoh, the king, began having dreams also. So troubled was he that he called in all his magicians and wise men to try to find their meaning, but no one could give any help.

All of a sudden the chief butler remembered the young Israelite who had helped him when he was in jail. Immediately Joseph was sent for, cleaned up and given a change of clothes, and brought before Pharaoh. When the king asked him if he could tell the meaning of dreams, Joseph answered, "The power is not in me; God will give the answer to you through me."

Pharaoh did not know about the God Joseph worshiped, but he was desperate to know the answer to his dreams. "I dream of seven fat cows and of seven poor, lean cows who eat up the fat ones. In my other dream, seven poor, empty ears of corn eat seven full ears that are already on the stalk. What can this mean?" Pharaoh begged of Joseph.

Through God's power, Joseph could see that these dreams had the same meaning. He told Pharaoh that Egypt was going to have seven years of plenty—there would be more food than the people could eat. But after that, there would be seven years of famine when no food would grow. "I suggest that Pharaoh find a wise man and put him in charge of storing food during the years of plenty in order that the people will have something to eat during the years when nothing is growing," Joseph said.

Pharaoh was impressed by Joseph and decided to make him the ruler over the storing of food. From his own hand, the king took a ring and gave it to Joseph; then he gave him a fine robe and put a gold chain around his neck. A new Egyptian name was given to him, as well as a lovely Egyptian bride.

What changes came about that day! From a prison cell to next in command to the king of Egypt, Joseph had advanced. God's plan for his life was becoming more clear.

Questions:

1. To whom was Joseph sold as a slave? 2. Did Joseph do his work well? 3. Why did Potiphar put Joseph in prison? 4. What were the butler's and baker's dreams? 5. What was Pharaoh's dream? 6. Who told him what it meant? 7. What did the king do for Joseph?

Joseph's Brothers Learn the Truth

And Israel said, It is enough; Joseph my son is
yet alive: I will go and see him before I die.
Gen. 45:28

AS next in command to the Egyptian Pharaoh, Joseph had a very important job. He had told the king that there would be seven years of plenty followed by seven years of famine, and it was his duty to buy food and store it for the years of famine. Great storehouses were built and filled with grain as he directed.

Just as God had said, the years of plenty ended and nothing would grow. Then Joseph opened his storehouses and sold the grain that he had been saving. The people of Egypt began to look to him as their savior.

The famine spread to countries around Egypt, and people began coming long distances to buy grain from Joseph. Even the grazing lands of Canaan grew barren and dry. Old Jacob and his eleven sons had practically no food left.

Jacob called his sons in and said, "I hear that there is food in Egypt. Some powerful governor there had stored food and is selling it now. Go down and buy some grain, only leave Benjamin with me. He is my youngest and I cannot bear to see him go."

In Egypt the ten brothers were led to Joseph to purchase grain. During the years they had been separated from their

Joseph and His Brothers

brother, he had grown from a boy to be a great man, dressed in kingly robes; and they did not recognize him. But Joseph recognized them right away. However, he pretended not to know them and spoke harshly, accusing them of being spies.

The ten were dismayed at being called spies and tried to convince this mighty lord that they were honest men, trying to buy food to take back to their old father and a younger brother.

What news this was to Joseph! After twenty years, to find that his father, Jacob, was still alive! And Benjamin! Joseph began to form a plan in his mind so that he could see his precious younger brother.

"You still do not convince me that you are not spies," he told them. "In order to prove that you are honest, one of you must stay here in prison while the rest go home and bring your younger brother to me." But he could hardly continue talking about his long-lost family, and he had to leave the room so they would not see him cry.

Very worried, the brothers finally decided to let Simeon stay in Egypt while they took the grain home. Then on the way home they found the money they had paid for the grain still in the sacks, as Joseph had secretly told the workmen to leave it. They could not understand what was happening, but they were afraid that God was bringing trouble upon them because of the way they had once treated their own brother.

As much as his sons tried to persuade him, Jacob refused to let them take Benjamin back to Egypt. But the sacks of grain did not last forever, and again Jacob's house had no food. This time the sons, remembering the strange ruler and their brother Simeon still in prison, refused to go for more grain until Jacob gave permission for Benjamin to go also. One of the brothers, Judah, promised to take special care of Benjamin.

This time, the Israelite men took a number of gifts with them to Egypt, too. As they bowed low before Joseph again, Joseph could hardly bear to look at his younger brother without telling them who he was. But instead, he asked that they have dinner with him in his home. Afraid of what this meant, the men approached Joseph's house trying to make explanations for the money they had found in their grain sacks on the last trip. Instead of receiving a scolding, they had their brother Simeon given back to them.

During the dinner, Joseph tried to remain calm as he asked about the health of their old father and as he met Benjamin; but once again he had to leave the room to keep them from seeing the tears of excitement in his eyes.

This time when they left for home, he not only had his servants put their money back in their sacks, but he also had his own silver cup placed in Benjamin's sack. After he had given them time to be on their way, he sent his servants to search them and to find the cup.

The brothers told the servants over and over that none of them had stolen the cup; and when it was found in the sack, they were terrified. After they were led back to Joseph's house, they fell before Joseph trying to explain.

"Take any of us prisoner except Benjamin. If he does not return, our old father will surely die."

As they told the story of the old man's love for his son, Joseph could not control himself any longer. He held out his arms to them and cried, "I am Joseph!"

They stared, not believing him, but when they saw that indeed it was so and that he still loved them, they began begging his forgiveness.

"Do not be afraid of me or think that the thing you did was so bad," Joseph told them. "It was God's will that I come to Egypt so I could save you from hunger when the famine came. He had guided us all. Now go back to Canaan and bring our father here also."

So Jacob and his sons packed all their belongings and gathered together all their flocks and moved to Egypt, where they could find food until the famine was over. Because he thought so much of Joseph, Pharaoh gave them a special part of land at Goshen on which to settle. There Joseph was able to visit with his father and brothers often. Finally old Jacob died; but because he had asked it, his sons took his body back to Canaan and buried it in the cave with Abraham and Sarah, Isaac and Rebekah.

Questions:

1. What was Joseph's important job? 2. Why did his brothers come to Egypt? 3. How did Joseph make sure that they brought Benjamin? 4. Why were the men dragged back to Joseph by his servants? 5. Was Joseph still angry? 6. What did Joseph's family do?

A Princess Finds a Baby

And the child grew, and she brought him unto Pharaoh's daughter, and he became her son. And she called his name Moses: and she said, Because I drew him out of the water.
Ex. 2:10

WHEN Jacob moved his family down to Egypt during the famine, they intended to stay only until the grass began to grow on the grazing lands in Canaan again. But the longer they stayed, the larger their families grew and the harder it was to move back. Because he liked Joseph so, Pharaoh had given them a good place to live in Goshen; and they were soon well settled there. Finally Joseph grew old and died, and the Pharaoh he had served died also. The new Pharaoh had not known Joseph, and he treated Joseph's people unkindly.

By this time many years had passed and there were thousands of people whose grandfathers or great-grandfathers had been one of the twelve sons of Jacob, or Israel. The Egyptians called them Israelites, or Hebrews. Because there were so many Israelites the Egyptians grew afraid of them—afraid that they might someday turn against them. They were afraid of the powerful God that the Hebrews worshiped. So the new Pharaoh made slaves of the Hebrews. He had them to build great cities of brick for him, and he put officers over them who made them work harder and faster than ever.

Discovering the Baby Moses

Pharaoh's plan to weaken the Israelites did not turn out as he had hoped, however, for the harder he made them work, the stronger they became. He had to think of a new way to keep them from growing in number. The plan he finally decided upon was more horrible than the Hebrews could believe. Pharaoh commanded them to drown each baby boy that was born to them!

What a terrible command this was to try to obey! One Hebrew couple who had a baby boy born to them decided that they just could not kill their little child. He was such a fine little fellow! For three months they did not let anyone know that they had him; they hid him when anyone came to their house. Finally, the mother decided that she could not keep him hidden any longer. He wanted to be awake more now and to play.

So this mother, named Jochebed, made a waterproof basket of reeds and plastered it with pitch. Inside the little ark, she made a soft bed and placed her baby in it. Then she and her little girl carried it to the river Nile, and put it to float among some reeds. It was hard for the mother to leave her baby, but the little boy's sister stayed behind to watch what happened to the baby, afloat on the river.

Miriam, the sister, did not have long to wait before she heard voices approaching. As she peered through the tall reeds, who should she see coming but the daughter of the wicked Pharaoh. She and her maids were coming down to bathe in the river. As she stood in the water washing herself, the princess spied the floating basket and sent one of her maids to bring it to her. She was curious to know what was in it.

As she turned back the covers in the basket, the baby began to cry. Watching, Miriam held her breath. What would the princess do? The sight of the sweet baby crying touched the heart of the princess. "Why, he is a Hebrew baby whose mother is trying to save him," she cried. "He will come home with me and be my child. I will name him Moses because it means 'drawn out' and I have drawn him out of the water."

Miriam stepped out from behind the reeds and with a bowed head she approached the Egyptian princess. In her mind whirled a bold plan. If only it would work!

"Would you like for me to get a Hebrew nurse for the baby?" Miriam asked the noble lady. "I think I know where I can find one."

The princess was delighted to hire one of the child's own people to take care of him, but little did she know that the nurse Miriam brought to her was the baby's own mother! Yes, Moses' mother came to the palace and helped the princess take care of him.

Questions:

1. Why were God's people living in Egypt instead of their home in Canaan? 2. Why was the Egyptian king afraid of them? 3. How did he plan to make them weak? 4. What other command did he give when his first plan did not work? 5. How did one family save their baby boy? 6. Who found him on the river? 7. How did Moses' own mother get to take care of him?

Moses, an Egyptian Prince

Who made thee a prince and a judge over us? Intendest thou to kill me, as thou killedst the Egyptian?
Ex. 2:14

ALTHOUGH Moses was reared as an Egyptian prince and a grandson of the Pharaoh himself, his mother served as his nurse and taught him that he was really an Israelite, not an Egyptian. She taught him the Hebrew language that she spoke, and she told him the stories of his people. He heard about the early fathers of his nation—Abraham, Isaac, Jacob, and Jacob's twelve sons—and he learned of the one true God Whom they had worshiped. Moses' mother told him that some day their God was going to lead them away from Egypt and back to the land that He had promised them, a land where they would be free.

Meanwhile, the princess saw that Moses was treated just as any royal son would have been. He lived in the palace, wore splendid robes, and studied with special teachers. Until he grew to be a man, this was the only life that he knew. But when he was old enough to leave the palace, Moses began to learn of the way his own people were being treated by the Egyptians. As he visited the cities and fields where they were working under the whips of Pharaoh's officers, he saw that their life was hardly any better than the oxen and cattle Pharaoh owned. In fact, they were treated like animals.

Moses Kills an Egyptian

One day, Moses saw an Egyptian beating a Hebrew. He got very angry at the unfair way his fellow Hebrew was treated; and before he really thought, he killed the Egyptian. Seeing no one around, he hid the body in the sand.

The next day Moses saw two Hebrews fighting with each other, and he stepped in to stop the fight. The guilty man looked at him angrily and said, "Who made you our ruler and judge? Do you intend to kill me as you killed that Egyptian yesterday?"

Moses was stunned at these words. The news of his murder was known! The Israelites did not understand that he was only trying to help them; they thought he was someone from the palace whom they could not trust. And Pharaoh—he would hear the news soon! He would have Moses put to death when he heard of it.

So Moses fled from Egypt. Across the desert to the east, he hurried to hide in the wilderness of the land of Midian. The family he had grown up with in the palace would turn against him now because he had killed one of their people, the Egyptian. But the Hebrew people did not know if Moses stood with them either, for they knew him as a royal prince, one like Pharaoh's own sons. Now he had no one to turn to but the God his mother had taught him to worship long ago, when she was his nurse.

Questions:

1. What did Moses' mother teach him? 2. What things did the princess do for Moses? 3. What did Moses find out when he grew up and visited away from the palace? 4. What mistake did he make? 5. Why did he run away from Pharaoh?

The Burning Bush

And he said, Draw not nigh hither: put off thy shoes from off thy feet, for the place whereon thou standest is holy ground.
Ex. 3:5

IN the land of Midian, far away from the angry Pharaoh who wanted to take his life, Moses made friends with Jethro, the priest of Midian, and his family. Moses helped Jethro tend his flocks and he made his home with the old man. After some time had passed, he chose one of Jethro's seven daughters to be his wife. Her name was Zipporah.

Moses' life in Midian was different from the one he had lived in the Egyptian palace. He wore the rough robes of an outdoor man, and he grew tanned and tough as he stayed out in the wind and sun, watching Jethro's flocks. On his long, lonely journeys, guiding the sheep to far away pastures, he would remember his people back in Egypt. As he thought of them, he probably prayed to God to take away their suffering.

Meanwhile, back in Egypt, the king who had wanted to kill Moses died, and a new Pharaoh took his place. This one was even more cruel than the others, and the Israelites suffered worse than before. As they cried for help, God heard their prayers. He remembered the promise He had made to Abraham, Isaac, and Israel; and He decided that now He would take their people, the Israelites, back to the land He had promised them.

Moses and the Burning Bush

One day Moses was alone with his father-in-law's sheep, far away from home, near Mount Horeb. Suddenly, before his eyes he saw a bush bright with flames of fire, yet not burning up. He took a step forward to take a closer look when a voice came to him from the bush: "Moses! Moses! Come no closer! Take off your shoes for you are standing on holy ground."

Moses recognized the voice immediately. This was the same voice that had spoken to Adam and Eve in the garden, to Noah, to Abraham, Isaac, and Jacob; it was the voice of God. Now it was speaking to him!

"I have heard my people crying in Egypt, and I am going to rescue them from their suffering and take them back to the land I promised them," the Lord said. "Moses, you are the one I have chosen to lead them out of Egypt."

"Oh, Lord," Moses said humbly, "who am I that I could lead them?"

"I will be with you, Moses. I will help you bring them some day to this very mountain to worship me," the voice told him.

Then Moses asked, "What if the Hebrews ask me who appointed me to be their leader?"

"Tell them it is I who sent you, the God who has always lived and the One who spoke with their fathers."

"But, Lord, they do not know me. They will never believe me or trust me to lead them."

"What is that in your hand?" God asked Moses.

"A rod, my shepherd's staff," Moses answered.

The Lord commanded Moses to throw it down; and when he did, it became a snake. When Moses ran from it, the Lord told him to reach out and take it by the tail. When he obeyed, he found that he held only the rod in his hand again. Then God had Moses place his hand inside his robe. When he took it out, it was white and covered with the sores of leprosy, a terrible disease. But after he laid it inside his robe again, it came out healed, as it was before.

God told Moses that he could use these same signs to prove to the children of Israel that he had been chosen by their God to lead them. As a third sign, Moses would have the power to turn water into blood.

Still Moses had an excuse. "Oh, my Lord," he pleaded, "I cannot speak well enough to do this great work. I cannot make my mouth say what I mean to say."

"Did I not make your mouth?" the voice insisted. "I will help you with the things you say."

"Please, Lord, send someone better than I." Moses began again to make excuses, but the Lord was growing impatient. He said, "Your brother Aaron is a fine speaker. I will send him with you. Right now he is coming across the wilderness to meet you."

Surely enough, led by a message from God, Aaron left Egypt and traveled toward Midian, where Moses was. Sure that the Lord would give him strength to lead the Israelites, Moses returned to Jethro and asked for permission to leave him. Then, Moses and his family set out for Egypt. In his hand, Moses carried the shepherd's staff through which God had worked miracles. In his heart was the desire to be a leader from God to his people. He was sure now that God had saved him as a baby that day in the river Nile for just this reason.

On the journey, Moses met Aaron and they traveled toward Egypt together.

Questions:

1. What did Moses do in Midian? 2. What strange thing did Moses see on the mountain? 3. Name two signs God showed Moses to prove that He was God and that He would be with Moses. 4. What was Moses' last excuse? 5. Whom did God give him to help him overcome this?

A Stubborn King

And the heart of Pharaoh was hardened, neither would he let the children of Israel go; as the Lord had spoken by Moses.
Ex. 9:35

THE Lord had given Moses a great task—to lead His people, the children of Israel, from the land of Egypt back to Canaan. At first, Moses thought it was too hard for him to do, but the Lord gave him the power to do miracles and gave him his brother Aaron to be his helper and speaker. Knowing that God was with him made Moses brave enough to return to his people in Egypt. When he showed them the miracles the Lord had shown him and Aaron told them of the Lord's appearing to Moses in the burning bush, the Israelites believed that at last the Lord had heard their prayers and was going to take them away from their life as slaves to the Egyptian king.

Feeling that the people would follow them now, Moses and Aaron went to the court of the Egyptian king, who was known as Pharaoh. Dressed in their simple, rough robes, they looked odd in the middle of the riches of the palace. On his throne, Pharaoh looked with disgust upon the Hebrew shepherds. At first, they did not ask that Pharaoh let the people leave Egypt forever; instead they said: "Our Lord says that Pharaoh is to let His people go into the wilderness for three days to worship."

John H. Eggers Publications and The New York Public Library

The Israelites' Last Supper in Egypt

Pharaoh's look became one of scorn. He was not going to let his army of slaves leave. Where else would he find such able workers to build his great cities? His voice rang out, "I know why the Israelites are eager to go and worship—they do not have enough to keep them busy. I will see to it that they have more to do!"

So Pharaoh gave his officers the command that the Hebrews would not only have to make bricks, but that they would also have to find their own materials for making them. At the same time, he wanted as many bricks made as before. This was very hard on the Israelites. Often they could not do all that their masters demanded, and they were beaten badly. They became angry at Moses and Aaron and accused them of making their lives worse instead of better.

A second time, the brothers returned to Pharaoh. This time Moses showed Pharaoh the miracles the Lord had shown him in the wilderness. When Aaron threw his shepherd's staff upon the floor, it turned into a writhing snake. Pharaoh merely called in his wise men and magicians, who changed their rods into snakes also. Then, before their eyes, the snake from Aaron's rod swallowed up all the others.

The next morning, the Lord directed Moses and Aaron to show Pharaoh still another sign. As the king was walking out near the water, Aaron held his wonderful rod over the water. When he did, it turned into blood. A terrible smell rose from the bright, thick liquid; and the fish began to die. Cries arose from those gathering water to drink. Pharaoh returned with disgust to his house, but he would not change his mind about letting the Hebrews go. For seven days, the Egyptians did without water, then the Lord took away the blood and let the clear water return.

Again Moses stood before Pharaoh. "Will you let my people go now?" he asked. "Our God has more troubles in store for you unless you give us permission to worship Him." But Pharaoh refused and would not let them go.

This time when Aaron stretched out his rod, the Lord sent frogs upon all the land. Millions of frogs came up from the water and went into every house in Egypt. People found them in their ovens, in their dishes, and in their beds. Everywhere they stepped outside, there were frogs.

Pharaoh grew uneasy. He did not like these signs. He called to Moses and said, "If you will remove these frogs, I will let your people go." So Moses prayed to God, and He caused the frogs to die. There were so many that the Egyptians piled them up in great heaps and burned them. When Pharaoh saw that they were gone, he changed his mind and decided not to keep his word after all.

Then the Lord commanded Moses and Aaron to hit the ground with the rod; and when they did, the dust became lice. The little insects covered every man and every animal, but Pharaoh remained stubborn. Next, the Lord sent great swarms of flies, so that they filled the houses and the sky. Where the Israelites lived, in the land of Goshen, however, there were no flies.

At this, Pharaoh began to give in a little. He called Moses and said, "Why can you not worship here in Egypt?"

"It would make the Egyptians angry to see us making our sacrifices here in their land," Moses answered.

"All right. You may go and worship, but you must not go far away and you must come back," said Pharaoh. "Now, pray to your God to take away these terrible flies."

Once more Moses asked God to remove the plague; and when He did, Pharaoh again broke his promise.

Other torments were sent by God upon Pharaoh and the Egyptians—diseases on all their herds and flocks, boils on every person, hail that ruined every field, locusts that ate everything the hail had spared, and a thick darkness for three days and nights. Only God's chosen people in the land of Goshen were saved from the plagues.

Finally, after the three days of darkness, Pharaoh became very angry. When Moses came before him again, he could not bear to hear any more about the Hebrews and their God. "Get out of my sight!" he shouted to Moses. "If I see you again, I will have you killed!"

"Very well," said Moses. "You have seen me the last time."

Then God told Moses that there would be only one more plague—a plague so terrible that Pharaoh would change his mind and let the people go. "The time has come," the Lord said, "for the Israelites to get ready to leave Egypt."

Questions:

1. How did Moses show the Israelites that God had sent him to lead them? 2. Why did Pharaoh not want the people to go? 3. Name the plagues God sent to try to make Pharaoh let the people go. 4. Did Pharaoh keep his word to Moses?

Blood on the Doorposts

And when I see the blood I will pass over you, and the plague shall not be upon you to destroy you, when I smite the land of Egypt.
Ex. 12:13

ALTHOUGH the people of Israel had wondered about Moses at first, it soon became clear that God was with him. Whenever Moses and Aaron used their wonderful rod, the Lord sent all kinds of plagues upon the enemies of the Israelites—the Egyptians. And while there was hail in Egypt, the Israelites' homeland had fine weather; when the diseases came, they stayed healthy; when the darkness covered Egypt, they worked in bright sunshine.

Now the time had come for them to prepare to leave Egypt. The Lord had told Moses that He was about to send His last plague upon Pharaoh. At midnight He was going to pass through the land and the oldest son in every house would die. This plague was going to be so terrible that Pharaoh was going to change his mind and send the Israelites away.

In order to keep the death plague from hurting them, God told Moses some special things He wanted His people to do. Each family was to take a lamb and kill it as they would for a sacrifice. Then they were to take its blood and sprinkle it at the doorway of their house, on the frame over the door and on each side. When the Lord came, He would pass over the houses where He saw the blood of the lamb,

The Death of the First Born

and no child would die there. The lamb itself was to be cooked with some vegetables and prepared for a big dinner. When the family ate the dinner, they were to be dressed with their shoes and coats on, ready to leave Egypt at any moment.

Quickly the Israelites set about to obey the commands of God. The lamb was cooked and its blood sprinkled on the doorposts. Each family sat down, dressed for traveling, to eat the lamb and little flat wafers, specially prepared for the dinner. The dinner or feast, was known as the first Passover, for it was eaten on the night when the Lord *passed over* the Israelites and struck the homes of the Egyptians. It became a great feast for the Hebrew people, and they ate the same kind of dinner every year afterward, as they were commanded. It reminded them of the wonderful way God saved them.

Promptly at midnight, death rushed through the land. Not one house of the Egyptians was missed. In every home, from Pharaoh's palace to his lowest servant's cottage, the oldest boy fell dead. A cry went up from the Egyptians as their children were taken from them. In the middle of the night Pharaoh sent for Moses and Aaron and said, "Take your people and go. Take everything you have and get out of our land. And pray to your God to harm me no more."

Moses and Aaron hurried back to their people. This was the time for which they had been waiting! Four hundred and thirty years had passed since Jacob took his family down into Egypt to be with Joseph during the famine. Now that family of twelve sons had become a nation of more than a million people, divided into twelve tribes, according to the son from which they came.

What a procession the group made! Thousands of people, from babies to grandmothers, many with packs of clothes or dishes or food upon their backs, marched out of Egypt as God led them. Behind them came cattle, sheep, and goats, braying and bleating in their attempt to follow the crowd. Gone forever were the days of slavery in Egypt, for their God was leading them home to the land He had promised their fathers long before.

Questions:

1. Had the plagues God sent bothered the Israelites? Why? 2. What was the last and most terrible plague going to be? 3. How were the Israelites going to stay safe from this plague? 4. What was the name of the special dinner, or feast, they ate that night? 5. How were they dressed when they ate it? 6. What did Pharaoh do when this last plague came? 7. Were there many Israelites to leave Egypt?

The Sea Opens Up

And Moses stretched out his hand over the sea; and the Lord caused the sea to go back by a strong east wind all that night, and made the sea dry land, and the waters were divided.
Ex. 14:21

AT last the Israelites were on their way from Egypt to the land of Canaan, the land God had promised them long ago. During the four hundred years that the family of Jacob and his twelve sons had spent in Egypt, each father had told his children of the blessings that God had given his special people through Abraham, Isaac, and Jacob. Each child wondered if he would be one of those to see the green grazing lands where Abraham had first heard the promises. Now that time had finally come.

Instead of following the shortest road to Canaan, the Lord told Moses to lead the people toward the Red Sea and the wilderness around it. He did this so that they would not have to pass through the land where the warlike Philistines lived. Moses knew this country near the Red Sea, for it was here that he had watched over Jethro's flocks. At the head of the long parade of Israelites Moses marched, with the Lord leading the way in a pillar of cloud by day and a pillar of fire at night.

When Pharaoh realized that the Israelites had gone, he was sorry that he had no more slaves to do his hard work. News reached him that they had made their way into the wilderness and were hemmed in by the mountains and the

Crossing the Red Sea

Red Sea, and he decided to follow and recapture them. Calling his captains, he commanded them to prepare the war chariots for battle.

In their swift chariots and on trained horses, the army of Pharaoh soon caught up with the Israelites, who had been walking. When the Israelites looked up and saw the dust stirred up by Pharaoh's army in the distance, they grew very frightened. "Are we any better off now than we were in Egypt?" they cried to Moses. "It would have been better to have stayed there as slaves than to come into the wilderness only to be killed."

But Moses remembered the wonders that the Lord had done in Egypt, and he knew that some way the Lord would help them now. "Do not be afraid," he told the people. "The Lord is going to fight for you."

Then as the night fell, the pillar of cloud that had been guiding the Israelites moved between them and the Egyptians so that the Egyptian army could not see ahead. They pitched camp for the night, planning to attack the Israelites in the morning. But in the Israelite camp, no one settled down to rest. By Moses' order they prepared once again to march. Right up to the bank of the Red Sea they went.

Then a marvelous thing happened. Moses held his rod above the waters of the sea, and a strong wind began to blow. It blew so hard that the water parted right down the center, making a path of dry ground walled in on either side by great banks of water. With Moses leading the way, the Israelites walked straight across the Red Sea.

When the Egyptians saw the Israelites marching into the sea, they quickly jumped onto their horses and into their chariots and followed. But as they entered the path through the sea, the Lord looked down from the pillar of cloud and made it difficult for the Egyptians to make their chariots go. Wheels began to fly off; and as they looked at the mighty walls of water surrounding them, they became afraid. "Let us forget the Israelites!" they cried. "Their God is too powerful and strong for us to fight."

By this time, the last of the Israelites had reached the shores on the other side of the Red Sea and were watching the Egyptian army coming after them. Once more, at God's command, Moses stretched forth his rod over the sea. The walls of water trembled, leaned, and then with a mighty roar they collapsed, swallowing up the Egyptian army with one crushing blow. As the Israelites watched the bodies of the soldiers rising with the waves, they bowed their heads in silence at the great power of their God.

Then Moses began to sing, and all the voices joined in with the words:

"I will sing unto the Lord, for he has triumphed:
The horse and his rider He has thrown into the sea.
The Lord is my strength and my song,
And He has saved me."

Questions:

1. Why did the Israelites not take the shortest way to Canaan? 2. What did Pharaoh do when he realized his slaves were gone? 3. Why could the Egyptian soldiers not see the Israelites preparing to cross the Red Sea? 4. How did the Israelites get across the sea? 5. What happened to Pharaoh's soldiers when they tried the same thing?

Food from Heaven

And Moses said unto them, This is the bread which the Lord hath given you to eat.
Ex. 16:15

IN order to reach the promised land of Canaan, the Israelites had to travel through miles of desert and across many mountains. With so many thousands of people and great herds and flocks, food and water became very scarce. Sometimes the water that they found was not clean enough to drink. One time God had Moses cast a tree into some bitter water, and it became clear and sweet for drinking.

But they had to move on from the good streams, and the paths grew rougher as they approached the great Mount Sinai. Grumbling began to arise from the crowds of people. They complained to Moses and Aaron that their food had been better back in Egypt, even though they had been slaves. "When you speak like this to us," Moses told them, "you are really speaking against the Lord. Do you not remember that He is leading us and taking care of us? He will not forget us now."

The Lord did not forget them. He said to Moses: "I will send food from heaven to you—bread each morning and quail, a kind of bird, each evening. Every day you are to gather just enough for one day, for it will not keep without spoiling. On the sixth day of the week, however, I will let you gather enough for two days because I will not send any on the seventh day. It is to be your day of rest."

John H. Eggers Publications and The New York Public Library

Gathering of the Manna

Just as the Lord said, the next morning when the people woke up, they found little white flakes like frost or snow on the ground. They turned to each other and asked in the Hebrew language, "What is it?" The word for this is "Manhu" and some think that this was the reason they afterward called it "manna."

Moses told them, "This is the bread which the Lord has given for you to eat." Everyone got a basket and began gathering the manna. When they tasted it, they found that it tasted like wafers flavored with honey. It was delicious cooked many different ways; and no matter how much a man gathered, there was plenty for his family. When the sun came up bright and strong, what was left on the ground melted like frost.

Some were greedy and disobeyed God by gathering too much. The next day they found that it was rotten and spoiled and smelled bad. God wanted them to trust in Him to send their food each day.

In the evening, quail came up and covered the camp, so the Lord provided meat for His people also. Six days every week, the Israelites received food from heaven, and on the seventh day they ate the extra that they had gathered the day before. Once a week, God let them keep more than they needed without having it spoil. This way they learned that one day in the week they were to rest as God did on the seventh day of His creation. This day was a holy day to God, and the Israelites called it the Sabbath, which means "day of rest."

The manna continued to fall day by day as long as the Hebrews traveled in the wilderness. Not until they reached the land of Canaan forty years later did God cause it to stop.

Questions:

1. Was the trip to the promised land an easy one? 2. What was especially hard to find? 3. Why did the people want to go back to Egypt? 4. What food did God send? 5. When did the manna come and what did it look and taste like? 6. How much were the people supposed to gather? 7. When could they gather more? Why? 8. How long did God send the manna and quail?

God Speaks from the Mountain

And the Lord said unto Moses, Lo, I come unto thee in a thick cloud; that the people may hear when I speak with thee, and believe thee for ever.
Ex. 19:9

AFTER three months in the wilderness, camping in several places, the Israelites came to the foot of Mount Sinai. Here they pitched their tents and made a more permanent camp where they could stay for a while. Moses looked fondly around the mountain, for it was nearby that he first talked with God in the burning bush. It was nearly impossible to believe that he had really led the Israelites safely out of Egypt since he had last been here.

Then the voice of God spoke to Moses from the mountain: "These people are a treasure to me. I am going to make them a holy nation. Tell them to clean themselves and wash their clothes and prepare their minds, for in three days they are going to see my glory on this mountain. Make a line around the mountain so that no person or animal will cross it and touch the mountain while I am here."

God's people did as they were told, and they were waiting and praying when the third day arrived. Then suddenly there was lightning and loud thunder from the mountain, a large cloud settled on the very top, smoke began pouring forth as though it were on fire, and the whole mountain shook. A sound of trumpets came, louder and louder, until the people grabbed one another in fear before God.

John H. Eggers Publications and The New York Public Library

Moses Breaks the Tablets

Then out of the cloud came the voice of God, announcing Himself so that all could hear: "I am the Lord your God, who brought you out of the land of Egypt, out of the house of bondage." Then He gave them the rules they were to follow as His people. These rules, known as the Ten Commandments, are like this:

I. Thou shalt have no other gods before me; or, I am the one true God, the One you must worship.

II. Thou shalt not make unto thee any graven image; or, you must not worship idols or gods made by men.

III. Thou shalt not take the name of the Lord thy God in vain; or, you must not speak or think lightly of the Lord.

IV. Remember the Sabbath day, to keep it holy; or, you must rest and worship the Lord on the seventh day.

V. Honor thy father and thy mother; or, love and obey your parents.

VI. Thou shalt not kill; or, you must not take the life of any person.

VII. Thou shalt not commit adultery; or, husbands and wives must love and be faithful to one another.

VIII. Thou shalt not steal; or, you must not take things that are not your own.

IX. Thou shalt not bear false witness against thy neighbor; or, you must not tell a lie about anyone.

X. Thou shalt not covet; or, you must not want something that is not yours.

After God had given these rules and His voice had died away, the people were still afraid. They said to Moses, "Let

God speak to you, Moses, and you tell us what He says, for we fear His voice."

"He came to you this way in order for you to know His power and be afraid to disobey Him," Moses explained. Then, taking only Aaron, Aaron's sons, seventy of the wisest and oldest Israelites, and his special helper Joshua, Moses began to climb the mountain. After they got far enough up to see a little of the glory of God, Aaron and his sons and the elders went back down to the camp. Only Joshua and Moses continued climbing higher. At last Moses left Joshua on the side of the mountain and disappeared into the cloud that covered the top. For forty days and nights, he stayed with God alone on Mount Sinai. God gave him many other rules for the Israelites to follow. Most of them told how they should treat one another and how they should worship Him. He also gave Moses two tables of stone on which He had written the Ten Commandments.

The people had not expected Moses to be gone so long, and they began to think that he was not coming back. They begged Aaron to make them a god they could see. So Aaron took the gold jewelry that they gave him, melted it, and shaped it into a golden calf. The Israelites were pleased with the idol; and they declared a holiday and began worshiping it with songs and games, the way they had seen the Egyptians do.

While Moses and Joshua were coming down the mountain, they heard the cries of the people, dancing and singing around the golden calf. When they caught sight of the camp, Moses became so angry and discouraged that he threw down the tables of stone on which the Ten Commandments were written, and they broke into little pieces.

The Israelites were punished for having disobeyed God's second commandment so soon. Those who started the calf worship were killed, and Moses took the golden calf and broke it to pieces. Then he ground it into a fine powder, mixed it with water, and made the people drink some of it as part of their punishment.

But Moses loved these people that he had brought from Egypt, and he went back up on the mountain to ask God to give them another chance. God did forgive them and wrote the Commandments again on new tables of stone. Moses stayed with Him for another forty days and talked with Him as a friend, closer than any other man ever did. When he came down from the mountain, his face was shining from having been so close to God. It was so radiant and bright that he had to put a cloth over it when he talked with the people.

Questions:

1. How did God come down on Mount Sinai? 2. What happened to the mountain? 3. Can you name the ten rules, or commandments, God gave the people? 4. Why did the people want Moses to go and talk with God? 5. How long did Moses stay with God on the mountain? 6. What did God give him? 7. What did the people do while Moses was gone? 8. How were they punished?

A Place for Worship

Then a cloud covered the tent of the congregation,
and the glory of the Lord filled the tabernacle.
Ex. 40:34

ONE of the things that God spoke to Moses about when they were on Mount Sinai together was the way He wanted His chosen people to worship Him. All of the people the Israelites had ever seen worshiped carved statues, or idols. But God's second commandment had said that they were not to bow down to other gods nor to make any idols. The one true God is a spirit and lives everywhere, so we do not have to have a statue to remind us where He is.

But God knew that it would be a long time before the people could understand this, and He gave them a place for worship that they could see, one that would remind them that He was with them at all times. Because the Israelites were camping in the wilderness, traveling from place to place when the pillar of cloud and fire moved, the place of worship was to be something like a tent. It was called a tabernacle. Every part of it was to be made in such a way that it could be quickly taken down, packed up, and carried to a new camping ground.

The directions for making the tabernacle and all that went with it were given to Moses while he was on the mountain; then he told the people exactly what God

John H. Eggers Publications and The New York Public Library

Making the Tabernacle

wanted. He saw that it was going to take much expensive material—gold, silver, bronze, fine linen, goats' skin, wood, oil, spices, and precious stones—so he simply asked the people to give for the tabernacle as they felt in their hearts they should. No one was commanded to give any particular amount, but they brought so much that the builders had to ask Moses to make the people stop.

Not only did the people give the materials for making their house of worship, they also gave their time. Those who had the ability built the frames, wove the curtains, molded the metal, or sewed the priestly robes. In charge of it all were two skilled workers, Bezalel, of the tribe of Judah, and Oholiab, of the tribe of Dan. These two put on all the finishing touches, did the elaborate weaving, and carved the figures in the wood and metal. For nearly a year the Israelites camped near Sinai, building the house of worship.

When all the separate parts of the place of worship were ready, the tabernacle was set into place. This was done on the first day of the first month of the year, the second year after they left Egypt. When it was finished, the tabernacle looked something like this:

Surrounding the tabernacle itself was a courtyard, built exactly in the center of the camp. Outside its entrance was the tent where Moses lived. The courtyard was open, but it had a high curtain around it, hung from bronze poles. The curtain was made of bright colored linen and was higher than a man's head, although there was an opening on one side where the priests could enter.

MANCHOLA

Lot and His Daughters

GAULLI

The Sacrifice of Isaac

MURILLO

Jacob and Rachel

CORNELIUS

Joseph Makes Himself Known

IHLEE

Moses in the Bulrushes

FETI

Moses Before the Burning Bush

Rembrandt

Moses Breaks the Tablets

REMBRANDT

Balaam and His Donkey

BLOCH

Samson at the Treadmill

Poussin

Ruth and Boaz

VICTORS

Hannah Brings Samuel Before Eli

RUBENS

Solomon's Judgment

Near the entrance, inside the court, stood a large altar. The altar was the place on which the Israelites laid their offering and worshiped God by burning it. It was usually made by piling up stones or by carving a place to build a fire out of a large rock. This altar, however, was built of wood, covered inside and out with bronze so the wood would not burn. It had no bottom or top, but there was a grating inside on which to build the fire and lay the offering. The ashes would fall on the ground underneath. Rings of metal were fastened on each corner; and when camp was moved, poles were placed through the rings and the priests could carry the altar on their shoulders.

Beyond the altar was a large basin called a laver. The laver held water with which the priests washed the offerings.

The laver was near the door of the tabernacle itself. The tabernacle looked like a large tent, but its walls were made of board covered with gold and mounted in silver frames. These frames could be taken apart and carried about, but they made the tabernacle sturdy. The boarded walls made up three sides of the tent, but the front was covered only with a curtain. Several curtains made the roof of the tent. The inside one was beautifully woven and decorated; the outside one was of goats' skin to protect the tabernacle from the weather.

The inside of the tabernacle was divided into two rooms. The front one was twice as large as the other and was called the Holy Place. It contained a table covered with gold, on which were placed twelve loaves of bread to represent the twelve tribes; a golden lampstand with seven branches; and an altar of incense, where gum was burned to give off a sweet odor.

The smaller room was called the Holy of Holies, and only the high priest entered this room once a year. It held a wooden chest, covered with gold and intricate carving. Inside the chest lay the tables of stone with the Ten Commandments written upon them. Over the chest two figures called cherubim were carved. This was the place where God Himself was to dwell.

When the tabernacle was in place and the last curtain was hung, the pillar of cloud settled over the tent and the glory of the Lord filled it. Throughout the rest of their journeys, this was where the pillar of cloud by day and of fire by night remained. Whenever it moved, the Israelites knew that they were to leave and follow.

Questions:

1. Who told the Israelites how to make their place of worship? 2. What was it called? 3. Why was it built so it could be moved about? 4. Did Moses have trouble getting the people to give money and goods so that the tabernacle could be built? 5. Name two things that were in the courtyard of the tabernacle. 6. How many rooms were in the tabernacle? 7. Where did God stay?

Two Spies Against Ten

If the Lord delight in us, then he will bring us into this land,
and give it us; a land which floweth with milk and honey.
Num. 14:8

AFTER the tabernacle, the new house of worship, was finished, the pillar of cloud that stayed over it moved one day. The Israelites knew that the time had come for them to leave Mount Sinai and continue on their journey to the land God had promised them. For several months they traveled, walking for a few days, then camping and resting for a while, gradually coming closer and closer to the border between the desert and the promised land.

At last they pitched camp at Kadesh-barnea, right on the border of Canaan. Now the land of Canaan was not empty and simply waiting for the Israelites to move in. People were living there who had been there for many years and had built fine cities. God suggested that Moses select some men to go over into Canaan and see what it was really like. Then they could return and tell the other Israelites about it. This seemed better than marching right in without knowing what to expect.

Moses chose a leader from each of the twelve tribes to go into Canaan. He told them to be sure and remember the kind of land that they found there, the food that could be grown, the kind of people living there, and the cities they had built.

John H. Eggers Publications and The New York Public

The Grapes of Canaan

In the fall of the year, just as the grapes were ripening, the men left on their scouting trip. For forty days they walked all over the land of Canaan, noticing the things that Moses had mentioned. Before they came back to their camp again, they cut a cluster of grapes that was so large it had to be carried between two men on a pole. They also brought back some figs and pomegranates, special fruit grown in that land.

When the men returned, all the people gathered to hear what they had learned. The men said, "This is as good a land as God told us it would be—see these grapes that we gathered in its vineyards? But the people who live there are stronger than we are, and the cities are so protected that we could never capture them."

Caleb, one of the spies, broke in: "The land is wonderful, as you have said. And with the help of God, I know that we could take it. Let us get ready to go at once."

But all the other scouts except Joshua disagreed. "No," they said, "there is no use to try to make war on those people. They are so big they make us look like tiny grasshoppers."

This message made the people scared. They, too, were afraid that they could not take the land. They did not believe that God was strong enough to help them overcome any enemy. All night they complained to Moses and Aaron. "Why did we ever leave Egypt?" some asked. "God brought us into the wilderness only to let us die here. Let us choose another leader who will take us back to Egypt."

Joshua and Caleb stood before the people and did everything they could to persuade them to go on into the new land. But the people became so angry with them that they wanted to kill them.

Just then the glory of the Lord, which stayed in the tabernacle within the Holy of Holies, shone from the tabernacle so that everyone could see it. God was so disappointed in the people that He wanted to leave them. But because Moses prayed for them and begged God to forgive them God changed His mind.

But God did not let the people go unpunished. The ten spies who had been afraid were killed. All of the other people who were over twenty years old were told that they would never get to go into the promised land of Canaan. They would have to stay in the wilderness another forty years, one year for each day the scouts spent in Canaan, until their children grew up in their place. Of the adults then living, only Joshua and Caleb, the faithful spies, would live to enter the land of Canaan.

God knew that Moses could teach the children as they grew up to love and trust Him more than their parents had and that he could also train them for war. They would never remember the life of slavery in Egypt that had made their parents so weak and unsure.

Some of the people decided to march upon the land of Canaan anyway; but the Lord did not go with them, and they were killed in battle. The others turned toward the desert again, and there they stayed for forty years.

Questions:

1. Why did the Israelites not cross the border and go right into Canaan? 2. What were the scouts supposed to do? 3. What was the report they brought back? 4. Which two spies were not afraid? 5. Why was God angry? 6. How did He punish the people? 7. Who was going to get to go into Canaan?

An Animal Speaks

And Balaam answered and said unto the servants of Balak, If Balak would give me his house full of silver and gold, I cannot go beyond the word of the Lord my God, to do less or more.
Num. 22:18

AFTER the long journey through the wilderness to the border of the promised land, the Israelites became afraid to go across. They believed the ten foolish scouts who told them that the Canaanites were too mighty for them to fight. They did not believe that God could make them strong enough to go ahead and take the land. So God punished them by sending them back into the wilderness to live for forty years.

During this long period of time Moses stayed with the Israelites and was their leader. He settled the problems and quarrels that came up. Aaron and his sons were God's priests and served Him in the tabernacle. They helped the other Israelites make sacrifices there. God sent manna and quail for the people to eat, and He also made sure that their clothes and shoes never wore out.

Over the years, those who had been afraid of the Canaanites died, and their children grew up and became the new leaders. While they were young, these Israelites had been trained for war and had been taught by Moses to believe that God could help them do anything. They were glad one day to see the pillar of cloud leave the place where it stayed over the tabernacle and lead them once again toward the land of Canaan.

John H. Eggers Publications and The New York Public Library

Balaam and the Donkey

This time, the people wanted to go to Canaan through the land of the Edomites, who came from Esau's family. When the Edomites would not let them, they went all the way around their land because they did not want to fight with their kinsmen. Remember that Esau was Jacob's twin brother and all the Israelites were from Jacob's family.

But when the Amorites would not let them pass through their land, the Israelites fought with them and won their first battle. They even killed Sihon, the king. Later they won a battle with the people of Bashan and killed Og, their king.

After this, the news began to travel that the Israelites were coming and that their God was making them strong in battle. Balak, the king of the Moabites, saw that they would try to pass through his land next. He was afraid to fight with them, so he sent for a prophet named Balaam. He wanted Balaam to put a curse on the Israelites and make them weak. When the king's messengers found Balaam, he told them that they would have to spend the night with him while he thought about King Balak's problem. During the night, God appeared to Balaam and told him that the Israelites were His people and for Balaam not to curse them. When morning came Balaam sent the messengers back to Balak with this message: "I cannot curse these people. The Lord has blessed them."

When Balak heard that Balaam would not come curse the Israelites, he sent some more messengers to the prophet. These were princes and more noble men than the others had been. With them, they brought many gifts to Balaam.

They urged Balaam to take the gifts and to come with them to King Balak. Now Balaam did not really love God and he wanted to take the presents and go with the men, but he knew that God was very powerful. He said, "It would not matter if the king gave me his palace full of silver and gold; if God does not want me to curse these people, I cannot do it." Then he asked them to stay all night while he asked once more if he could go. This time God agreed that he could go with the princes if he would be careful to do only what God told him.

The next morning Balaam saddled up his ass and he and two servants rode away with the messengers. On the way some strange things began to happen. An angel of the Lord, with a sword in his hand, appeared in the middle of the road, but only Balaam's ass saw it. The frightened animal turned off the road and went running across a field, much to Balaam's surprise. Holding onto her tightly, Balaam hit the ass and finally led her back to the road.

Later on, as they were going through a narrow passage through a vineyard, with walls on either side, the ass saw the angel again. This time she pushed up against the wall, pressing Balaam's foot between her and the wall. Once more Balaam got angry and hit the animal to make her move.

Then the angel went on ahead and stood in the road at a narrow place where there was no room to turn at either side. When the ass came upon the angel there, she lay right down in the middle of the road with Balaam on her back.

Now this made Balaam very angry. What was wrong with this ass? How was he ever going to get to King Balak? He began beating the animal with a stick.

Then the Lord did a strange thing—he gave the ass the power to speak. The ass asked Balaam, "What have I done to make you beat me three times?"

"Why, you have made fun of me," Balaam replied. "If I had a sword right now I would kill you!"

"Have you not been riding on me for a long time, Balaam?" the donkey asked. "Have I ever done like this before?"

"No," Balaam admitted, and when he looked up, he, too, saw the angel with the sword standing in the way. He bowed before the angel and said that he had not seen it before. He offered to go back home again if the Lord did not want him to go to see Balak.

"Go ahead," the angel replied. "But remember not to say anything except that which God tells you."

When Balaam reached the king, Balak took him to a high mountain where they could see the Israelites camped below. They built altars and made sacrifices and then Balaam knew it was time for him to curse the Israelites. But when he opened his mouth, he could only say good things about them.

Balak was displeased at the prophet and he took him to another mountain and gave him another chance. Still he could only bless God's people. A third time Balaam tried, at another place, and again the Lord only sent blessings to his mouth.

Now Balak was very angry at Balaam for blessing his enemies instead of cursing them. "I will not give you the presents I had for you," he told Balaam.

But it seems that Balaam had said the words of God only because God had not let him say anything else. He was sorry that he could not have the gifts Balak had for him. He helped King Balak think of another way to harm the Israelites. Together they planned to make the Israelites bow down to idol gods. Was not that a terrible thing for Balaam to do when he knew that the God of the Israelites was the only true God? God punished him for it by letting him be killed when the Israelites finally fought against the Moabites.

Surely Balaam would have been better off if he had followed his animal home instead of ever going to see Balak.

Questions:

1. Against whom did the Israelites win their first battle? 2. How was King Balak going to try to make the Israelites weak? 3. Why did Balaam not go to the king as he had been asked? 4. What strange thing happened on the trip when Balaam finally did go? 5. Did Balaam do as Balak asked? Why not? 6. Was Balaam really a good man? How do we know?

An Old Leader and a New One

And there arose not a prophet since in Israel like unto Moses, whom the Lord knew face to face.
Deut. 34:10

DURING the years that the Israelites lived in the wilderness, Moses was a good leader. He tried always to make the people obey God and the laws God had given them while they camped at Mount Sinai. But Moses was just a man, and like everyone, he made mistakes. One day he made the bad mistake of disobeying God before all the people. God had told Moses to speak to a certain rock and water would come forth for the people to drink. Moses was not content just to speak to the rock, however; he took his rod and hit it, too.

God was displeased that Moses had acted in this way. He told Moses that, like the other disobedient ones who had come from Egypt, he was not going to be able to go into the promised land. Moses was sorry, but he knew that he had done wrong. Still, it was sad for him to know that after all these years of waiting in the wilderness, he was not going to get to go into Canaan with those he had trained to capture it.

By the time the Israelites had fought the Amorites and the Moabites and made their way right up to the Jordan River and the land of Canaan, only three men were living

John H. Eggers Publications and The New York Public Library

Moses Sees the Promised Land

of all the grown men who had marched out of Egypt —Moses, Joshua, and Caleb. Joshua and Caleb had been the only scouts who had given a good report when they had spied out the land of Canaan forty years before. At that time, God had promised them that they would live to go into the land.

Moses was one hundred twenty years old at this time, and his work was over, for he had led God's people from Egypt to the land God had promised them. God was going to choose another younger man to lead the Israelites in the battles to capture Canaan.

Moses called the people together and told them the things he wanted them to be sure to remember. He told them about the things God had done for them. He gave them once more the laws God wanted them to obey. He reminded them to teach their children to worship God and keep His commandments. Then he sang a farewell song and taught it to the people.

Finally, he laid his hands on the new leader God had chosen. It was Joshua, the faithful scout and Moses' good friend who had gone with him up on Mount Sinai. The power of God's Spirit that had been with Moses went to Joshua.

All alone, Moses left the camp and climbed to the top of Mount Nebo. Here God let him see the land of promise, even though he could not cross over to it. He saw the mountain where Abraham, Isaac, and Jacob were buried, the pasture where they had fed their cattle, the city of Jerusalem, and far away, the Great Sea. Moses was thankful that his people were at last going to live in this place after spending so many years as slaves and wanderers.

While he was alone with God on the mountain, Moses died; and God Himself buried him in a place that no one knows.

The Israelites were very sad that Moses had left them, and they mourned for many days. They knew that no other would quite be able to take his place, for the Bible tells us that no other man talked with God so freely, as a friend. But they trusted their new leader, Joshua, and they knew that he, too, would lead them as God led him.

Questions:

1. Why did Moses not get to go into the promised land? 2. Who were the only ones who came from Egypt who did get to go in? 3. Why did they get to? 4. What did Moses say to the people before he left them? 5. Who was chosen to be the new leader in Moses' place? 6. What did God let Moses see before he died? 7. Who buried Moses and where?

A Narrow Escape

And it shall be, when the Lord hath given us the land, that we will deal kindly and truly with thee.
Joshua 2:14

FORTY years had passed since Joshua and Caleb and the other ten scouts had made their trip through the land of Canaan. As the new leader of the Israelites, Joshua knew that things had probably changed in Canaan since he had been there. Different people had come there to live; cities had been built where there had been none before. The Israelites themselves had now won some battles and the news had spread. Joshua wondered just what the Canaanites had heard about them.

Across the Jordan River from the place where the Israelites were camped stood the city of Jericho, surrounded by high walls. Before they could take the rest of the country, they had to capture this city which stood in the way. Joshua sent two men across the river secretly to find out something about Jericho.

The two spies slipped in through the gates in the great wall of the city among the crowds that went in and out. They found a house inside where they stopped to eat and rest. But they had not been as smart as they thought they had. Someone had spotted them as strangers and reported them to the king.

©

John H. Eggers Publications and The New York Public Library

The Flight of the Spies

Immediately the king sent messengers to the woman who owned the house where they were staying. Her name was Rahab. When she saw the officers coming, she rushed the Israelites up onto the roof of her house. There she had stalks of flax spread out to dry so that she could make them into cloth one day. The men lay down on the flat roof and she covered them with the flax. Then she went down to meet the officers.

"Rahab!" the soldiers called out. "The king demands that you turn over to him the two strangers that came into your house. They are known to be spies from Israel."

"Oh, it is true some men were here earlier today," Rahab answered, "but I did not know that they were spies. They left about dark, so if you intend to catch them, you will have to hurry. They have already had time to get a head start."

Hurriedly, the men rode off through the city gates, heading toward the river where they had seen the Israelites camped. But naturally, they never found any trace of the men.

When she knew the messengers had gone, Rahab climbed back onto the roof and told the spies that it was safe to come down.

"Tell us why you hid us and saved our lives," they asked her.

"I know that your God has promised to give you this land. Everyone here in Jericho knows it, and they are afraid. We all heard of the way your God held back the waters of the Red Sea while you crossed over and we heard of the battle you won over the Amorites. We know that He will help you take our city, for the God you worship is truly God in heaven above and on earth beneath."

"Please," she begged, "when you return to take this city, save me and my family. Promise me you will do this."

"Our lives for yours," they promised. "If you will not tell anyone about our being here, we will remember you when we come back to the city."

Now Rahab's house was built right into the wall of the city, and it had a window facing outside the wall. Through this window she dropped a strong cord, a brilliant red piece of rope. Before the men slid down the rope to safety, they reminded Rahab, "Gather all your family into your house before we return. That way they will be saved with you."

"How will you remember which house it is?" she asked.

"Keep this red rope hanging from the window, and we will find you," they answered.

Then she lowered them on the rope and left it tied tightly to the window. "Go to the hills and hide for three days until the king stops looking for you," she called softly to them through the darkness of the night.

After three days the king's officers returned to Jericho to report that they had not been able to capture the spies. It was safe then for the men to come down from the hills and return to their camp across the river. Excited by their adventure, they hurried to Joshua and gave him this message: "The people of Jericho are afraid of us and will not fight against us. It is time to attack!"

Questions:

1. Why did Joshua want to send more spies into Canaan? 2. Did anyone find out that the spies had come to Jericho? Who? 3. Where did the men hide from the king's officers? 4. What reward did Rahab want? 5. How were the men going to remember where she lived? 6. Did the men go straight back to camp? 7. What did they tell Joshua?

The Promised Land at Last

And the priests that bore the ark of the covenant of the Lord stood firm on dry ground in the midst of Jordan, and all the Israelites passed over on dry ground, until all the people were passed clean over Jordan.
Joshua 3:17

AFTER the spies came back from Jericho and told Joshua that the people there were afraid, Joshua gave the command for the Israelites to pack up their camp and move to the banks of the Jordan River. The tents came down; the tabernacle was taken apart. The priests ran poles through the rings in the corners of the Ark of the Covenant and lifted it to their shoulders. You will remember that the tables of stone on which God had written the Ten Commandments were in the Ark, and it was very precious to the Israelites.

This was during the spring of the year, and the Jordan River was flooded by spring rains. With a powerful current it ran swiftly down to the Dead Sea. It was so broad and moved so fast that only a very strong man could have swum it. The Israelites stood near its banks and looked at it and then they looked at the land of Canaan on the other side. How were they going to get across? There were no bridges and they had no boats.

Then Joshua gave commands to his officers and they moved through the crowd, shouting orders. "When you see the priests carrying the Ark of the Covenant, follow behind them."

Crossing the Jordan

The priests moved among the people and marched with the Ark to the edge of the water. Joshua gave them the command, "Wade into the water!" When the feet of the priests touched the water, God caused a wonderful thing to happen—up the river the water stopped flowing as if an invisible dam held it back. The people saw it rise and pile up without flowing down. Below, the water that was already there flowed onward toward the Dead Sea until the river bed lay dry and the stones on its bottom were uncovered.

The priests moved out into the very center of the river bed and stood with the Ark on their shoulders. Past them marched all the people of Israel, following Joshua safely to the other side of the river, exactly as their parents had followed Moses across the Red Sea. God had shown them that His Spirit was going to be with Joshua as it once had been with Moses.

When all of Israel had crossed to the other side, Joshua called a man from each of the twelve tribes and said, "Each of you gather a large stone from the river bottom where the priests are standing and pile them in a heap here on the bank. Later on when your children ask you why the stones are here, you can tell them how the Lord made the river dry. They will help you remember this wonderful thing."

Then Joshua himself set up twelve stones in the middle of the river bed. When the two piles were made, one on the bank and one in the river, Joshua gave the command for the priests to join them on the bank. As the feet of the priests touched the shore, the river began suddenly to flow as before, its water tumbling down from the hills, racing for the Dead Sea.

Israel camped that night on the shore of the promised land for the first time since they had left Egypt. They kept thanking and praising God every time they looked back at the swift river and thought of having walked through it on dry ground that very day.

The new camp, set up near the heap of stones from the river bed, was named Gilgal. It became the main camp during the time that Israel fought for the land of Canaan. While the Israelites camped here, they ate the Passover feast, as their parents had done for the first time the night before they left Egypt. They made their bread for the feast from grain growing there in the land of Canaan. When they did the manna, food from heaven, that God had sent for forty years quit falling. The days of wandering were over.

Questions:

1. What was keeping the Israelites from going into the promised land now? 2. What happened when the priests stepped into the water? 3. What were they carrying? 4. Why did Joshua have the twelve men pile up the stones? 5. What was the new camp named? 6. What happened once the people were safe inside Canaan?

A Strange Battle

Joshua said unto the people, Shout; for the Lord hath given you the city.
Joshua 6:16

THE Israelites camped at Gilgal, inside the land of Canaan, waiting for God's commands. One day Joshua, their brave leader, was out walking along where he could see the great city Jericho. As he walked, he came face to face with a man carrying a sword. "Are you a friend or an enemy?" Joshua boldly asked.

"I am neither," the stranger replied. "I have come to you as the commander of the army of the Lord."

When Joshua saw that it was an angel, he fell to the ground and bowed low before him. "What message do you have from my Lord?" he asked.

Then the angel gave him the plans that God wanted the Israelites to follow when they attacked the city of Jericho. Joshua had never heard such strange plans of war, but he remembered exactly what the angel had said. He returned to camp, knowing that he would try to do just as he had been told because he felt that the Lord knew better than he. What the Lord said, he would obey.

Now the people of Jericho had become very frightened when they saw the Israelites camped within sight of their city. They closed their city gates tight, and no one came in or went out. Toward this walled city Joshua commanded the people to march. First came a special group of armed

The Walls of Jericho

soldiers; then followed seven priests with rams' horns. Behind them came more priests carrying the precious Ark of the Covenant, covered and riding on poles on their shoulders. Last of all, came the rest of the people, marching in order.

All the way around the walls of the city the Israelites marched. No one talked or shouted. The only noise was the sound of the rams' horns being blow by seven priests. Then they returned to their camp. The next morning they did the same thing. For six days the strange group made one trip around the city.

Inside the city, the people of Jericho were puzzled. They had expected to have to fight thousands of armed soldiers. What could this mean? Even the Israelites wondered what was about to happen. But Joshua knew that this was what the Lord had told him to do, and he was going to obey.

On the sixth night, he called all the people together. "Tomorrow," he said, "we will march around the city not once, but seven times. Then when the rams' horns give a long blast, everyone is to shout. If we do this, the Lord has promised to give us the city. Remember, though, that God wants us to destroy every living thing in the city except those we find in the house of Rahab, for she saved our spies. You can tell her house because there is a red cord hanging from the window. All the gold and silver that is in the city must go into the treasury of the Lord."

The next morning the Israelites got up early and formed their strange parade. Again they marched toward Jericho and around its city walls—once, twice, three times, and up to seven times. Then the marchers stopped still. The priests blew loud and long upon their horns, and Joshua's voice rang out, "Shout, for the Lord has given you the city!" All the people answered with a great wild shout; and when they did, the walls of the city began to crack and crumble. They trembled and leaned, and then they fell crashing to the ground.

The Israelite army began climbing over the ruins to fight the people inside the city; but they found them so frightened by the collapse of the walls that they hardly had to fight at all. The two spies found Rahab's house with all of her family safe inside, and they took them back to the Israelite camp to wait until the battle was over. Rahab stayed and made her home with the Israelites, for she had chosen to serve their God. Later on, she married a fine Israelite named Salmon, and she became a great-great-grandmother of David, into whose family Jesus Christ was born.

After the battle of Jericho, the fame of Joshua and the Israelites began to spread throughout the land of Canaan. Others dreaded the day they were going to have to fight against this army whose commander was God.

Questions:

1. Who told Joshua how to capture the city of Jericho? 2. In what order did the Israelites march? 3. How many days did they march around the city? How many times? 4. What happened on the seventh day? 5. Who was the only one in Jericho that was saved?

Fighting for Canaan

And Achan answered Joshua, and said, Indeed I have sinned against the Lord God of Israel.
Joshua 7:20

GOD had given his people, the Israelites, some rules to follow while they fought for the promised land. First, they were to destroy everyone in the cities they captured. You see, these people worshiped idols instead of the true God and God knew that if they lived, they would make the Israelites turn away from Him. Besides this, the Israelites were supposed to bring all the gold and silver and treasures that they found for the treasury of the Lord. No one was supposed to have any of it for his own because it belonged to God.

After the battle of Jericho, Joshua followed these rules. Only Rahab and her family were saved because it had been promised when she hid the two spies. All the treasure from the city was put in the house of the Lord, or so Joshua thought.

Beyond Jericho stood a smaller city named Ai. Joshua's spies came back from Ai and said, "Ai is such a small city that we can easily capture it without taking the whole army there." So Joshua just sent part of his army up to fight at Ai, expecting them to win. Before long, however, the Israelites came running back. The men of Ai had beaten them and driven them away.

The Sun Stands Still

Joshua and all the people were frightened when their soldiers did not win the battle at Ai. With the help of God they had won all their other battles, but now it seemed that God had left them. They were afraid the other Canaanites in the land would hear about it and come and destroy them.

Then God gave Joshua the reason why his army could not win. "Israel has done wrong," the Lord said. "You took some of the treasure from Jericho and kept it for yourselves. I am not going to be with you in battle again until the stolen things are found." Then he told Joshua how to find out just who had done this wicked thing.

The next morning Joshua had all the Israelites parade in front of him—every tribe and every family in each tribe. From all these people God showed Joshua which one had sinned. It was a man named Achan.

Joshua said to him, "My son, tell me now what you have done. Do not try to hide it from me."

"It is true that I disobeyed God," Achan replied. "When we were capturing Jericho, I saw there a beautiful garment and some silver and gold that I wanted for my own. So I dug a hole in my tent and buried them there."

Joshua sent a messenger to Achan's tent, and sure enough, there lay the treasure Achan had taken from Jericho. Then, because Achan's sin had made all the people suffer, he and his stolen treasure and all his family and goods were destroyed. God did this to show the Israelites that He meant for them to obey every commandment He had given them.

After this, Joshua sent another army up to Ai; and they captured the city just as easily as they had taken Jericho. They saw now that when they did right, God was with them; but that it was terrible to do wrong and find themselves without Him.

For many years Joshua led the Israelites through Canaan, fighting to take the land for their own. The people who were living in Canaan did not know what to think of these strangers who had suddenly entered their country and taken city after city. Some tried to fool Joshua with tricks in order to save their people. Some kings banded together with other kings so that they would have a very strong army to fight against the Israelites. One day when Joshua fought against five kings, God caused the sun to stand still in the sky and kept the night from coming until His people had won the battle. He also helped them by sending a hail storm on the enemies. The five kings ran and hid in a cave but Joshua found them and killed them.

Later Joshua won another battle against the kings of the north and took their land. All these battles took many years, but finally it seemed that Israel had captured nearly all the land and were ruling the people who were left. The Israelites themselves were growing tired of fighting, so Joshua divided the land among all the twelve tribes. Each family got a section for its own where the family could settle down, build a home, and grow a garden. How happy they were to be finally in a home of their own! But before they separated and went to their own places, Joshua reminded them that the land would not have been theirs if it had not been for God's help. He warned them not to leave God and turn to the foolish idols that the Canaanites worshiped.

It was easy then for the Israelites to promise that they would do as Joshua said because they could remember the battles God had helped them win and they loved Joshua so. And as long as the people remembered Joshua, they kept on serving the Lord, but a time was going to come when these promises were broken.

Questions:

1. Name two rules God's people had to follow in the battles they fought in taking Canaan. 2. Why did Joshua's soldiers lose the battle at Ai? 3. What had Achan taken from Jericho? 4. What did this teach the people? 5. What did Joshua do for the people after most of the land had been captured? 6. What did the people promise to do before they separated?

Two Women Free the Israelites

And Barak said unto her, If thou wilt go with me then I will go; but if thou wilt not go with me, then I will not go.
Judges 4:8

WHEN Joshua had conquered most of the land of Canaan, he went ahead and divided the land among the people. Some of the Canaanites were still living in the land, but the Israelites moved right in with them. Because these Canaanites worshiped idols, the Israelites needed a strong leader to remind them that they were to worship only the one true God. As long as Joshua lived, the people worshiped as he led them; but after everyone who remembered Joshua died, the Israelites began worshiping idol gods. When they forgot about God this way, He punished them by letting their enemies come in from lands around and conquer them. For years the Israelites slaved for their enemies, but then they began to remember how God had once helped them. They remembered how strong they had been when they obeyed God. When this happened, they began once again to pray to God and to ask Him to forgive them. God would hear their prayer and usually He would send a great man to lead them in battle against their masters.

One time when the Israelites sinned, the Lord let the Canaanites from the north, some that Joshua had never

John H. Eggers Publications and The New York Public Library

A Heroine of Israel

taken, come down and conquer them. Jabin, the ruler of these Canaanites, had nine hundred chariots of iron, and the Israelites were afraid of them, for they made it very hard to fight against Jabin.

For twenty years Jabin ruled the Israelites and treated them cruelly. At this time, there was a woman judge ruling Israel. Her name was Deborah. She did not have an army or fight battles, but she was a very smart woman and the people saw that God was with her. She sat out under a palm tree and the people would bring her their problems and questions. She gave them good advice and helped them.

One day Deborah sent for a brave man she had heard of named Barak. She told Barak that God wanted him to gather an army and go fight against Sisera, the commander of Jabin's army. God had promised to help Barak win the battle.

But Barak was not quite sure that he would be able to do this alone. He told Deborah, "I will not go unless you come with me."

Deborah was not afraid to go to battle against Sisera. "I will go with you," she told Barak, "but because you did not trust in God to help you, the honor of capturing Sisera is going to be given to a woman."

So Barak and Deborah gathered up an army and rode out to meet Sisera, who had heard that they were coming. This time the iron chariots did not frighten the Israelites. They fought bravely and soon had Sisera's army running in every direction.

When Sisera saw that he had no chance of winning the battle, he jumped from his chariot and ran away as fast as he could. At last he came, panting, to a tent that stood all alone in the deserted countryside. A woman named Jael lived with her husband in the tent, but at this time she was there all alone. She recognized the weary general and said to him, "Stop here a while, my lord; you will be safe in my tent."

Sisera was glad to find a place to rest. He lay down on the floor of Jael's tent and she covered him with a blanket. Sisera asked her for a drink and she brought him some milk. By this time Sisera was very drowsy, but before he went to sleep he called to Jael, "Stand near the door of the tent. If anyone comes looking for me, tell them I am not here." Then he fell fast asleep, being very tired from fighting and running.

Now Jael was not an Israelite, but she was a friend of the Israelites. Once Sisera was asleep, she slipped into the tent and killed him by driving a tent pin through his head.

Before long, Barak, commander of the Israelites, came looking for Sisera. Jael ran to meet him and said, "Come and I will show you where Sisera is." Then she pulled aside the door of the tent and there lay Sisera on the floor.

Barak and Deborah praised Jael for this brave deed. They sang a song, praising God for helping them win the great battle. All the Israelites were thankful to Jael and Deborah, two women who helped set them free from the wicked Canaanites.

Questions:

1. Who led the Israelites away from God? 2. What happened to them when they did wrong and worshiped idols? 3. What were the leaders called who helped them fight their enemies and led them back to God? 4. Name a woman judge. 5. Whom did she ask to be the commander of the Israelite army? 6. Was he as brave as he should have been? 7. Who won the battle against the Canaanites? 8. What happened to Sisera, the Canaanite general?

Gideon, a Fighting Judge

When I blow with a trumpet, I and all that are with me, then blow ye the trumpets also on every side of all the camp, and say, The sword of the Lord, and of Gideon.
Judges 7:18

FOR a while after Deborah and Barak fought the Canaanites, the Israelites obeyed God; but after many years passed, they forgot about the way God had helped them. They began bowing down to strange idols instead of praying to God. When God saw this, he allowed the wandering tribe of Midianites to come into the land of the Israelites. Every time the Israelites would grow crops, the Midianites would come and steal what they had grown. For seven years, the Midianites lived on what the Israelites grew, and their cattle ate all the grass in the Israelites' pasture land. Finally, the Israelites had to run from their homes and farms and hide from the wicked Midianites in caves in the mountainside. They had no food except that which they had hidden from the Midianites. They were so poor and starving that they began to remember the true God who helped them and cared for them when they obeyed Him. They prayed to Him to save them from the Midianites.

God heard the prayers of His people and He was sorry for them. He chose a new leader, or judge, to help them take their land away from the Midianites. This leader was a brave farmer named Gideon. At first Gideon could not

Gideon and the Three Hundred

believe that God had really chosen him to fight the Midianites—he did not feel that he was strong enough or important enough. But God showed Gideon a strange miracle. Then Gideon believed that God was truly with him and that together they could do anything.

Before Gideon could lead the Israelites with God's help, he had to destroy the idols that the people had been worshiping. Two of these idols stood right by his own father's house. Because he was afraid of what the people would do if they saw him, Gideon waited until nighttime. Then he and ten of his servants crept out and tore the great idols down. In their place Gideon built an altar to God and offered a sacrifice upon it.

In the morning when the people came out to bow down before their idols, they were furious to find them broken. They asked around until they found out that Gideon had done it. They were so angry they wanted to kill him. They went to his father's house to find him. Gideon's father told them: "Why are you fighting for your strange god named Baal? If he is a god, why do you not let him punish Gideon?" But, of course, Baal was really not a god and nothing ever happened to Gideon.

After this, the people saw how foolish they had been. They turned back to God and they trusted Gideon to lead them the way God wanted him to. When Gideon sent out word that he was calling together an army, Israelites from everywhere came to help him fight against the Midianites.

Before he led all the people to fight, Gideon wanted to be sure once more that God was going to be with him. That night he lay a lamb's skin, fleecy with wool, on the ground. He asked the Lord to let the fleece be wet with dew but to keep the ground around it dry. In the morning, the fleece was so wet that Gideon wrung a bowlful of water from it. But all around the ground was dry.

Then Gideon said, "Lord, do not be angry with me, but I ask you to show me one more time that you are going to help me. This night, let the fleece be dry and the ground around be wet with dew."

The next morning Gideon found it just as he had asked. Then he was sure that God wanted him to lead His people. Gideon prepared the army to attack the Midianites. But the Lord told Gideon, "Your army is too large. If you were to take this many men to fight, then you would feel like you had won the battle by yourselves instead of with My help. Let everyone who is afraid and does not want to fight go home."

Gideon sent word to his men that anyone who was afraid could go home. The soldiers thought that this was very strange. Already they had fewer men than the Midianites. But of the 32,000 men in the army, 22,000 went back home. This left a small army of 10,000.

Again the Lord spoke to Gideon: "You still have too many soldiers. Take them all down to the brook to drink and I will show you which ones to keep." When they got to the brook, three hundred drank from their hands, lapping the water like a dog, still keeping their eyes ahead to see what was happening. But the rest of the men knelt down and put their heads to the water to drink.

"Send everyone home except those who lapped from their hands," the Lord told Gideon. This left only three hundred men! Truly they looked like a small group camped on a hill above the large camp of the Midianites.

That night Gideon and a servant crept down very close to the Midianite camp. There they heard two soldiers talking. One told the other that he had dreamed that God was going to help the Israelites defeat the Midianites. This made Gideon feel good. He hurried back to his camp, anxious to start the fight.

Gideon's men prepared to attack in a strange way. First, Gideon divided them into three groups, each group having one hundred men. Then he gave each man a trumpet, a pitcher, and a torch. The men were to light the torches and then cover them with the pitchers. In the night the three companies crept down the mountainside to the Midianite camp. The groups stayed very quiet and did not wake any of the Midianites while they took their places on the three sides of the camp.

When everyone was in place, Gideon blew loud on his trumpet. Then he hit his pitcher against a stone and it broke, letting the torch shine through the night. Immediately all the soldiers answered with their trumpets. They broke their pitchers and light flashed in every direction, as they shouted, "The sword of the Lord and of Gideon!"

The Midianites awoke with a start when they heard the trumpets and the shout. They were horrified to see the lights and their enemies everywhere they turned. They were so confused and afraid that they turned and ran in every direction. In the dark and in their hurry to get away, the Midianites even began fighting one another. Soon their camp was deserted. But the Israelites in other places had been warned and they caught the Midianites as they ran toward the Jordan River.

After this, Gideon became a very famous man and the Israelites wanted to make him their ruler. "No," Gideon said, "God is already your ruler." How good it would have been if the Israelites had only remembered this!

Questions:

1. What were the Midianites doing to the Israelites? 2. Whom did God choose to be a new leader for the Israelites? 3. What did Gideon do to the idols? 4. What two signs did God show with the fleece? 5. How did Gideon make his army smaller? 6. Why did he do this? 7. What three things did the Israelites carry in the battle? 8. Were the Midianites afraid? What did they do?

A Lion and a Riddle

And he said unto them, Out of the eater came forth meat, and out of the strong came forth sweetness. And they could not in three days expound the riddle.
Judges 14:14

AFTER the time of Gideon, one of the enemies who conquered the Israelites when they sinned was the Philistines, a strong nation that lived near the Great Sea. For forty years the Israelites served the Philistines, and the Lord sent no one to save them. Finally, an angel appeared to an Israelite woman and told her that she was going to have a son who would rescue God's people from the Philistines. This boy was to be specially given to God from the time he was born. The woman was not to eat any unclean thing or drink any wine, and the little baby was never to have his hair cut, for he would be a Nazirite. To the Israelites, a Nazirite was one who let his hair grow and drank no wine to show that he belonged to God.

The woman hurried to tell her husband Manoah of the wonderful news, but he could hardly believe it. It was too good to be true! He prayed that God would send the angel again, so they would be sure to understand how they were to treat their special son.

This time the angel appeared to Manoah and his wife while they were out in the fields. Manoah had many questions to ask the angel, but the angel only repeated the same message he had told the woman before. Manoah was so

Samson Kills a Lion

grateful that he offered a sacrifice to God there. When the flame from the altar rose, the angel ascended to heaven in the fire.

In time, the promised son came; and the happy parents named him Samson. They took good care of him and saw that he never ate anything unclean and that his hair was never cut. As Samson grew up, his long hair was not the only strange thing people began to notice about him. He was a very strong boy and could do things no one his age, or even those older, could do. But sometimes it seemed that Samson was not serious enough, for he would use his strength just to show off.

When Samson was old enough to get married, he came to his mother and father and told them that he had seen a Philistine woman in the town of Timnath that he wanted to be his wife. Manoah and his wife were very disappointed that Samson had chosen a Philistine instead of one of the Israelite girls. They could not know, of course, that God was using this way for Samson to bring much harm to the Philistines. Finally, however, they made a trip with Samson down to Timnath to see about the marriage.

During the journey, Samson and his parents became separated. Perhaps Samson wandered off alone, away from the road, to explore the wilderness. While he was alone, a lion leaped out at him, ready to attack. In a second, Samson caught the lion and killed him with his bare hands, leaving him in many pieces on the ground. But he never told his parents or anyone else about this.

Plans for the marriage were made and Samson and his family went back home. Then at the time planned, he returned to Timnath for the wedding. On the trip, he thought again of the lion he had killed, and he wandered into the brush to look for what was left of it. He found that the body of the lion had been eaten by wild beasts and birds, and only its bones were left. But then he noticed that among the bones some bees had made a honeycomb and left some honey in it. He reached into the honeycomb and took some of the honey to eat. It tasted good to him as he walked along on his long journey.

After the wedding, it was the custom in those days for there to be a long wedding feast or celebration. At Samson's wedding the celebration lasted a whole week. During that time, Samson and the other young men entertained themselves with riddles and guessing games. Samson thought and thought and then he said: "I will give you a riddle. If you can answer it within these seven days, I will give you each a new suit of clothes; but if you cannot answer it, you must give me thirty suits of clothes."

"Fine!" his companions declared. "Now, tell us your riddle."

So he said, "Out of the eater came something to eat. Out of the strong came something sweet."

For three days the men puzzled over Samson's riddle, but they could not find the right answer. Finally, they came to Samson's bride and told her, "Get Samson to tell you the answer to his riddle. If you cannot find out for us, we will burn your family's house."

So Samson's new wife begged and pleaded with him to tell her the answer to his riddle. Finally she began crying and said, "If you really loved me, you would tell me the answer." She bothered him so much about it that he finally gave in and told her about the lion he had killed and the honey he had found among its bones. Naturally, she gave the answer then to the other men.

On the last day of the feast, just as it was ending, the men came confidently to Samson. With a smile they said, "What is sweeter than honey? What is stronger than a lion?"

Samson knew immediately that they had gotten the answer from his wife. He was so angry that he went right out and killed the first thirty Philistines he found and used their clothes to pay his bet.

But this was only the beginning of Samson's trouble with the Philistines. The Lord had given him his strength to save his people from the Philistines—not with an army, but with his might alone.

Questions:

1. What special things did the angel tell Manoah's wife about the son she was to have? 2. How was Samson different from other boys? 3. What did Samson fight on the way to make plans for his wedding? 4. What had happened to it when he found it again? 5. What was Samson's riddle? 6. How did the Philistines find out the answer? 7. How did Samson pay his part of the bargain?

Samson's Secret

If I be shaven, then my strength will go from me, and
I shall become weak, and be like any other man.
Judges 16:17

AFTER his adventures with the Philistines, Samson became well known to all the Israelites. Everyone began looking to him as their leader and judge. They would bring their problems to him, and he would try to advise them the way the Lord would be pleased.

But Samson was restless and could not be still very long. Time and time again he would find an excuse to do some harm to the Philistines. One time he killed a thousand of them in one day with the jawbone of a donkey. Another time, they locked him within a city gate, thinking they had captured him. He not only escaped; he lifted the whole gate with its posts to his shoulders and carried it to a faraway hill.

Some of Samson's tricks make us think that he was not as serious about leading his people as he should have been. He seemed to enjoy playing jokes on his enemies more than leading his people back to God. But in all this time, he *had* obeyed the Nazirite law as the angel had told his mother he must. He had never cut his hair nor eaten anything unclean nor drunk wine.

Then, for the second time, Samson fell in love with a Philistine woman. Naturally, by this time the Philistine rulers were anxious to do away with this fellow who

Samson and Delilah

caused them so much trouble. They came to the woman with a bargain to make. "Delilah," they said, "if you can find out what makes Samson so strong and how we can overcome him, we will each give you eleven hundred pieces of silver."

It was a great amount of money. Delilah thought about it a bit, and she finally agreed to do as they said.

Now Samson thought that Delilah loved him as much as he loved her, and he never suspected that she would do anything to hurt him. Still, when she would coax him to tell her the secret of his strength, he would tease her. First, he told her that if he were bound with seven green twigs, he would not be strong any more.

The Philistines secretly brought Delilah the green twigs, and when Samson was asleep, she bound him with them. Then she called out, "Wake up, Samson, the Philistines are coming!" With that, he jumped up, breaking the twigs with ease. She knew that he had not told her the truth.

Samson thought that Delilah was playing some kind of a game; and the next time she begged him to tell her his secret, he told her that he would be weak if he were bound with new ropes. Taking new ropes, she bound him; and again he broke them as though they were threads.

Still playing a game, the next time Samson told her that his strength would leave him if his hair was woven in a loom. Delilah wove his hair into a loom during his sleep and then fastened it tightly with a pin. This time, when she called out to him, he stood up with the loom still fastened to his hair.

Delilah did not like Samson's game, for she was anxious to get her money from the rulers. She asked him, "How can you say that you love me when you will not tell me the truth?" Every day she would beg and plead with him until he got tired of listening to her. Finally he told her, "My hair has never been cut because I am a Nazirite and belong to the Lord in a special way. If my head were shaved, my strength would be gone."

This time Delilah knew that he had told the truth. She called the rulers to bring her their money. Then she had them wait in another room. When Samson fell alseep, she called in a man with a razor. As the hair fell from Samson's head, his strength began to fail. When Delilah called that the Philistines were upon him, Samson woke and found that the Lord had left him. The rulers drew aside the curtain that hid them and took him their prisoner. They put out his eyes and took him down to a jail. Here, poor, blind Samson pulled a millstone to grind wheat just as a donkey would have done.

But while Samson was in prison his hair began to grow again. And he had a lot of time to think. He probably prayed to God to forgive him for often wasting the marvelous strength that he had been given and then lost.

To celebrate the capture of Samson, the Philistines gave a great festival in the temple of their idol god, Dagon. During the celebration, some began to call for Samson. They wanted him brought out so they could make fun of him. Dragged from the prison, Samson was led between two great pillars so that all could see him. What a sight he must have made! Stumbling and ragged, he walked in while they laughed at him.

Then Samson asked the boy who was leading him about to show him where the two pillars were so he could rest. With his hands on the pillars Samson began to pray silently: "Lord God, give me my strength just one more time that I may repay the Philistines for the trouble they have caused me."

Then, grasping the two pillars tightly, he began to feel his old strength returning. "Let me die with the Philistines!" he cried; and with one mighty push, he cracked the two pillars and the temple collapsed. All the thousands who had been in the temple, including Samson, were killed. In his brave death, Samson killed more Philistines and did more to set his people free than he did during all his life.

Questions:

1. Name some things Samson did to make the Philistines angry at him. 2. What kind of bargain did the Philistine rulers make with Samson's lover? 3. What was her name? 4. How did Samson tease Delilah when she asked him what made him strong? 5. What really made Samson strong? 6. What did the Philistines do to Samson after they cut his hair and caught him? 7. How did the Philistines celebrate having captured Samson? 8. What did Samson do at the celebration?

A Love Story

And Ruth said, Entreat me not to leave thee, or to return from following after thee: for whither thou goest, I will go; and where thou lodgest, I will lodge; thy people shall be my people, and thy God my God.
Ruth 1:16

DURING the time of the judges, a famine came upon the land of the Israelites, as one had come in the time of Jacob. This meant that nothing would grow in the fields, and the pastures became dry and dusty. When food became scarce, a certain man named Elimelech grew worried about his family. He had two growing boys, as well as a wife; and there simply was not enough food to go around. Finally, Elimelech decided to leave his home in Bethlehem and go to the land of Moab to live until the famine was over. There he would be able to find work and food.

So Elimelech and his wife Naomi took their sons to Moab and made a home for them there. Moab is one of the countries through which the Israelites had to pass when Moses led them from Egypt to Canaan.

Poor Elimelech never got to see his home in Bethlehem again, for he died while the family was in Moab. Naomi continued to live there with her sons until they were grown.

The time came for the sons to choose wives, and naturally they each chose one of the Moabite women they knew. Chilion married a woman named Orpah; Mahlon's wife

Ruth

was called Ruth. The lovely brides helped make Naomi's life happier.

Then trouble came again. Both of the sons died. All three women were without husbands. The younger women stayed and lived with Naomi.

One day Naomi heard that the Lord had made the land of Israel green and beautiful once more and that food was growing there. She decided to return to her people. Both Orpah and Ruth made plans to go with Naomi on her journey, but Naomi would not hear of it. "My daughters," she said, "there is no reason for you to leave your families and your homeland. You are still young, and you have time to find another husband and have a family. Return to your father's house."

Tearfully Orpah kissed her mother-in-law and said goodbye, but Ruth would not leave. "Follow your sister-in-law," Naomi begged. "Return with her to your home."

Ruth had a beautiful reply: "Do not ask me to leave you or to quit following you. I want to go where you go and live where you live. Your people will become my people and your God, my God."

When Naomi saw that Ruth would not change her mind, she said no more. The two made the long trip to Bethlehem together.

News traveled quickly that Naomi was back in town, and many came out to greet her. "Is this Naomi?" they asked.

"Do not call me Naomi any more," she replied. "It means 'pleasant,' and my life has not been pleasant. A better name for me would be Mara, for it means 'bitter.' "

Now Naomi and Ruth returned at the time of the barley harvest, and Ruth went out in the fields to gather grain with the other reapers. These grain gatherers were called "reapers." It was the custom in Israel for the reapers to leave some of the grain for the poor people to gather, and this was what Ruth picked as she followed along.

It so happened that Ruth had chosen to gather grain in a field which belonged to a rich man of Bethlehem named Boaz. When Boaz came to look over his field, he noticed Ruth among the reapers. He asked the master of the reapers, "Who is the young woman there?"

"She is the Moabite woman who returned to Bethlehem with Naomi," the man replied. "She asked to glean here and has been here since yesterday."

Boaz went to Ruth and told her, "Stay here in my fields and glean for the rest of the harvest. I will see that everyone is kind to you. When you get thirsty, feel free to take some of our water."

Ruth bowed and thanked Boaz for his kindness to her, especially since she was a stranger in Israel. But Boaz said, "You are really no stranger for I have heard how good and kind you have been to your mother-in-law. I know that you left your home and family to come with her. May the Lord, in Whom you have come to trust, reward you." Then Boaz invited her to eat with his reapers. When she had finished eating and gone back to work, Boaz asked his reapers to let some of their barley fall on purpose so she could gather it.

That evening Ruth was excited when she returned to Naomi. "Look how much I have gathered today," she said. "I met the owner of the field, and he was the kindest man! He told me to gather there until the end of the harvest."

"Who is this man?" asked Naomi.

"He is called Boaz," Ruth replied.

"Why, he is my husband's near kinsman," Naomi exclaimed. "Stay in his field as he has invited you to do."

By the end of the harvest, Boaz had come to love Ruth; and when he got permission from the wise men of the city, he took her to be his wife. Naomi came to make her home with them; and when Ruth had a baby boy, Naomi was its nurse. "Once more," she said to her friends, "my life is pleasant."

The little boy born to Ruth and Boaz was named Obed. His own son was named Jesse, and Jesse was the father of David, the shepherd boy who became king. Thus Ruth, the young Moabitess who followed her mother-in-law to Israel, became the great-grandmother of Israel's great king.

Questions:

1. Why did Elimelech take his family away from the land of Israel? 2. How many were in his family? 3. What happened to Elimelech while he was in Moab? 4. What happened to his sons? 5. Who wanted to go to Israel with Naomi? 6. What did Ruth do so that she and Naomi would have some food? 7. Were the reapers and the owner kind to her? 8. How did the story end happily for Ruth and Naomi?

A Voice in the Night

And the Lord came, and stood, and called as at other times, Samuel, Samuel. Then Samuel answered, Speak; for thy servant heareth.
I Sam. 3:10

WHILE the judges ruled Israel, the house of worship stood at Shiloh, near the center of the land. The priests who served in the worship in the tabernacle lived in tents near it. All of the Israelites were commanded to come to Shiloh at least once a year and offer sacrifices on the altar that stood before the tabernacle, the tent of worship that Moses and the people had made in the wilderness.

There was a man named Elkanah living in the mountains not too far from Shiloh who always worshiped at the tabernacle. Every year he would bring his two wives and all his children with him to the Holy Place to offer sacrifices. Now all of his children belonged to one of his wives; the other, named Hannah, had none.

One year, while at Shiloh, Hannah prayed earnestly to the Lord to give her a baby boy. She promised God that if He would send her a son, she would give him to the Lord all the days of his life.

While she was praying, Eli, the priest, saw her and promised her that God would answer her prayer. In time, the baby was born and she named him Samuel, which means, "Asked of God."

Samuel Brought Before Eli

When Samuel was still a little boy, Hannah brought him to Eli at the tabernacle. "I am the woman you saw praying one day for a son," she said. "This boy is the one the Lord sent me. Just as I promised, I now want to give him back to God to serve Him all his life."

So Samuel came to live with Eli and grow up near the house of God. Every year his mother would make him a little coat like the one the priests wore and bring it to him at Shiloh. The Lord blessed Hannah and gave her three more sons and two daughters so she would not get lonesome for Samuel.

Eli was growing old and could barely see, so Samuel was a great help to him in the worship. Eli needed Samuel all the more because his own sons were very wicked. Even though they were priests of God, like Eli, they caused the other Israelites to sin when they came to worship. Eli had not made them obey him enough when they were young, and now they had grown too old for him to handle.

In those days, God had not spoken to any man, as He had to Abraham and Moses, for a long while. Then late one night when the only light still burning was the lamp in the house of the Lord, Samuel woke from his sleep, hearing someone call his name. He thought it was Eli and ran to his bed. "Here I am, for you called me," he said to the old priest.

"No, my son," said Eli, "I have not called you. Go back to your bed."

Back in his bed, Samuel lay, falling asleep, when the voice came again: "Samuel!"

Again he went to Eli, sure that he had been called; but Eli said, "I have not called you, Samuel. Lie down once more."

A third time Samuel heard his name called. This time he said to Eli, "Here I am. I know I heard you calling to me."

Then Eli realized that the Lord had been speaking to Samuel. He told Samuel to go back to bed; and when he heard the voice again, he was to say: "Speak, Lord, for I am listening."

Before long, the voice was heard once more: "Samuel! Samuel!" This time Samuel answered, "Speak, Lord, for I am listening."

Then the Lord told Samuel that he was going to punish Eli's sons for their wickedness.

Samuel lay in his bed until morning. Then he got up and went right to work, opening the doors of the tabernacle. He tried to stay away from Eli because he hated to tell him the sad news.

Finally, Eli called to Samuel and asked, "What did the Lord say to you, Samuel?"

Obedient as always, Samuel told Eli all that God had said. The message made Eli very sad, but he said, "Let God do what seems best to Him."

It did not take long for word to travel that God had spoken to Samuel. People began to respect him; and when he grew up, they looked to him as a prophet, one through whom God gives messages to His people.

God's promise to punish Eli's sons came true, for both of them were killed in a battle one day with the Philistines.

During the battle, the Ark of the Covenant, which held the tables of stone on which the ten commandments were written, was stolen by the Philistines. When Eli heard of all this, he, too, died.

Without the Ark and the priests, the tabernacle soon became shabby and fell into ruins. Samuel went to his father's home and lived until he grew up. Then he traveled among all the twelve tribes of Israel, giving them God's messages. He was the last judge, and he ruled the people in peace instead of leading them into battle.

Questions:

1. What did Hannah pray for when she went to the tabernacle at Shiloh? 2. What did she do with the little boy? 3. Why was Eli glad to have Samuel? 4. What did God tell Samuel one night? 5. Did this come true? 6. What did Samuel do after he grew up?

A Shy, Young King

And he had a son, whose name was Saul, a choice young man, and a goodly: and there was not among the children of Israel a goodlier person than he: from his shoulders and upward he was higher than any of the people.
I Sam. 9:2

ALTHOUGH Samuel was a good leader and judge over the Israelites, his sons were not truthful and fair. The wise old men of the Israelites went to Samuel's house at Ramah and told him that his sons were not good enough to rule when he died. "Let us have a king to rule over us like the other nations have," they asked.

Samuel was disappointed at this. He felt that the Lord God should be their only king. God had not meant for His people to be a fighting nation like the others around them once they had settled in Canaan. They were supposed to serve Him in a quiet, peaceful way; but instead, they had begun to want power and riches. Samuel prayed to God about this, and God told him: "Go ahead and give the people a king as they have asked. They are not turning away from you, Samuel; they are turning away from Me in wanting another to lead them. But before you appoint the new leader, warn the people of the lives they will lead if they have a king."

Samuel tried to tell the people that if they had a king, he would take their sons to be his soldiers and their daughters to work in his palace. They would have to pay taxes to him

Samuel Anoints Saul

and work for him. "Someday," he warned them, "you will cry to the Lord about your king, but then the Lord will not hear you."

But the people would not change their minds. "No, no," they cried; "give us our king! Give us a great leader to judge us and lead us in battle!"

So the Lord said to Samuel, "Do as they ask and appoint a king to rule over them." Samuel told the people that their wish would be granted and sent them home.

At this time, there was a powerful man of the tribe of Benjamin named Kish. He had a son named Saul, a handsome looking young man and a very tall one. In a crowd, his head and shoulders showed above everyone else. But although Saul was big and fine looking, he still was quiet and not boastful.

Now Kish, Saul's father, was a very rich man and owned many fine animals. One day some of his asses wandered away, and Kish sent Saul and a servant to find them. For several days they searched the countryside, but they found no trace of the lost animals.

"We had better go back home now," Saul told the servant. "My father will have quit worrying about his asses and begun to worry about us."

By this time they had come to Ramah, the city where Samuel lived. The servant had heard of Samuel, and he suggested that they stop and ask the man of God where they could find their asses. It was known that Samuel was a prophet and could tell what was about to happen through

God's power. Saul agreed after they found some money they could give Samuel as a gift.

Now Saul did not know that Samuel had been warned by God to expect him. The day before, God had told Samuel, "Tomorrow I am going to send a man to you from the tribe of Benjamin. He is the one you are to anoint as king over my people."

When Saul came to Samuel that day, he would hardly have been recognized as a king. He was dirty and tired from looking for the asses, and he only wanted to ask the great prophet a simple question. But Samuel heard God's voice speaking to him again: "This is the one I was speaking of. This is the future king."

Saul could not understand why Samuel treated him so well. Samuel insisted that Saul come to the feast he was attending and gave him the best food there. Then he invited Saul and the servant to spend the night at his house. That night Saul and Samuel stayed up late to talk of all the things that were going to happen in Israel.

The next morning, Samuel walked with Saul and the servant to the edge of the city. Then he asked the servant to go on ahead while he talked to Saul alone. When no one could see them, Samuel brought out a little bottle filled with oil and poured it on Saul's head. This was called "anointing." Then he announced to Saul, "The Lord has appointed you a prince over His people."

After this, he told Saul of three things that would happen to him on his way home. First, he would meet two men who would tell him that the asses had been found. Then he would meet three men who would give him some food. Finally, he would meet some prophets; and when God's Spirit had come upon him, he would be able to prophesy with them.

All these things happened just as Samuel had said they would.

When Saul finally reached home, an uncle met him and asked where he had been. Saul told him that he had seen Samuel, but he did not tell anyone that he had been anointed Israel's first king.

Then Samuel called all the Israelites together at Mizpah. "You have made God unhappy by asking for a king, but He has heard you and will give you that king. Now, let all the tribes of Israel, family by family, pass in front of me."

One by one, the tribes passed until Samuel chose the smallest and weakest, the tribe of Benjamin. Then of all the families of Benjamin, the family of Kish was singled out. Finally, Saul was called for. But Saul was not with his family! He had hidden from the crowd among the baggage.

Then someone ran and got him, and as he walked toward the people, they all looked eagerly to see what kind of man God had chosen. Everyone was pleased when they saw the tall, handsome young man. "Long live the King!" they shouted as they cheered their approval of Saul, the new ruler.

Questions:

1. What did the men of Israel ask Samuel to give them?

2. Why did Samuel not think that this was a good idea?

3. What did God tell Samuel to do? 4. What was Saul doing when he came to Samuel's house? 5. What did Samuel do to Saul before he left? 6. Why did Samuel call all the Israelites together? 7. Where was Saul when they tried to find him?

Success and Failure

And Samuel said to Saul, Thou hast done foolishly: thou hast not kept the commandment of the Lord thy God, which he commanded thee.
I Sam. 13:13

AFTER Samuel showed the Israelites that Saul was to be their king, Saul did not start acting as a king at once. For a while he went back home and worked in his father's fields as he had always done.

One day he came home from plowing to find his family and servants all sad and crying.

"What is wrong with you?" Saul asked.

"We have bad news about our Israelite kinspeople who live across the Jordan River," they answered. "The king of the Ammonites has told them that in seven days he will come and put out everyone's right eye and make them his servants. There are not enough of our people there to fight the wicked king."

This news made Saul very angry. He knew that God had made him a leader over all the Israelites. The time had come for him to take his place as king and save his people.

When Saul decided this, the Spirit of God came upon him and made him strong and brave. He took the oxen that had been pulling his plow, killed them, and cut them into twelve pieces. He sent a piece to each Israelite tribe with this message: "Come now and fight with Saul and Samuel, or this same thing will be done to your oxen."

Saul's Sacrifice

The strong words of their new leader made the Israelites want to obey. At once men gathered from all the tribes to help free their people on the other side of the Jordan River. When Saul saw that the people had answered his call, he sent messengers across the Jordan to tell the people there: "Tomorrow, by the time the sun is hot, we will come and save you."

Just as he had promised, Saul marched his army to the Jordan River, crossed it, and came upon the Ammonite army while it was still early in the morning. The two began to fight, but it was not long before Saul's army had completely beaten the Ammonites and had them running in every direction.

This battle made Saul the hero of all the Israelites. They met Saul and Samuel at Gilgal on their way home from fighting. There they offered sacrifices to God and crowned Saul king. It was a happy time for everyone—Saul was going to be a wonderful ruler!

After this Saul was known as the leader of the Israelite army. Since he was a good soldier himself, he knew what it took to make strong fighters. He looked throughout Israel for brave men, and then he took them and trained them to fight with him. He also trained his son Jonathan to be one of his generals. With this army Saul fought the enemies on all sides of the land of Israel.

The Philistines were the strongest of these enemies and Saul had to fight them over and over again. Before one important battle with the Philistines, Samuel asked Saul not to start fighting until he had come and offered a sacrifice and asked God to help them. But Saul thought that Samuel was taking too long to come. He was afraid the battle would begin without God's blessing; so he went ahead and offered the sacrifice, just as though he thought that he could do what only the priests were allowed to do.

No sooner had the sacrifice stopped burning, than Samuel arrived. "What have you done?" Samuel asked.

"I was afraid that my men might leave me or that the battle would begin, and since you were not here, I offered the sacrifice myself," Saul answered.

"That was a foolish thing to do," Samuel told him. "You disobeyed God. Because you did not obey Him, God is not going to let the kingdom stay in your family. Someday He is going to give your kingdom to a man who *will* obey Him."

Saul won the battle with the Philistines that day, but he had lost his kingdom. He had begun to think that he was strong and powerful and he had forgotten that God was the one who made him that way. Saul was not careful to do just what God told him if he wanted to do something else. This was the reason that God was going to let someone from another family be king after Saul instead of Saul's own son, Jonathan. How sad that Saul did not turn out to be the kind of king that everyone thought he would be! Samuel had warned the people that only God should be their king, and now they were finding out just what he meant.

Questions:

1. Did Saul become king right after Samuel showed the Is-

raelites that he was to be the new leader? 2. What news made him want to lead the people? 3. How did Saul get an army together? 4. Did he win his first battle? 5. Who were the worst enemies Saul had to fight? 6. What mistake did he make before an important battle? 7. How did God punish Saul for this?

A Singing Shepherd Boy

Now he was ruddy, and withal of a beautiful countenance, and goodly to look to. And the Lord said, Arise, anoint him: for this is he.
I Sam. 16:12

GOD did not take Saul's kingdom away from him as soon as he disobeyed and showed that he was not the right kind of man to lead God's people. Saul continued to be king and lead the Israelites in many battles; but Samuel, the prophet, knew that God's Spirit was not with Saul anymore. He waited for God to show him who the new king would be.

One day God sent Samuel down to the house of a man named Jesse. He told Samuel to take with him some oil like that which he had used to anoint Saul king. God was going to show Samuel whom He had chosen to be the new king.

Now Samuel knew that Saul would be very angry if he heard that he was going to anoint a new king; so when he went to Jesse's house in Bethlehem, he acted as though he was going just to offer sacrifices there.

When he arrived in Bethlehem, Samuel invited Jesse and his sons to come to the sacrifice. As Jesse walked in, Samuel was pleased to see that he had seven fine-looking sons with him. Surely one of these young men was the new king God had chosen. Starting with the oldest, the sons walked in front of Samuel. As each one passed, Samuel thought,

David the Shepherd

"This must be the one God wants me to anoint." But all seven passed by and God gave Samuel no sign.

"Are these all of your sons?" Samuel asked Jesse.

"No," answered Jesse; "there is one more, but he is very young. He is in the fields taking care of the sheep."

"Send for him," Samuel said. "I will wait until he comes."

After a while, the youngest son came in. He was handsome and strong, and he had a healthy color from staying outdoors all day. His name was David.

When David walked in, God told Samuel: "Anoint this one; he is the one I have chosen."

In front of his brothers and his father, David had oil poured upon his head by Samuel. The Spirit of the Lord that had left Saul came upon David. But no one else, especially Saul, knew about this new young king. He went back to his sheep in the fields to wait for the time to come when he would become the leader of God's people.

While David wandered about the hillsides and meadows watching his sheep, God was with him. He was strong and could protect his sheep from the wild animals that tried to eat them. But he also had time to sit quietly and think about God. He thought about the kind of man and king God wanted him to be, and the more he thought about this, the more God helped him to be just the way he should.

During these quiet times when he sat and thought, David would take his harp and make up songs about God and His goodness. He could sing and play very beautifully. The songs that David wrote are found in the "songbook of the Bible"—the Psalms. In one of them David talks about God being our shepherd and watching over us just as David did his sheep. You may be able to say the words to David's song yourself:

> The Lord is my shepherd, I shall not want;
> He makes me lie down in green pastures.
> He leads me beside still waters;
> He restores my soul.
> He leads me in paths of righteousness for his name's sake.
> Even though I walk through the valley of the shadow of death,
> I fear no evil; for thou art with me;
> Thy rod and thy staff, they comfort me.
> Thou preparest a table before me in the presence of my enemies;
> Thou anointest my head with oil,
> My cup overflows.
> Surely goodness and mercy shall follow me
> All the days of my life;
> And I shall dwell in the house of the Lord forever.

Questions:

1. Did Saul quit being the king as soon as he disobeyed? 2. Where did God send Samuel to find the new king? 3. Who was the one God had chosen? 4. Did everyone know that Samuel had anointed David? 5. What did David do while he waited to grow up and become king? 6. Name some of the things David did out in the fields. 7. Try to learn all or some of the words of David's song.

The Boy with a Sling

David said moreover, The Lord that delivered me out of the paw of the lion, and out of the paw of the bear, he will deliver me out of the hand of this Philistine.
I Sam. 17:37

WHILE David was still a shepherd boy and Saul was king, the Philistines came back to attack the Israelites. Saul had won battles over the Philistines before, but somehow they managed to recover and come back to fight again. As the army of the Philistines prepared for battle on one hill, the Israelites pitched camp across from them on another. The fight was to take place in the valley between them.

Before they had begun to fight, a soldier stepped out from among the Philistines, and what a soldier he was! This man, called Goliath, was truly a giant, for he was nearly twice as tall as a normal man. He wore a bronze helmet and heavy coat of armor, and in his hand he carried an enormous spear. Before him went his shieldbearer. To the armies of Saul, he shouted out a challenge for someone to come and fight him. If Goliath won, the Israelites would serve the Philistines; but if an Israelite conquered Goliath, the Philistines would be servants of the Israelites.

The Israelites were afraid when they heard this challenge, and no one dared to go out and fight with the giant. For forty days, Goliath came out and strutted before the battle

David and Goliath

lines, but never was an Israelite brave enough to answer him.

Now, David had stayed home to watch his father's sheep at Bethlehem as he was too young to be a soldier; but three of his older brothers were in Saul's army. According to the custom in those days, David's father sent him to the battle lines with food for his brothers; and, in turn, he was to come back and tell his father how they were doing.

When David finally found his brothers among the soldiers, he was able to overhear the giant Goliath making his challenge. David eagerly begged for a chance to fight the giant himself, but the soldiers made fun of him. He was so anxious, however, that eventually King Saul heard of it and sent for him. Saul tried to tell David that he was too young to fight the giant; but David answered that he had killed a lion and a bear that had attacked his sheep, and with God's help, he could conquer the giant, also. When Saul saw that David's mind was made up, he even tried to get him to use his own kingly armor. But David found that he was not used to it and that it only bothered him, so he gave it back to Saul. Instead, all he took with him were his shepherd's staff, his sling, and five smooth stones that he took from a brook and put into his shepherd's bag.

Goliath was angry when he saw the young man coming toward him, for he thought that the Israelites were trying to make fun of him. But David said, "You come to me with a sword and with a spear and with a javelin; but I come to you in the name of the Lord of hosts . . ."

Then, reaching into his bag, he took out one of the stones and placed it in the simple leather sling. With one expert throw, the stone struck the giant in the center of the forehead and he fell to the ground. David rushed up, took the giant's own sword, and cut off Goliath's head.

The frightened Philistines ran while the Israelites began to shout and praise the young hero, David. Little did they know that God had chosen him to be their next king. David himself, though, gave glory to God, for he knew that he had not won the fight alone. The God that he loved and served had been with him.

Questions:

1. Who was the Philistines' most famous soldier? 2. What did he ask the Israelites to do? 3. What was David doing at the place of battle? 4. Why was he not afraid to fight the giant? 5. Why would he not use King Saul's armor? 6. What did he take with him to meet the giant? 7. How did David win the fight?

A Story of Friends

And it came to pass, . . . that the soul of Jonathan was knit with the soul of David, and Jonathan loved him as his own soul.
I Sam. 18:1

AFTER David killed Goliath, Saul brought him to the palace to live. There, in Saul's house, David met one of Saul's sons, Jonathan. The two became very close friends, and each loved the other with all of his heart. They promised that they would always love each other; and to show his love, Jonathan gave David his robe, his sword, and his bow.

David did everything that Saul asked him to do very well, and it was not long before Saul appointed him to be one of his generals. David was a wonderful fighter, as he had shown when he killed Goliath, and he was very well liked by his men. He was the sort of man whom everyone admired.

On his return from one battle, the people came out to meet David singing,

"Saul has killed his thousands,
And David his *ten* thousands."

When Saul heard this, he became jealous of David. He didn't want David to be better liked than he was. He already knew that God was not going to let his son become king because he had not been a good ruler. Maybe he wondered if David was going to be the one to take the throne.

John H. Eggers Publications and The New York Public Library

Saul Throws Spear at David

But David had not told anyone that indeed he *was* the one God had chosen to be the next king.

Saul's worrying seemed to drive him nearly mad. The Spirit of God had left him, and the spirit that came over him made him very unhappy. Sometimes he would behave like a crazy man. Now you will remember that David was not only a shepherd and a fighter, he was also a musician. To try to make Saul feel better, he brought in his harp and sang some songs that he had written while he was in the fields. But while he was playing, Saul became very angry and threw his spear at David. David jumped aside just in time to miss being hit.

From that time on, Saul began to realize how powerful David was and that he was powerful because God was with him. He knew that David was really stronger than he was even though he was the king. He also knew that the people would not stand for him to kill David, so he sent him on dangerous missions, hoping he would be killed in battle. But David fought bravely every time and worked just as hard as ever for Saul, and God kept him safe.

Now no matter what Saul did, everyone spoke of wonderful David, instead. Finally, Saul made no secret of wanting to see David killed, but asked the wrong person to do it—Jonathan.

When Jonathan found out how his father felt, he went straight to David and told David to hide until the danger was over. Then he went to his father and begged for David's life. "Why do you want to kill David, Father? He has never done anything but good for you. Why, he even risked his life to kill Goliath and saved our whole nation. You, too, were proud of him then."

Saul loved his son, and he listened carefully to what Jonathan said. "I will not kill David," he promised.

But another battle with the Philistines broke out and David won a great victory. This time, in his jealousy, Saul became sicker than ever. When David came in to play and sing softly to calm him, he became so angry that he tried to pin David to the wall with his spear.

David ran from the palace to his house, but he was not safe there. Saul sent soldiers to find him, but David's wife helped him escape out the window.

This time David ran far away from Saul and came to live at Ramah with the prophet Samuel. Twice Saul sent messengers to find him, and once he went himself, but God protected David each time.

Although David was afraid to be seen near the palace, he and Jonathan planned a secret meeting out in the field. The two friends were glad to see each other after being separated for so long, but their meeting was not a happy one because they had to hide and keep their friendship a secret.

"What have I done?" David asked Jonathan. "Why is your father trying to kill me?"

"He has promised me that he will not hurt you, David," Jonathan said.

"But he knows that we are good friends," David replied. "Because of that, he will keep his plans from you."

"Tell me what I can do to help you," Jonathan asked. "I will try to do anything you ask."

"Go to the feast that the king is giving," said David, "but I will not attend. When King Saul asks for me, make some excuse—say that I had to go to Bethlehem. If he believes you, I will know it is safe to return; but if he gets angry, I will be certain that my life is in danger."

"Just as you say," Jonathan agreed. Then they arranged a way that Jonathan could signal to David about Saul when he returned.

The first day of the feast, Saul did not mention David's name. But on the second day, the question came, "Where has David been the past two days?"

"He had to make a trip to Bethlehem, Father," Jonathan replied.

Saul's eyes blazed with anger. He lashed out at Jonathan for being a friend to the very man who was going to take the throne away from them. He promised to find David and kill him. When Jonathan opened his mouth to speak a word for David, Saul became so angry at him that he hurled his spear at his own son.

Jonathan left the banquet and went back to the field where David hid. With his bow and arrows he signaled to David that his life was in danger. David came out of hiding and ran to kiss his beloved friend. The two stood and cried for they did not know if it would ever be safe for them to meet again.

"Go in peace," Jonathan told David. "The Lord shall be between us forever."

Then David hurried away to find a place to hide and Jonathan walked back toward the city and his angry father.

Questions:

1. Who was the friend David made in Saul's palace? 2. What jobs did Saul train David to do? 3. Was David good at fighting? 4. Why did Saul get angry at David? 5. Did Jonathan get angry, too? 6. Why did Jonathan and David have a secret meeting in a field? 7. Was it safe for David to see Saul again?

A Man in Hiding

And he said to David, Thou art more righteous than I: for thou hast rewarded me good, whereas I have rewarded thee evil.
I Sam. 24:17

AFTER Jonathan warned David that King Saul was going to try to kill him, David had to run away and hide. He lived the life of an outlaw—always wandering, never safe at any one place—for as long as Saul lived. David even had to find a place outside the land of Israel for his old parents to live so that they would be safe.

Traveling from place to place, living in caves or anything else he could find, David began to draw some followers. His brothers and cousins came to help him, as well as others in the land who were dissatisfied with King Saul. Soon, he led a band of about four hundred men.

Now King Saul had spies all over the land, looking for David. When he found out where David was hiding, he came with his army to capture him. Through the wilderness the two armies chased one another, but God always kept David safe. When at last Saul was closing in on him, a messenger came to Saul and told him that the Philistines had made a raid on the land of Israel. So with David as close as the other side of the mountain, Saul had to leave and fight the Philistines.

While Saul was gone, David and his men changed their headquarters to a huge cave in some wild country near the

The Death of Saul

Dead Sea. When Saul had finished with the Philistines, he brought three thousand of his best soldiers to this rocky country to find David. Over the rough ledges the men climbed, but no sign of David was seen. You see, David and his men were hiding far back in the dark corners of their cave.

After searching for a long time, Saul grew tired and decided to rest. Where do you suppose he lay down to sleep? In the very cave where David was hiding! While Saul was lying there, David sneaked up very quietly and cut off part of Saul's robe with his sword; then he went back to his hiding place.

"Why don't you kill King Saul now before he gets you?" David's men asked.

"No!" David answered, "I could not do anything to harm one whom God has anointed."

By and by Saul woke up and walked out of the cave. After he had gone a little distance, David ran to the mouth of the cave and called after him, "My lord, the king!"

When Saul looked around, David bowed to the ground to show that he still respected him. "What makes you think I am trying to hurt you?" he called to Saul. "Look, I had a chance to kill you today, but I would not do it. Here is a piece I cut from your robe, but I did nothing else because you are God's anointed. Can we not live in peace?"

Saul could hardly believe his eyes and his ears. "David," he called. "Is that you, my son?" Then he hung his head and the tears began to fall down his cheeks. "You are a much better man than I," he said to David. "You have repaid my evil with goodness. Today you could have killed me, and you let me go free. I know now that you are going to be king. Promise me that when you are king, you will not hurt my children."

David promised all that King Saul asked, but he and his men did not go back home right away. David knew that Saul might change his mind and turn against him, because he had done it before.

Surely enough, when Saul got home and began to think about it, he was sorry he had let David go. His ugly spirit came upon him and he came looking for David again. Once more David had a chance to kill Saul, but he would not do it even though he knew Saul would have killed him if he could.

Months passed and the two armies chased one another and fought small battles, but God still kept David from harm. Finally, David took his men out of the land of Israel, hoping that Saul would leave them alone.

About this time, the Philistines came with a big army to fight against Saul. In the battle, Jonathan and two of Saul's other sons were killed. Some Philistine arrows hit Saul, and he, too, lay wounded. "Kill me," Saul begged his armor bearer, "before the Philistines find me and torture me." But the servant would not do it. Then Saul took his own sword and fell on it, killing himself.

You might think that David was glad to hear that Saul was dead. Now he could come out of hiding and become king! But David was very sad to hear about Jonathan and Saul. He wrote a beautiful song about them. In the song he called Jonathan his "brother" and said that Saul was "mighty, . . . stronger than lions."

Questions:

1. Why did David have to hide? 2. How did David get a band of soldiers? 3. Where were David's headquarters? 4. Why did Saul come in David's cave? 5. Why did David not kill Saul while he had a chance? 6. What did he do instead? 7. What finally happened to Saul? 8. Was David glad to be rid of him?

Why the Prophet Told David a Story

And Nathan said to David, Thou art the man.
II Sam. 12:7

AFTER King Saul died, the commander of his army tried to make one of Saul's own sons king, but he did not succeed. God had told Saul that he would take the kingdom away from his family and give it to a man who would obey him. David was the man whom God had chosen. Instead of following Saul's son, people began to look to David to lead them.

Saul had not obeyed God and had been sick and worried while he was king, and he had not taken good care of the land of Israel. The Philistines had taken parts of it again. King David fought the Philistines and drove them away. He also fought other enemies and took lands around Israel to make it bigger and stronger than ever. Wherever he fought, David took silver and gold back to Israel to save to make a great house of worship.

David made Jerusalem the new royal city and lived there. He brought the Ark of the Covenant that had once been in the tabernacle to Jerusalem so that the people could worship around it. The Israelites remembered God and worshiped Him as David did. Because of this, God was with them and made them strong.

©

John H. Eggers Publications and The New York Public Library

David and the Prophet Nathan

After David had been king for several years and had led the Israelites in many battles, he began to stay at the palace in Jerusalem to take care of his kingly duties. He sent his general, Joab, to lead the armies.

One evening David was out walking on the roof of the palace. In those days roofs were flat and people enjoyed the sun or the breezes by walking or sitting on their rooftop. While he was standing there, David looked down and saw a beautiful woman in the courtyard of another house. David sent someone to find out who this woman was.

Word came back to David that the woman was named Bathsheba. She was married to a soldier in David's army. David was disappointed when he heard this news, for he had wanted to marry the woman himself. Then David had a wicked thought: "What if Bathsheba's husband were killed in battle? Then I could marry her!"

Even the best of us have bad thoughts sometime, but when we do we should never listen to them. David *did* listen that day and when he did, he forgot about obeying God.

David sent a letter to Joab, his general. "Put Uriah, Bathsheba's husband, in the middle of the hardest fighting," it said. When Joab did this, Uriah was killed just as David had planned. After a little while, David brought Bathsheba to the palace and she became one of his wives.

Now God was very displeased with the way David had acted. He sent a prophet named Nathan to David. At first, Nathan did not tell David just why he had come. Instead, he told David this story:

"Once there were two men who lived in the same city. One was very rich and had many flocks and herds, but the other was very poor—he had only one lamb. The poor man had taken care of the lamb from the time it was small; it ate out of his own dishes and sat on his lap. It was like his own child to him. One day a visitor came to see the rich man. Instead of preparing one of his own animals to feed the stranger, the rich man took the poor man's only lamb and killed it for his visitor's dinner."

This story made David very angry. "That rich man deserves to die!" he said. "He must give four lambs to the poor man as a payment for taking his only one."

Then Nathan looked at David sadly and said, "*You* are that man, David. The Lord made you king over all Israel, gave you a lovely palace home, and many wives—everything you could want. But you had Uriah killed so that you could take the only wife he had. You have done a very wicked thing and the Lord is going to punish you for it."

When David heard this, he realized how wrong he had been. He was very sorry.

"God will forgive you," Nathan told David, "but because you did such a bad thing, your and Bathsheba's baby will not live."

Surely enough, David and Bathsheba's baby became very sick. David was so sorry now that he had forgotten God and disobeyed Him. He cried and would not eat and prayed to God to save his baby. But just as God had promised, the baby died.

When the baby died, people were afraid to tell David, but he noticed everyone standing around whispering. Suddenly he knew what had happened.

"Is it true that my child is dead?" he asked.

"Yes," the servants sadly replied, wondering what David would do, now that he knew.

How surprised they were to see David quit crying and praying, wash himself, and go to the house of the Lord for worship. Then for the first time since the baby had been sick, he sat down to eat.

When David saw the servants looking strangely at him for acting this way, he turned to them and said, "While my child was alive I prayed, thinking that perhaps God would let him live. But now that he is dead, I cannot bring him back to life. He can never be here with me again, but I know that some day I can go and be with him in heaven."

Yes, David had done a very wicked thing, but he had been very sorry about it and had promised God never to do anything like that again. He knew that God believed his promise and would help him be strong enough to keep it, so that some day he could live in heaven with his child and with God Himself.

Later on, God gave David and Bathsheba another baby named Solomon. This boy grew up to be king after his father David.

Questions:

1. Name some of the things David did as king. 2. What did David see when he was out on his roof one evening? 3. How

did he plan to have Bathsheba for his own wife when she was already married? 4. How did God's prophet show David that he had done something very wicked? 5. Was David sorry? 6. How did God punish David? 7. How did David act after his baby died? Why?

Absalom, David's Disobedient Son

And the king commanded Joab and Abishai and Ittai, saying, Deal gently for my sake with the young man, even with Absalom.
II Sam. 18:5

WHEN David and Bathsheba had little Solomon, David already had other sons who were grown. One of these sons was named Absalom. Absalom was the most handsome man in all the land of Israel, and he had fine, long hair of which he was very proud. David loved Absalom very much, even though Absalom was often disobedient to his father and to God's law. Once Absalom killed his own brother and David had to send him away, but he loved him so much that he later forgave him and let him come back home.

You can see that Absalom did not have a loving heart like his father's—his was wicked and ungrateful. He began planning a way to become king in place of his father. In order to do this, he tried to get the people to notice him. He would ride around the city in his fine chariot with fifty men running before him. Naturally the people turned to look at him when he rode by. Another thing he did was to go to the city gates early in the morning and meet those who were coming to see King David. He would put his arm around their shoulders and act like he was their friend. "The King is too busy to see you," he would tell them. "If I were

The Death of Absalom

only king, I would take time to see everyone and act fairly toward them." Within a few years, everyone loved Absalom. They thought that he really wanted to be their friend.

Now all this time David was living in the palace and he did not know what Absalom was doing. One day Absalom came and asked his father if he could go to the city of Hebron to worship God. David was pleased that Absalom was going to worship and he gave his permission. Little did he know that Absalom had another reason for making the trip.

When he got to Hebron, Absalom sent word all over Israel that he had become king. He asked for his friends to join him there. When they heard the news, many of the people with whom he had been friendly flocked there to meet him. Some of the people who heard the news were still loyal to David. One of them hurried to Jerusalem to tell David what Absalom had done.

How shocked and sad David was to hear that his own son, whom he loved, was going to take the kingdom away from him. He did not know just what his son would try to do, so he gathered together all his family and escaped from the palace. They hurried to the banks of the Jordan River to wait and see what would happen.

About this time Absalom and his friends arrived in Jerusalem and found the palace empty. They took it themselves and began to plan how they would capture King David. One of Absalom's wise men suggested that they go after David right away. But another wise man named Hushai, who was really on David's side, suggested: "David and his men will be angry right now and may beat our men. Let us wait until we can gather a great, big army and then we will have a better chance." He knew that if he could convince Absalom to wait that David would have an opportunity to gather an army, too. Absalom decided to follow Hushai's plan, not realizing that he was giving bad advice on purpose.

Although many of the Israelites joined Absalom's army in Jerusalem, others of them loved David and knew that he was a good king. They could see that Absalom was a disobedient son. These Israelites came to David to fight in his army.

Finally the time came for the battle to decide whether Absalom or David would be king. David's generals insisted that he was too important to risk his life in the battle and made him wait at the city while they fought, but Absalom rode with his army. Before his commanders left, David told them: "I know that this battle must be fought, but it makes me very sad. While you are fighting, watch out for my son. I still love him, no matter what he has done."

That day David's army won a great victory. Thousands of Absalom's soldiers were killed. When Absalom saw what was happening, he turned his mule and tried to run away. As the mule took off in a gallop, it passed under a tree with low-hanging branches. Absalom's thick hair caught in the branches of the tree, and he was left hanging there when the mule ran on. One of David's soldiers saw Absalom hanging helplessly there, but he would not hurt him because of what David had said. He ran to tell Joab, David's general, instead. When Joab heard of it, he went and found

Absalom and thrust three darts into his heart. Then he and his soldiers threw Absalom into a big pit in the forest and covered him with stones. They knew they would make David unhappy when they did this, but they did it anyway because they hated the wicked son for causing his good old father so much trouble.

David was sitting by the city gate when he saw messengers coming toward him from the direction of the battle. The first one ran up saying, "All is well; we have won the battle!" But David was not interested in the battle—he wanted to know how his son was. Then a second messenger arrived with news that Absalom was dead. When he heard of it, David began to cry: "O my son Absalom, my son, my son! If only I could have died for you."

You see, no matter what Absalom did, David never stopped loving him, just as God loves even his disobedient children. How much happier it would have made David if Absalom had done the right thing, and Absalom would not have had such a sad life either. In the same way, God is pleased and we are happier when we obey Him.

Questions:

1. Did David have other sons beside Solomon? 2. How did Absalom get the people to notice him and like him? 3. Why was he doing this? 4. What did David do when he heard that Absalom was going to try to become king? 5. Why did Absalom not fight David right away? 6. What happened to Absalom in the battle? 7. Was David glad Absalom was gone so he could have his kingdom back?

The King with an Understanding Heart

Give therefore thy servant an understanding heart to judge thy people, that I may discern between good and bad.
I Kings 3:9

DAVID was a good king and reigned over Israel for forty years. Most of the time he was king he spent fighting first one enemy and then another. But because he was so successful in his battles, he made Israel strong and powerful. A time of peace came after he died, for the other nations around were afraid to fight the strong Israelite nation King David had made.

Young Solomon, David and Bathsheba's son, became the ruler when his father died. He took over the throne that David had built in Jerusalem. Since the prophet Samuel's death, the altar of the Lord had been moved from his home in Ramah to Gibeon, a few miles away from Jerusalem. When Solomon became king, he realized the tremendous task he had as leader of God's chosen people and he went out to Gibeon to offer sacrifices and to pray to God for help. As Solomon prayed, the Lord heard him; and later He appeared to Solomon in a dream, saying, "Ask me for any gift and I will give it to you."

There were so many things that he could have chosen—what do you think he asked for? Maybe it was not what

The Wisdom of Solomon

you would expect, for this was what he said: "Lord, I know so little about ruling this wonderful nation. Give me an understanding heart so that I might know how to make the best decisions and be a good leader."

God was pleased with Solomon's request. He answered: "Because you asked for this instead of for long life or riches or victory in battle, I am going to grant your wish. You will have a wise mind and be able to tell what is right and what is wrong more than any other man who has ever lived or will live after you. More than that, I am also going to give you the things for which you did *not* ask. You will have riches and honor, and if you serve me as your father did, I will grant you a long life, too."

It was not long before Solomon had a chance to use the wisdom God gave him. Two women and a baby were brought before Solomon. The two women lived together and each one claimed that the baby was her own. You see, one woman's baby had died and she had taken the other woman's child, so no one could tell who the real mother was.

The two stood before King Solomon arguing, "This child is mine," one would say. "No," the other would reply; "the dead child was yours, and this one is mine."

Solomon looked from one to another, then he finally said, "Bring me a sword!" When the sword was brought, he pointed to the baby. "Cut the child in half and give half of it to each one."

When she saw the sword, one of the women gave a loud cry and fell to her knees. "Oh, my lord," she begged, "do not cut the baby in half. Give it to the other woman, but let it live."

But the other woman stood agreeing with Solomon. "That is a good suggestion," she said. "Divide the baby in two, and let us each have half."

This was all Solomon needed to know. "Give the child to the first woman," he said. "She is its true mother for she could not stand to see it killed."

When the people saw how wisely Solomon had found the answer to this question, they knew that indeed God had granted him an understanding heart.

Questions:

1. Why did Solomon have a strong kingdom to rule? 2. What did Solomon pray for? 3. Did God give him what he had asked for? 4. What else did God give him? 5. What were the two women arguing about? 6. How did Solomon tell which one was telling the truth? 7. What did this show about Solomon?

The House of God

And, behold, I purpose to build an house unto the name of the Lord my God.
I Kings 5:5

NOW David had wanted to move the Ark of the Covenant and the altar to Jerusalem and build a great Temple for worship to God, but God had not let him do it. David's reign had been a time of war, and God wanted His house built during peaceful times. However, even though he could not build the Temple, David had collected gold and silver and wood and stone to be used when it was built.

Because Solomon was at peace when he was king, the Lord let him build the wonderful building that David had planned. It stood high on Mount Moriah in Jerusalem. Treasures were brought from all over the world to add to those David had gathered. From King Hiram of Tyre came cedar trees found in the beautiful forests of Lebanon. These logs were made into rafts and were floated down the Great Sea until they were carried ashore and taken to Jerusalem.

For seven years, skilled workmen carefully made each portion of the great building. It was something like the tabernacle that Moses and the Israelites built to worship in while they were in the wilderness. It, too, had a court, containing the altar for sacrifices, and a building, consisting of the Holy Place and the Holy of Holies. Here in the Holy of Holies, the Ark was kept. You will remember that the Ark

Solomon's Temple

was very important to the Israelites, for it was the chest that held the tablets on which the Ten Commandments were written by God. Of course, the Temple was larger than the tabernacle, large enough for the people to gather in the court; and it was a strong building of wood and stone rather than a tent. It even had rooms where the priests could live.

When it was finished, Solomon's Temple was the most splendid building ever seen in those days. Its walls were red cedar wood and its floors shiny marble. Everywhere one looked there was elaborate carving covered with gold and sparkling with precious stones. The Ark stood behind an embroidered scarlet and purple curtain that divided the Holy Place from the Holy of Holies.

When the Ark was brought from Gibeon to be placed in the Temple, it was a time of great celebration for the Israelites. The priests were all dressed in white and sang in a beautiful chorus. The same cloud of glory that had hovered over the Tabernacle filled the new house of worship with a heavenly light. Together, the Israelites and King Solomon prayed for God to bless the great house and make it holy by His presence there.

Besides the Temple, Solomon built splendid palaces in Jerusalem. Within his palace, his throne was made of ivory, covered with gold, and had carved lions on each side. Many other beautiful homes and gardens lined the streets of the city. Israel had never been so rich and great before.

Naturally, news traveled to other lands about Solomon's magnificent kingdom. Kings from other countries came to see this wealthy and wise ruler. With them, they brought treasures of gold and gifts for Solomon.

One of the rulers who visited Solomon was the Queen of Sheba, a country in faraway Arabia. She had heard of Solomon's riches and also of his understanding heart. She came to talk with Solomon about many hard questions that were troubling her. She knew that God could help Solomon give her the right answers. After they had talked, Solomon showed the queen the glory of his palaces and the Temple, his many servants, and his delicious food. The queen had never seen anything so marvelous before. "I had heard about your wisdom and your greatness," she said, "but I could not believe it. Now that I have seen them, I know that they are really far beyond what I had heard. Not half has been told!"

It is sad to know that Solomon was not always as true and faithful to God as he was when he prayed in the new Temple. As he grew older, he began to listen to some of his foreign wives and he worshiped their idol gods. God grew angry when Solomon turned from Him after He had given him so much. He told Solomon that He was going to take all the kingdom except one tribe from Solomon's son. Indeed, the mighty kingdom did begin to fall apart after Solomon died. Solomon's reign had been the greatest time of power and glory that the Israelites had ever known, and they were never able to reach it again.

Questions:

1. Why had King David not built the Temple? 2. Where did

Solomon build it? 3. How was it like the tabernacle? 4. What kind of service was held when the Temple opened? 5. Who came to see Solomon? 6. What did she think of his kingdom? 7. What did Solomon do wrong as he grew old?

No Rain in Israel

And the ravens brought him bread and flesh in the morning, and bread and flesh in the evening; and he drank of the brook.
I Kings 17:6

DAVID had conquered many lands around Israel and made it a strong and rich nation for his son Solomon to rule. But the time of glory while Solomon was king was short—it did not last beyond Solomon himself. Besides disobeying God and worshiping the idol gods of his many wives, Solomon had taken much money from the people to build the Temple and keep up his great kingdom. When Rehoboam, Solomon's son, became king, he asked the people for even more money. The ten tribes who lived north of Jerusalem decided not to follow Rehoboam and they named a young soldier, Jeroboam, to be their leader. Only the tribes of Judah and Benjamin stayed loyal to King Rehoboam in Jerusalem. You see, the capital city of Jerusalem was in the part of the land that belonged to the tribe of Judah.

Young Rehoboam wanted to fight the ten tribes who had broken away from the kingdom and bring the Israelites together again, but God sent a prophet to him. The prophet brought this message: "Do not go up and fight against your brethren. It is God's will that there be two kingdoms." God had seen that the Israelites had grown to be a rich and mighty kingdom and that this had become more important to them than being good people and obeying God's law.

Elijah Fed by the Ravens

God thought that if they were not so great and powerful, perhaps they would depend upon Him more.

So now there were two kingdoms—Israel and Judah. As king of Israel, Jeroboam the soldier led his followers away from the worship of God and they began to worship idols. The kings who came after him grew worse and worse, until finally the people of Israel had forgotten all about being God's chosen people.

Ahab, the sixth king after Jeroboam, was more wicked than all the kings before him. His wife Jezebel taught the Israelites to worship idol gods called Baal and Asherah. Jezebel so hated even the mention of the true God of Israel that she tried to kill the prophets who taught the people about Him. To save their lives, the prophets had to hide in caves.

Now these things greatly displeased the Lord. One day without any warning, He sent a prophet named Elijah right into the presence of King Ahab. Wearing a rough coat of animal skins and looking rather wild, Elijah marched bravely up to Ahab and declared to him that the Lord was going to send no more rain until he, Elijah, asked for it again. Then he disappeared as strangely as he had come.

Surely enough, no rain nor dew fell from that time on. Elijah was led by God to a hidden place by a little brook. Here he drank from the stream and ate food that the ravens brought him.

Because there was no rain, after a while the brook from which Elijah drank began to dry up. But God was taking care of His servant, and this time He sent him to a kind lady who lived in a town that did not belong to the Israelites. You see, Elijah had to stay away from the land of Israel because Ahab was looking for him, as he blamed the prophet for the dry fields and streams that covered his country.

When Elijah finally reached the town where the lady lived, he found her gathering firewood. "May I have some water and a little bread?" he asked her.

"You may have some water," she replied, "but I do not have any bread. All that I have left in my house is a little meal and oil. I was going to make that up into a little cake for me and my son; but when it is eaten, we shall starve."

"Do not be afraid," Elijah told her. "Go ahead and make something for all three of us. The Lord will see that there is always enough meal and oil until the rain comes again and the crops grow."

Surely enough, no matter how much oil or meal the lady took each day to prepare dinner, there was plenty left. She and her son and the hideaway prophet always had enough to eat.

While Elijah was living with the lady, her son became very sick and died before anyone could do anything to help. Now the lady knew that there was something very powerful about Elijah—something she thought was magic. When her son died, she thought that Elijah had done it. "Why did you cause my son to die?" she cried to him.

"Give the boy to me," Elijah said. Then he took the child in his arms and carried him to his own room. Here he laid the boy upon his bed and began to pray to God. He stretched himself upon the body of the boy and asked God to let him live again. Three times he did this, trying, it seemed, to warm the body of the child with his own.

The Lord heard Elijah's prayer and made the boy live again. When the woman saw her son well and happy, she turned and looked at Elijah with wonder. Who was this man who had come to live with her? "Truly, you are a man of God," she finally said.

Questions:

1. Explain the difference in Rehoboam and Jeroboam. 2. Who followed the new leader? 3. Who stayed loyal to Solomon's son? 4. How did King Ahab and Queen Jezebel disobey God? 5. Whom did God send to Ahab and what did he say? 6. Who fed Elijah by the brook? 7. How did the kind woman have enough food for Elijah? 8. What did Elijah do for the woman's son?

Elijah's Strange Contest

And when all the people saw it, they fell on their faces: and they said, The Lord, he is the God; the Lord, he is the God.
I Kings 18:39

FOR three years, no rain nor dew fell upon the land of Israel, just as the prophet Elijah had promised King Ahab. The rivers dried up to a slow trickle and then disappeared. The fields where the Israelites had grown their food became dry and brown. There was no grass for the cattle. At last, the people began to run out of the food they had saved. They cried to King Ahab because they were hungry.

Now among Ahab's servants there was a good man called Obadiah. Once he had hidden some of the prophets of God that Queen Jezebel wanted to kill. While Obadiah was out looking for water one day, he saw Elijah on his way to see the king. He ran back to the palace himself to tell Ahab that Elijah was coming.

King Ahab blamed Elijah for the trouble his people had suffered during the three years without rain. Actually, it was God who was punishing the king and his people, but he had spoken the words of the curse through Elijah. When Ahab saw Elijah coming toward him, he called him a "troubler of Israel."

"*You* are the troubler of Israel," Elijah told the king.

Elijah on Mt. Carmel

"You and your wife Jezebel have brought it upon your people by worshiping Baal."

Then to prove how foolish it was to worship idol gods, Elijah challenged Ahab to a strange contest of prayer. Ahab was to command the people to assemble on Mount Carmel. Then he was to bring the four hundred fifty priests of Baal and four hundred priests of Asherah to meet Elijah there. The king agreed to the meeting.

Several days later the Israelites came together on Mount Carmel. Elijah stood before the crowd and said, "You have changed back and forth from God to Baal long enough. Today both the prophets of Baal and I will call for fire from our God, and the one who sends it will be Lord indeed, whether he be Baal or our Father in heaven."

The people agreed that it was a fair test. Two oxen were prepared and one placed on the altar to Baal, but no fire was lit. Then the prophets of Baal stood around their altar and called to their god to send fire down upon the altar. "O Baal, answer us," they cried from morning until noon; but there was no reply.

"Cry louder!" Elijah called to them. "Maybe your god is away on a journey, or maybe he is asleep and you will have to wake him."

The prophets of Baal, who were already tired, became furious when they heard this. Because they did not know what else to do, they began cutting their bodies with knives until they bled, while they chanted their heathen prayers louder and louder.

By the middle of the afternoon their altar stood just as it had at the beginning of the day. No fire had come to burn the sacrifice. Then the people turned to Elijah. Solemnly he placed twelve stones, one for each tribe, to form an altar. Then he prepared his oxen for the sacrifice and laid it upon some wood. Next he called for water and three times poured it over the altar, the wood, and the sacrifice, soaking them thoroughly. Lifting his eyes toward heaven, he began to pray: "O Lord, God of Abraham, Isaac, and Israel, let it be known today that you are the God of Israel, and that I am your servant and follow your word."

Suddenly the answer came—flames fell from the sky in fiery sheets that burned up the offering and the wood and even the altar and the stones on which they were laid. Every drop of water around the altar disappeared in the fierce flames. The people fell on their faces when they saw this terrifying sight. "The Lord, He is God; the Lord, He is God," they cried over and over.

When this happened, the prophets of Baal began to run away, but Elijah called out: "Take the prophets of Baal; do not let them escape!" So the people followed them and killed them at the foot of the mountain.

Then Elijah had one more prayer to make on that great day—this time for rain. Before Ahab's chariot had driven him from Mount Carmel back to the palace, the dark clouds rolled overhead and the huge drops began to fall. It had been a victorious day for Elijah and his God.

Questions:

1. Why had no rain fallen on Israel in three years? 2. Why

did Elijah challenge Ahab to a contest? 3. What did the priests of Baal do to try to bring fire from their god? 4. What did Elijah do? 5. Who won the contest?

Seven Dips in the Jordan

And she said unto her mistress, Would God my lord were with the prophet that is in Samaria! for he would recover him of his leprosy.
II Kings 5:3

IN the days of the great prophet, Elisha, the Syrians and the Israelites of the Northern Kingdom made little attacks on one another even when the two were not really having a war. The two peoples lived right next to one another, and usually these attacks were made on the towns along the border between them. Bands of soldiers would suddenly storm into these villages, rob the people of their grain and cattle, and take away captives to be sold as slaves. During one raid, a little Israelite girl was taken from her family by the Syrian soldiers. She was carried with them back to their country, and she became a servant in the house of a great Syrian captain, Naaman. Probably she was sad and lonely away from her family, but God always lets things happen for good, and this small girl was able to do great good in this strange land.

Naaman, the servant girl's master, had won many battles, and he was a favorite of the king of Syria. But this brave and strong soldier became sick with a terrible disease called leprosy. Naaman and his family were distressed and the king was sorry because there was no way to cure leprosy. A person who had leprosy got terrible sores on his body and eventually he would die. No one wanted to come near

Naaman in the Jordan

a leper for fear he would get the disease, too. Even though Naaman was a great man, he was sure to die.

The little Israelite girl that lived in Naaman's house had not forgotten about God and the prophets of God who lived in her own land. She felt sorry for her master, but she was too timid to go to him. Instead, she went to Naaman's wife, her mistress, and told her that in Israel there was a prophet of God who could cure Naaman.

When Naaman heard of this prophet, he went straight to his king and told him about it. The king was interested and gave Naaman a letter to take to the king of Israel, asking that he try to heal the captain. Besides the letter, Naaman took along many servants and gifts on his trip to Israel.

When Naaman gave the king of Israel the letter, the king was worried. He knew that he could not heal the man. He was afraid the king of Syria was only trying to stir up trouble.

Elisha the prophet heard that the king of Israel was worried, so he sent word that Naaman was to come to him. When Naaman and his servants came to the prophet's house, Elisha did not even come out to meet him. He simply sent word by his servant that Naaman was to wash seven times in the Jordan River and he would be well.

Naaman grew very angry when he heard what Elisha wanted him to do. He had expected the prophet to come out and do some wonderful thing to heal him. "Why," he said, "the rivers of my own country are better than the Jordan! Why should I wash there?"

But Naaman's servants were more thoughtful than he was. They asked him, "Master, would you not have done some great thing if he had asked you to? Why not do this simple thing?"

Naaman listened to his servants and thought it over. Finally he drove down to the Jordan River and stepped out of his chariot. Into the water he went and dipped himself—once, twice, up to seven times. As he came out of the water the last time, every bit of his leprosy was gone. His skin that had been covered with sores was as smooth and clean as a baby's soft skin. God had performed another wonderful miracle through the great prophet Elisha.

When Naaman hurried back to thank Elisha, Elisha would not take the rewards and gifts Naaman offered him. He had not healed Naaman for money. He had wanted to teach him of the wonderful God of the Israelites. Naaman gave him the best gift when he told him that he would never again pray to any god except the true God that had given the waters of the Jordan the power to make him well.

Questions:

1. Why was an Israelite girl living in Naaman's house? 2. What was wrong with Naaman? 3. What did the little girl tell Naaman's wife? 4. Why was the king of Israel worried when Naaman came to him? 5. Who came to the king's rescue? 6. What did he tell Naaman to do? 7. What happened to Naaman when he did what Elisha said?

Elisha Helps a Friend

And she said unto her husband, Behold now, I perceive that this is an holy man of God, which passeth by us continually.
II Kings 4:9

ALL of his life Elijah the prophet tried to bring the Israelites of the north and their wicked kings back to the worship of the true God. He taught other prophets to help him in his work. Among these, his closest friend and helper was Elisha. When Elijah was old, Elisha saw God carry him to heaven in a fiery chariot, pulled by horses of fire and carried upward in a whirlwind. As Elijah climbed into the chariot and it began to fly toward heaven, his coat fell at Elisha's feet, showing that God had chosen him to take Elijah's place.

After this, Elisha began traveling from place to place, helping the people, teaching them of God, and leading them in their worship. One day Elisha visited a little town named Shunem, and a rich woman there invited him to eat with her. He enjoyed himself so much that afterward, whenever he passed by Shunem, he always stopped to visit and eat with the kind lady.

One day the lady said to her husband: "It seems that this man of God passes our way often. Let us build a little room for him upstairs that he can stay in whenever he comes." So they built a nice clean room, and in it they put a bed, a table, a chair, and a lamp to make Elisha feel welcome.

Elisha and the Shunammite Woman

Elisha was very pleased with the room that was his own. He enjoyed staying in it, and he was thankful to the lady for building it for him. He told her, "You have been very kind to me. Now what can I do for you? Shall I ask the king or the commander of the army for some favor for you?"

"No, thank you," replied the lady. "I am happy here with my own people."

Elisha tried and tried to think of something he could do for the lady. Then his servant, Gehazi, had an idea. "The lady's husband is old and she has no one else, no children at all," he told Elisha.

So they called the woman up to their room. As she stood in the doorway, Elisha told her, "This time next year you will have a baby boy."

How happy the woman was to hear this! All year she waited and prepared things for the baby that was coming. Then, just as Elisha had promised, a baby boy was born to her. He was his mother's and father's greatest joy.

Several years later, when the boy had grown old enough, he went out with his father into the field. As he was standing there in the hot sun, he suddenly cried out, "Oh, my head! My head!"

Seeing that his son was very sick, the father said to his servants, "Carry him in to his mother." The mother held her boy in her lap all morning, and she did everything she could for him, but about noon he died.

The sad lady carried him upstairs to Elisha's room and laid him on the bed. Then she hurried downstairs. "I am going to see the prophet," she told her husband, and she left on an ass the servant had saddled for her.

When Elisha saw the woman riding fast toward him, he sent Gehazi out to meet her. "Is everything all right with you? How are your husband and your child?" Gehazi asked. But the woman would not even stop. "Everything is fine," she told him, and kept right on going until she reached Elisha. Then she got off the ass and bowed down and began sobbing, but she did not tell Elisha what was wrong. Elisha knew that she was very sad, but he waited quietly until she finally spoke: "Did I ask you to give me a son?"

Immediately Elisha knew that something had happened to the boy. He sent Gehazi to the woman's house, and he and the woman came behind.

Before Elisha and the lady reached the house, Gehazi came running back to them. He had already gotten to the house and seen the boy. "The child did not awaken," he whispered to Elisha. Surely enough, Elisha found the child lying dead in his room. He closed the door so that he and the child were alone. Then he lay down on the bed on top of the child. He put his mouth and eyes and hands upon those of the boy, and the boy's body began to feel warm just as Elisha's was.

Elisha got up and walked around the room a bit and then lay down upon the child again. Suddenly the boy sneezed seven times and opened his eyes. Elisha called to the lady, "Come and get your son!"

The lady could hardly believe it when she saw her son sitting up and looking about. She fell at Elisha's feet, thanking him again and again. Then she lovingly picked up her son and carried him downstairs.

Questions:

1. How did Elijah go to heaven? 2. Whom did God choose to take his place? 3. What did a kind lady do for Elisha? 4. How did Elisha thank her for doing this? 5. What happened to the lady's son when he was in the field? 6. To whom did she go for help?

Jonah Tries to Run Away

Now the Lord had prepared a great fish to swallow up Jonah. And Jonah was in the belly of the fish three days and three nights.
Jonah 1:17

DURING the time when the prophets Elijah and Elisha lived, the Syrians were the greatest enemies of the Israelites of the north, the ten tribes who had not followed Solomon's son. But as Elisha promised just before he died, the Syrians were finally defeated.

A new nation called Assyria became powerful after Syria went down. The Assyrians moved into all the nations around them and conquered them; and those in the land of Israel knew that they, too, would have to fight before long. Many stories were told about the mighty Assyrians, especially about their great city, Nineveh, so huge that it would take a man three days to walk around it.

One day the Lord called a new prophet from the Israelites, a man named Jonah. He gave Jonah a strange message: "Go to Nineveh and preach to the people. Tell them that I am displeased at their wicked ways."

"Nineveh?" Jonah asked himself. "Surely the Lord could not have meant for me to go to Nineveh. The Israelites are God's only chosen people. The people in Nineveh are idol-worshipers. They are not even worth my trouble."

But Jonah was not really sure that he should not go. Perhaps he knew that he was doing wrong, because he

The Prophet Jonah

felt like he wanted to run away and hide. Instead of going to Nineveh, he went the other direction, toward the Great Sea. Finally he came to Joppa, a seaport town, and made arrangements to board a trading ship headed for a faraway port.

No sooner had the ship set sail when a terrible storm arose. The ship rolled and tossed as great waves broke over the deck. Trying to save it, the sailors threw all the goods overboard so that the load would be as light as possible. Still the boat rocked as though it might go under at any moment. In terror, the sailors fell to their knees and began praying to their idol gods.

Now all this time Jonah had been asleep in his room below deck. The captain went down and shook him awake. "How can you sleep?" he asked. "Begin praying to your God also; perhaps He can save us." But Jonah's prayers did no more than the others and the storm roared on. Finally someone decided, "There must be a man on this ship who has done wrong and brought this danger upon us. Let us cast lots and find out which of us it is."

When the lots were cast, Jonah was the one found guilty. The sailors turned to him and began asking: "Who are you? Where are you from? What business do you have here? What have you done to bring about this storm?"

Jonah told them that he was an Israelite and that he was running away from a job that God had given him. Sadly he told them that the only way they could save their ship would be to throw him overboard.

At first the sailors were not willing to do as Jonah said. Instead, they tried hard to steer the ship to safety themselves. But at last they saw that it was no use, and they tossed Jonah over the side of the ship.

When Jonah fell into the sea, the storm suddenly grew calm. The sailors, looking on, fell to their knees in worship of the powerful God whom Jonah the Israelite served.

Under the water Jonah's body plunged, but God's mighty hand caused a giant fish to pass that way at that moment. The fish opened its huge mouth and sucked Jonah, alive, right into its stomach. For three days and nights Jonah lived in the slimy darkness of the fish's stomach. Most of that time he spent praying to God to forgive him and save him. Then suddenly the fish opened his mouth and threw up Jonah, right onto a dry beach.

As he stood in the sand, smoothing his ragged clothes and wiping off his skin, he heard the call of the Lord again: "Go to Nineveh and preach." This time he did not wait, but hurried as quickly as he could to the great city.

In Nineveh, Jonah told his message to everyone he met. "Unless you turn from evil, the Lord is going to destroy your city," he warned the people as he walked up and down each street.

To Jonah's surprise, the people believed what he said. They listened as though they had been just waiting to know how they could save themselves. They grew sorry for their sins, and even the king ordered that everyone pray to the Lord God for forgiveness.

When the Lord saw this, He forgave the people of Nineveh and decided to save their city. But this made Jonah very angry. He was disappointed that God wanted to save these foreign people. In his heart, he wished that God had gone ahead and destroyed them.

Sulking and stubborn, Jonah marched out of the city. He built himself a little shack on the edge of town and sat down to wait and see whether or not the Lord would destroy the city.

One day God caused a plant to grow up beside Jonah's little shelter. It had big leaves that threw shade across Jonah and he rested happily out of the hot sun. Then in the night a worm ate the plant and killed it. As the hot wind and sun hit Jonah the next day, Jonah cried for his shade vine. He said that he would rather die than suffer in the heat.

Then God spoke to foolish Jonah: "How can you cry over a little plant that came and went in one day and then show no pity for a great city where thousands of helpless children live?"

Jonah realized then that people are the most precious thing in the world and that God cares for every person, even those who never had a chance to know about Him. Most of the Old Testament tells of God's concern for His chosen people, the Israelites, but the story of Jonah shows us that He is a God of all nations and that everyone falls under the power of His love.

Questions:

1. Who were the Assyrians? 2. What did God ask Jonah to

do for the Assyrian people in Nineveh? 3. What did Jonah do instead? 4. Why was Jonah thrown off the ship? 5. In what strange place did Jonah live for three days? 6. What did the people of Nineveh do when Jonah finally came and preached to them? 7. Why did this disappoint Jonah? 8. How did God show Jonah that the people of Nineveh were important to Him?

One Good King

Turn again and tell Hezekiah the captain of my people, Thus saith the Lord, the God of David thy father, I have heard thy prayer, I have seen thy tears: behold, I will heal thee.
II Kings 20:5

EVEN though the Lord sent prophets like Elijah and Elisha to the ten tribes of Israel in the north, not many of the people were led back to the worship of the true God. Most of them followed their wicked kings and worshiped idol gods. Without God's help, they became weaker and weaker. Finally, the mighty Assyrians came down, captured the king, and took most of the Israelites back to their own country.

These captive Israelites stayed in the cities of the Assyrians and mixed with them. After several years had passed, one could not even tell who was an Israelite and who was an Assyrian. Ten tribes of Israel were lost forever. It is sad to think that so many of God's people were too wicked for Him to let them stay in the land He had given them.

The tribes of Judah and Benjamin who had remained loyal to Solomon's son in Jerusalem had some kings who worshiped idols, but they had some good kings who served the Lord, too. These people of Judah were the people God planned to keep separate from others as His chosen people, although they were only a small part of the twelve tribes that had served Him in the beginning. Usually these two

Isaiah and King Hezekiah

tribes were known simply as Judah because Judah was the larger tribe, and sometimes this was shortened to "Jews." Their land was called Judea.

After several wicked kings had ruled over Judah, the nation was almost as bad as the ten tribes who had been carried away. Then one of the wicked kings died and his son, Hezekiah, became king. Hezekiah was not like his father—he did what was right before God. He was one of the best kings Judah had.

While the evil kings had ruled, the beautiful Temple that Solomon had built had become shabby and dirty. The priests who took care of it had been made to leave, and no one came there to worship. The first thing Hezekiah did when he became king was to open the doors of the Temple. He called the priests to come back and clean the building. When the priests went in they found dirt and rubbish everywhere. For eight days they cleaned and scrubbed until the altar and all the dishes used for worship were ready to be used again. Then Hezekiah and many of the people went to the Temple and offered sacrifices. The priests sang some of the songs David had written in praise to God. Everyone was thrilled to worship the Lord again, although it was a little strange since they had not done it for so long.

When King Hezekiah saw how good it was to serve the Lord and that the people were willing to do it, he decided to observe the Passover that year. You remember that the Passover was a feast to remind the Israelites of the way the Lord passed over on the night they left Egypt. God had commanded them to eat this feast every year, but for many years no one in Judah or Israel had remembered it. Hezekiah sent letters all over the kingdom inviting the people to come to Jerusalem for the Passover feast. He even invited those who were left of the ten tribes in the north, but they would not come. However, the people of Judah did come, and they enjoyed the feast and the worship so much that they stayed a week longer than they had intended.

Because Hezekiah loved God and tried to urge the people to worship Him, the little kingdom of Judah was kept safe during his reign. Even the Assyrians, who were capturing all the nations around, were stopped by an angel of the Lord when they tried to attack Jerusalem.

About the time that Hezekiah was trying to keep the Assyrians from taking his land and people, he became very sick, so sick that he was about to die. A prophet of God named Isaiah came to him and said, "Get ready to leave your family and kingdom, because the time has come for you to die."

When Hezekiah heard this he became very sad. He turned away from Isaiah and the tears began to roll down his cheeks. He felt that his people really needed him a little while longer. Earnestly he began to pray: "O God, remember how I have tried to be faithful and do what was right in your sight. Please let me live."

The Lord heard Hezekiah. Isaiah, who was still on his way home, turned back toward the palace. "Tell Hezekiah," the Lord said to Isaiah, "that I have heard him and seen his tears, and that I will make him get well. He will live another fifteen years."

Surely enough, in three days Hezekiah was well enough to go to the Temple and worship. For another fifteen years he ruled over Judah. He was very rich and happy and the people honored him as the best king Judah had ever had.

Questions:

1. What happened to the ten tribes of Israel in the north? 2. Who was left of God's chosen people? 3. Had the people of Judah always stayed faithful to God? 4. What was the Temple like when Hezekiah became king? 5. Why did Hezekiah invite the people to come to Jerusalem? 6. What sad message did Isaiah bring to Hezekiah? 7. How did God answer Hezekiah's prayer?

Captives in Babylon

And at the end of ten days their countenances appeared fairer and fatter in flesh than all the children which did eat the portion of the king's meat.
Daniel 1:15

HEZEKIAH was one of Judah's good kings, but there was only one more good king after him—Josiah. The rest were wicked and led the people away from God. Again and again prophets like Isaiah and Jeremiah told the people that God would punish them, just as Elijah and Elisha had warned the Israelites in the north, but the foolish Jews paid no attention.

By this time the Assyrians, who had captured the Israelites, were not the strongest nation in the world. Their great city, Nineveh, where Jonah had preached, had been destroyed. The newest power was Babylon and Nebuchadnezzar was its king. King Nebuchadnezzar fought the strong countries around him and conquered them all. Finally, he brought his mighty army to Judah and captured the weak king who was ruling. He carried the king, his noblemen, and many of the best people in the land back to Babylon with him. He also took the golden dishes from the Temple to use in his idol temples.

Now the people of Judah were captives just as the people of Israel had been. Nebuchadnezzar's soldiers made them walk the hundreds of miles to Babylon and it took a long, long time. They were sad to leave their homes and they

Shadrach, Meshach and Abednego

cried when they thought that they might never see Jerusalem again. But the best thing about the people of Judah was this: their troubles made them remember God. Because they did not feel sure of themselves any longer, they turned to God for help.

Jeremiah the prophet was among the few people Nebuchadnezzar left in Jerusalem. God told him that those who had been captured were the people who were going to stay faithful to Him and bring a blessing on the tribe of Judah. He told Jeremiah to write letters to the people in Babylon and tell them that if they were true to God, He would let them return to their own land in seventy years.

The Jews in Babylon were glad to hear from Jeremiah. Actually they were finding their captivity better than they thought it would be. They discovered that Nebuchadnezzar meant to be kind to them. He let them build their homes and raise their own crops. But no matter how successful they were, these captives were thankful to know that God was going to let them go back to Jerusalem some day. They reminded their children of this and taught them to worship God instead of the Babylonian idols.

Nebuchadnezzar knew that he had brought princes and noblemen from Judah, and he wanted to use them in his kingdom. He told one of the men who had charge of his affairs to choose some of the Jewish noblemen to come to a special school at the palace. He wanted young men who were smart and handsome and well-mannered.

Among the princes who were chosen for this honor were Daniel, Shadrach, Meshach, and Abednego. For three years they studied and trained before they were taken to the king.

While serving the king, the four young men were given some of the same food that was served to his majesty as a special treat. But the Jews had laws that Moses had given them about the kind of food they could eat, and the young men knew that the food of the king was the wrong kind for them.

Daniel and his friends decided that they could not disobey God and eat the king's food. They went to the chief nobleman and told him this. The nobleman was kind to listen to them, but he said: "If you do not eat the king's food, I am afraid you will look pale and thin and the king will notice it. He will blame me for not taking care of you and have me killed."

"Just let us try something," Daniel begged. "For ten days give us only vegetables to eat instead of the king's rich food. At the end of that time, see if we do not look as healthy as the other young men."

The man agreed to let Daniel and his friends try this plan; and at the end of ten days, the four looked better than all those who served the king. When all the young princes who had been trained in the palace school came and stood before Nebuchadnezzar, he chose Daniel, Shadrach, Meshach, and Abednego to take the highest positions in his court.

Questions:

1. Who was Nebuchadnezzar? 2. How had the Babylonians become the strongest people in the world? 3. What did they

do when they came to Judea? 4. What did Jeremiah write to the Jews in Babylon? 5. How were the Jews treated in Babylon? 6. Who was chosen to go to the king's school? 7. Why did Daniel and his friends not want to eat the king's food? 8. Did not eating this food make them look any different?

The Fiery Furnace

He answered and said, Lo, I see four men loose, walking in the midst of the fire, and they have no hurt; and the form of the fourth is like the Son of God.
Dan. 3:25

AFTER Daniel, Shadrach, Meshach, and Abednego came to the palace to serve King Nebuchadnezzar, the king had a dream. Like the people of those days, the king thought his dream had a meaning, but he could not even remember what the dream was. He called in his magicians and wise men and asked them to tell him what his dream meant.

"O king," the wise men said, "if you could tell us about your dream, we could tell you what it means."

"I do not remember the dream!" the king said in anger. "Either you tell me my dream and its meaning or I will have you torn limb from limb."

The wise men looked at one another, but none knew what to say. King Nebuchadnezzar grew more and more furious, waiting for them to answer. Finally, he sent them from the room and ordered that they all be killed.

Now Daniel and his friends were known as wise men, and the captain of the king's guard arrested them so he could kill them, too.

"Why is the king so angry with us?" Daniel asked in surprise.

When he found out what the trouble was, he asked to see the king himself. "Great Nebuchadnezzar," he said,

©
John H. Eggers Publications and The New York Public Library

In the Fiery Furnace

"give me a little time, and I will ask my God to show me the meaning of your dream. Please do not kill the wise men yet."

So Nebuchadnezzar agreed to wait and gave Daniel a time to come back and tell him of the dream. That night Daniel, Shadrach, Meshach, and Abednego prayed and prayed to God to show them the meaning of the king's dream. At last, God showed Daniel clearly what he was to say to the king.

When Daniel came back to the king, he told him all about his dream. It was a strange dream about a statue and it told of the kingdoms that would rule the world in the future.

Nebuchadnezzar was surprised that Daniel knew all of these things, and he could tell that they were true. Even though he was the highest ruler in the land, he bowed before Daniel and said, "Truly your God is the God of all gods to have shown this mystery to you."

But Nebuchadnezzar did not really understand about the true God that the captives from Judah worshiped. He was used to the many idol gods of Babylon, and he thought that the Israelite God was just another of these, even though He was a great One. He did not understand that He was the *only* One.

Knowing this, we can understand why Nebuchadnezzar built idol gods for his people to worship. One of these was a great gold statue that stood in a field so that everyone could see it. Nebuchadnezzar thought that this god had helped him become a great king; and in order to please it, he ruled that everyone bow down to it. All over the kingdom it was proclaimed: "When you hear the sound of all the musical instruments, you must fall down and worship the gold idol of King Nebuchadnezzar. Anyone who disobeys will be thrown into a fiery furnace."

After that, whenever the music sounded, everyone looked toward the great golden statue and bowed his head toward the ground. That is, everyone but three bowed to the ground. Yes, Daniel's three friends stood straight and tall even when they heard the music. They bowed only before the true God.

When Nebuchadnezzar heard that Shadrach, Meshach, and Abednego had disobeyed his command, he grew very angry.

"I will give you one more chance to obey me and bow down to this idol," he said to them. But the three men still refused to worship the golden statue.

This made Nebuchadnezzar angrier than ever. "Make the furnace seven times hotter than ever before," he commanded, "and throw these men into it!"

So Shadrach, Meshach, and Abednego were tied and thrown into the furnace. When the door was opened to toss them in, the heat was so terrific that it burned to death the soldiers that were holding them.

Nebuchadnezzar stood at a distance and watched as the three men were shoved into the flames. Then he stepped as close as he could and looked in again through the open door. Something was very strange!

"Did we not throw *three* men into the furnace?" he asked those who stood around him.

"That is true, great king," they replied.

"Well, I see *four* men in there now!" he cried. "They are loose and walking around, as if they are not hurt. One of them even looks like a god!"

Then Nebuchadnezzar called out, "Shadrach, Meshach, and Abednego, servants of the most high God, come out of there."

The three young men stepped from the furnace and walked toward King Nebuchadnezzar. Everyone gathered around them, but they could see that neither their clothes nor their bodies were burned a bit. They did not even smell like smoke.

Then Nebuchadnezzar turned to the crowd around him and said, "Blessed be the God of these men, the One who sent an angel to save them when they refused to worship any other. Hear this: anyone who speaks against the God of Shadrach, Meshach, and Abednego shall be punished, for there is no other god who can do a thing like this."

Afterward, Nebuchadnezzar promoted the three captives from Judah to even higher positions in his court.

Questions:

1. Why did Nebuchadnezzar order that the wise men be killed? 2. How did Daniel know the meaning of the king's dream? 3. Why did Nebuchadnezzar become angry with Shadrach, Meshach, and Abednego? 4. How did he plan to punish them? 5. How hot was the furnace? 6. What did Nebuchadnezzar see in the furnace?

The Handwriting on the Wall

Then Daniel answered and said before the king, Let thy gifts be to thyself, and give thy rewards to another; yet I will read the writing unto the king, and make known to him the interpretation.
Dan. 5:17

NEBUCHADNEZZAR was a strong king and he was usually kind to the captives from Judah. He brought Daniel and some other Jewish men to the palace to help him rule his kingdom. When Nebuchadnezzar died, several others served as king, but none of them could do as well as he. Babylon was still the strongest nation in the world, but it became weaker while these other kings reigned. Finally a man called Belshazzar became king of Babylon. He was not a wise ruler, and he did not feel that he needed Daniel to hold an important position in his kingdom.

Now Belshazzar liked to give big parties for the Babylonians who were his friends. On one particular night he gave a dinner for a thousand of his lords. The dinner was held at a temple to one of the idols they worshiped. To make the dinner look finer and grander, Belshazzar served his friends with the golden dishes that had been stolen from God's Temple in Jerusalem.

While the guests were still around the tables, laughing and drinking wine from the beautiful golden cups, something very strange happened. High on the wall a hand appeared, writing words that no one could read or understand.

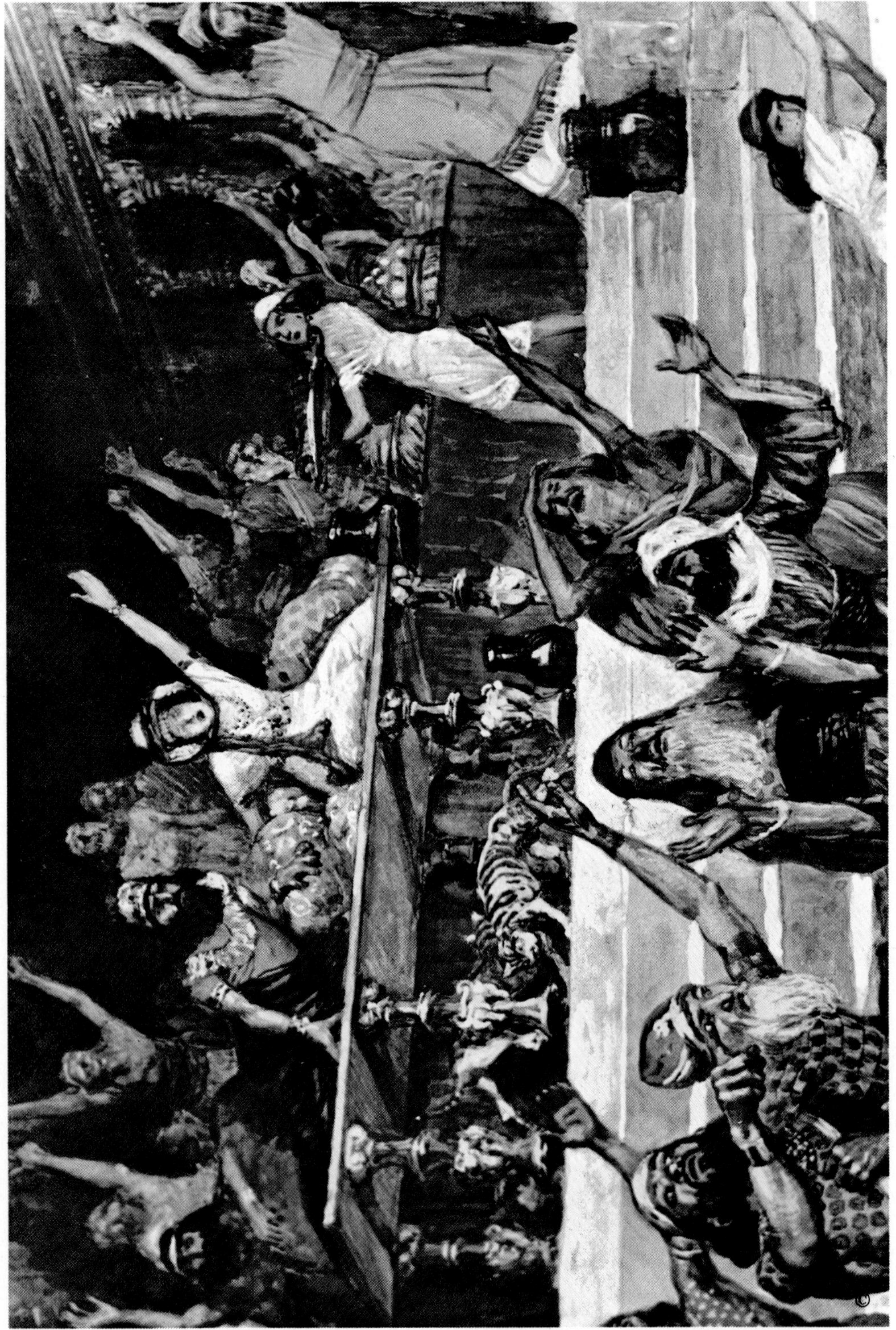

John H. Eggers Publications and The New York Public Library

The Handwriting on the Wall

Everyone in the room grew still and quiet when they saw the hand slowly moving across the wall. The king was so frightened that his knees began to shake. No one knew what to do.

Finally Belshazzar thought enough to say: "Bring the wise men and magicians here to tell me what this means. Whoever can read this writing may have a scarlet robe and a chain of gold around his neck and may be the third ruler in the kingdom."

The wise men and magicians hurried to the banquet hall when they heard this. They looked and looked at the strange writing on the wall, but none of them could read it.

King Belshazzar was more dismayed than ever. He did not know where to turn and yet he felt that it was important for him to find out what the words said. Finally the queen remembered something. She turned to Belshazzar and said, "There was a man who served Nebuchadnezzar who could tell what dreams meant. He had the spirit of a holy God within him. His name was Daniel. Let us call him here to tell us the meaning of this strange writing."

So Daniel was sent for. When he came into the great hall, the king asked him: "Are you the Daniel who was brought with the captives of Judah by Nebuchadnezzar? I have heard that you have the spirit of God and can understand dreams. If you can read this writing, I will give you a scarlet robe to wear, a golden chain to put around your neck, and you shall be the third highest ruler in my kingdom."

"You may keep the gifts or give them to someone else," Daniel told the king. "I do not want them, but I will tell you the meaning of this writing."

"O king," he continued, "Nebuchadnezzar was a powerful ruler because God permitted him to be. The true God in heaven rules over all earthly kings. Even though you knew this, you brought the dishes from the Temple of the Lord here for your princes to drink wine from. You worshiped idol gods instead of the one God who gave you this kingdom and all that you have."

"Now God has sent you this message written upon the wall. It means that your kingdom is going to end. It will be taken from you and given to the Medes and Persians. You have not measured up to what God expected of you."

The message was a terrible one to King Belshazzar, but he had promised Daniel a reward. Sadly he called for a robe and necklace and pronounced Daniel the third highest ruler in the kingdom.

But no sooner had this happened when shouts and noise were heard outside in the streets. They were the sounds of soldiers marching and running, coming nearer and nearer. Suddenly the gates of the hall were thrown open and the Medes and Persians rushed in.

Yes, these mighty soldiers had been waiting outside the walls of Babylon that very evening. While Belshazzar was having the dinner, they had made a passage under the city walls and crept into the city.

There was no escape for the king and his guests, although Daniel did get away safely. The kingdom of Babylon ended that night. Now the Medes and the Persians, together, were the strongest nation in the world.

Questions:

1. Who became king after Nebuchadnezzar? 2. What dishes did Belshazzar use at his dinner party? 3. What happened during the dinner? 4. Whom did the queen suggest that Belshazzar send for to tell the meaning of the writing? 5. What did Daniel say that the message meant? 6. How did it come true that very night?

In a Den of Lions

And the king spake and said to Daniel, O Daniel, servant of the living God, is thy God, whom thou servest continually, able to deliver thee from the lions?
Dan. 6:20

AFTER Nebuchadnezzar died, the kingdom of Babylon began to fall. Several other kings reigned, and finally one named Belshazzar came into power. Belshazzar was an unwise ruler and he even served his banquet guests with the golden dishes that had been stolen from the Temple at Jerusalem. During the feast, God's hand wrote a strange message on the wall that only Daniel could read. It told that Belshazzar's kingdom was going to be taken from him by the Medes and Persians, and it truly was that very night.

The Persians who captured Babylon and killed King Belshazzar at his feast had the mightiest kingdom ever known. It was stronger and bigger than either the Assyrians' or the Babylonians'. It covered all the lands of the Bible people. Its ruler, King Cyrus, sent an old man named Darius to rule over Babylon where the people of Judah were still captives. Daniel, who was now old himself, served King Darius as he had King Nebuchadnezzar.

Daniel did not merely serve the king—he was the most important of all the king's officers. Of course, some of the other princes were jealous of Daniel. They knew that he was not really a Babylonian, but a Jewish captive, and they thought that he should not be so important. So these men tried to find something wrong with the man of God

John H. Eggers Publications and The New York Public Library

Daniel in the Lions' Den

so they could report it to the king. This one thing they knew: three times every day Daniel opened his window and looked toward Jerusalem while he prayed to God. Planning their trap, the other officers asked Darius to make a law that everyone should bow down only to the king for thirty days or be thrown into a den of lions. Darius was foolish and proud, and he agreed to sign the law.

When Daniel found out about the law, he still continued to pray every day to the true God. The princes stood by his window and watched him open it to pray as usual; then they went and told the king that Daniel had disobeyed him.

Now Darius was sorry that he had signed such a foolish law, and he tried to find some way to save Daniel, but there was no way to do it. The law had been made. Finally Darius sent Daniel to the den of lions. In his heart, he hoped that the God Daniel served would save him, because he thought a great deal of Daniel and knew that he was a good man.

Now in those days hungry lions were kept in a sealed pit to be used as a special punishment. As the soldiers led Daniel toward the pit, the lions' roars were muffled; but how loud and fierce they came when the stone covering the den was opened! The guards threw Daniel in quickly and covered the opening with the stone again.

All night the king worried about Daniel. He could not even sleep or eat his food. When morning came, he hurried to the lions' den and took away the stone.

"Daniel, was your God able to save you?" he called hopefully.

From deep inside the darkness of the pit, Daniel answered, "My Lord sent an angel who has closed the mouth of the lions, O King, so that you could see that I meant no wrong."

How happy Darius was! He had Daniel taken from the den, and the jealous princes were thrown in instead. This time, the lions were not guarded by any angel and the men were killed.

Daniel continued to serve in the palace all the days of his life and he continued to make his wonderful prophecies about the kingdom of God which was to come.

Questions:

1. What job did Daniel have in the new kingdom of the Persians? 2. Why did the other princes want to trap Daniel? 3. What foolish law did they get the king to sign? 4. Did Daniel obey the new law? 5. What was his punishment? 6. What happened in the den of lions that night? 7. What happened to the jealous princes the next day?

Home Again!

And all the people shouted with a great shout, when they praised the Lord, because the foundation of the house of the Lord was laid.
Ezra 3:11

WHEN the Persians killed Belshazzar and began to rule Babylon, God's people, the captives from Judah, had been there many years. Those who had been young when they were brought to Babylon, such as Daniel, were now quite old. Some of the people had died while they were in Babylon and many babies were born who had never lived in Judea at all. But the older people remembered their homeland and their wonderful city, Jerusalem, and they told the children all about it. This made the children want to go there some day.

Cyrus was the mighty king of the Persians, and when he became ruler of Babylon, God put it in his heart to make a new law. The new law of Cyrus said: "God has given me all the kingdoms that I rule. Now he wants me to build him a house of worship in Jerusalem. All the captives from Judah may now go back to their home in Jerusalem and build this house. Those who choose to stay in Babylon must give money and silver and gold and food to help those who make the long journey."

When the Jews heard of and read the new law, they were excited and glad. At last they were going home to build a temple of worship to the God they served. Do you remem-

Rebuilding the Temple

ber that the prophet Jeremiah had written letters to Babylon when the Jews first came there and told them that they would get to return to Jerusalem in seventy years? Well, when Cyrus made this law, that promise came true, for seventy years had passed.

Many of the Jews began to get ready for the long journey ahead. Those who were too old or too young to make the trip and those who wanted to stay in Babylon helped those who were going. They brought gifts of gold and silver to use in building the new Temple. They prepared food for the trip and gave animals for people to ride on. Even Cyrus the king gave something—all the golden dishes from the Temple of God that Nebuchadnezzar had stolen.

With all this treasure, the Jews set out on their journey. What a happy group they made! Beside the river they walked and rode, singing as they went. At night they made a camp and slept in tents. Finally they crossed the mountains and made their way down to their own land, the land of Judea. But here they met an unhappy sight. The beautiful city of Jerusalem had been burned by Nebuchadnezzar and it was in ruins. The walls around it were crumbled and broken down, and the Temple of God that Solomon had built was nothing but ashes.

The first thing the people did was to clear away enough of the rubbish to find where the altar had stood. Here they built a new altar with stones and offered sacrifices to God. The priests continued to make these offerings every morning and evening, while the people began building homes for themselves. After the people had found their land and built homes, they began building a new Temple.

The man whom Cyrus had named to rule in Judea was a prince from King David's family named Zerubbabel. Zerubbabel himself led in the building of the new Temple. He had priests, who served in the Temple worship, and carpenters and bricklayers to help him. When the first stones of the building were laid, there was a great celebration with music and singing. But some of the old people who were there could remember the old Temple as Solomon had built it. These people cried a little because they knew that the new Temple could never be that beautiful.

Now in the country of Samaria, right above Jerusalem, there lived some of the Israelites whose fathers had been in the ten tribes that the Assyrians captured. These Samaritans were jealous of the Jews because God was still with them. They tried to worry the Jews and keep them from building the Temple. When King Cyrus died, they wrote a letter to the new king and said: "The captives who came back to Judea are trying to build the town of Jerusalem again. Once they get it built, they are going to turn against you and quit serving you."

When the king read this letter, he sent an answer back to the Samaritans: "I command that the building of the city of Jerusalem stop."

The Samaritans hurried with this letter to Jerusalem and made the Jews stop working. The Temple stood bare and unfinished during the time that this king ruled.

Then a new king began to reign. God sent two prophets, Haggai and Zechariah, to call the people back to work. Zerubbabel and his helpers began building harder than ever. When the enemies of the Jews told the new king about it, he looked back in the records to see what he could find out about the case. When he found that Cyrus had given the Jews the command to build the Temple, he told the enemies to help the Jews build instead of fighting them.

So after about twenty years, the new Temple was finally finished. It was a little larger than the one Solomon had built, but it was not as beautiful or as richly decorated. Even so, the people were glad to have a new house of worship and were thankful to God for bringing them home to build it.

Questions:

1. What new law did King Cyrus make? 2. What prophet had said that this would happen? 3. How did the Jews in Babylon help those who made the trip? 4. How did the city of Jerusalem look when the Jews got there? 5. Who led in building the new Temple? 6. Why did the work on the Temple stop? 7. How long did it take to build the new Temple? 8. How did it look?

A Queen Saves Her People

And who knoweth whether thou art come to the kingdom for such a time as this?
Esther 4:14

CYRUS, the Persian king who conquered Babylon, made a law allowing the Jews to go back to their home in the land of Judea and the city of Jerusalem. Many Jews returned, but others had been living in Babylon for so long that they decided to stay there. One of these was a man from the tribe of Benjamin named Mordecai. He lived with his young cousin, Esther, whose own parents were dead, in the new capital city of Persia at Shushan.

By this time, King Darius, who had put Daniel in the den of lions, had died; and in his place, his son Ahashuerus was ruling. During a great dinner that Ahashuerus gave for his princes and noblemen, he asked that his beautiful wife Vashti come before the group. When Vashti refused to come as he had asked, he became very angry. He decided that she would no longer be queen, but that he would have a contest and select the most beautiful girl in his kingdom to take her place.

Among the girls brought to the palace from whom Ahashuerus would select his new queen was the Jewess, Esther. Her heart was as pure and lovely as her face; and when the king saw her, he loved her. She was the one he chose to be his bride.

Esther Becomes Queen

Now Mordecai could no longer visit with Esther after she went to the palace to live because she was the queen, but he sent her messages and she sent messages to him. Esther had come to mean as much to Mordecai as a daughter, and he missed her very much.

One day Mordecai overheard two men plotting to kill the king, and he reported it to Esther. When she told the king, he immediately took the men and punished them, and he wrote down Mordecai's brave deed in his books of records.

Now the greatest man in the kingdom, next to Ahashuerus, was Haman, chief of all the princes. He thought he was very important and loved to see all the people bow down when he passed by. Mordecai, however, worshiped only God, and he would not bow when he saw Haman. This made Haman very angry. When he found out who Mordecai was and that he was a Jew, he determined to do away with all the Jews.

Haman told the king that the Jews were causing trouble by refusing to obey the laws of the land, and he got permission to kill all of them. The king really did not know anything about the Jews or who they were, and he never dreamed that his own queen was one of them.

The day was set for the killing of the Jews, the law was written commanding their death, and copies were sent throughout the kingdom. When Mordecai and the other Jews heard of it, they put on torn clothes and roamed about the city, speaking loudly against the new law. When Esther heard of Mordecai's strange actions, she sent a servant to find out what was wrong with him. Mordecai told the servant of the terrible command and sent Esther a copy of the law. He asked that she go to the king and ask him to save her people.

When Esther heard of all this, she was greatly distressed also. She sent a message back to Mordecai, saying: "No one in the kingdom may go to the king in his courtroom unless he sends for him. Anyone who tries to do so will be killed unless the king holds out his golden scepter. I, the queen, have not even been called for in thirty days now."

But Mordecai sent word back again, "Do not think that you will be safe just because you are inside the palace. You, too, are a Jew. Whether you help us or not, God will find some way to save us; but perhaps this is the very reason He allowed you to come into the kingdom as queen."

This time Esther's reply was for Mordecai and the Jews to pray for her as she and her own maidens would do. Then she would go to the king in three days.

On the third day, Esther dressed in her loveliest robes and walked through the palace halls to the entrance to the throne room. As she stood in the doorway, the king, across the room on his throne, smiled at her and held out his scepter to her. Humbly, she walked across to him and touched the scepter.

"What do you want, Esther?" the king asked. "I shall give you anything, up to half my kingdom."

But Esther did not ask for the wish of her heart at first. Wisely, she asked Haman and the king to come to a dinner she was having for them.

Haman was very pleased that he, alone, was invited to eat with the king and queen. As soon as the dinner was over, he went straight home to tell his wife and friends of the wonders of palace life. But on the way he saw the hated Mordecai standing tall as he passed by, and it changed his happy mood. That day, he ordered the gallows, or tall posts, to be made on which he would hang Mordecai.

On that same night the king was listening to his book of records read and he remembered the time Mordecai had saved his life. The next day he got Haman to suggest some way to honor a man who had pleased the king very much. Now Haman thought that the king was probably talking about him, and he proudly suggested that the man be dressed finely and then ride on the king's own horse throughout the city with a nobleman walking ahead to announce his good deed.

How astonished Haman was when he learned that the one the king wanted to honor was Mordecai the Jew! He could hardly raise his head as he walked about the city, calling to all of the honor of Mordecai. Here he was, the chief prince, praising the very enemy for whom he had built tall gallows the day before!

Afterward, he hurried to the second dinner Esther had prepared. At the dinner, the king looked at his beautiful wife and was pleased. "Tell me, Esther," he said, "what would you like for me to do for you?"

Solemnly, the queen replied, "My life, O King, and the lives of my people is what I am asking for. We are about to be killed, all of us."

"Who would dare to such a thing?" Ahashuerus demanded.

Esther turned and looked past the king to the guilty one. "Our enemy—this wicked Haman!" she answered.

Haman at once began begging for his life, but the king was too angry to listen. He ordered Haman to be hanged on the gallows that had been built for Mordecai.

On that day, Mordecai took Haman's place as chief of the princes. The law for killing the Jews could not be changed, but the king made a new law which allowed the Jews to fight against anyone who tried to kill them. Most of the people were too afraid to fight them, but the ones who did were quickly destroyed by the Jews.

So instead of a sorrowful day, the day named for the killing of the Jews turned out to be a victorious one. The people celebrated a feast of thanksgiving to God for saving their lives, and the Jews today eat that same feast, the feast of Purim. When they do, they remember the beautiful queen who saved their people.

Questions:

1. Why did King Ahashuerus want to choose a new queen? 2. Who did he think was the most beautiful in the land? 3. How did Esther's cousin, Mordecai, make Haman angry? 4. What law did Haman get the king to make? 5. What did Esther do when she found that she and her people were going to be killed? 6. What did the king do when she came to him? 7. Why did the king honor Mordecai? 8. What happened to Haman when Esther told the king how wicked he was? 9. What happened to the Jews?

A Man Who Loved God's Law

Then arose Ezra, and made the chief priests, the Levites, and all Israel, to swear that they should do according to this word.
Ezra 10:5

EVEN though the building of the new temple was finally finished by Zerubbabel, Jerusalem was still not the strong, rich city it once had been. Its walls were crumbled and broken so that robbers and thieves could easily slip in. There were not a great many people in the city, and they were quite poor. Although some of the Jews had come back to Jerusalem when King Cyrus told them they could, most of them had decided to stay in Babylon. Still others moved on to other foreign lands, so that Jews were living in many parts of the world.

News began to travel to these scattered Jews about the hard times the people in Jerusalem were having. Now just because these Jews had chosen to stay away from Jerusalem does not mean that they were also unfaithful to God. Many still served God and they felt that it was their duty to help their kinspeople who had gone back to Judea.

One of the people who felt this way was Ezra, a prophet still living in Babylon. Ezra loved God's word, but at that time there were no copies of the law of Moses as we have it now in the Old Testament. The books that make up our

Ezra Explains the Law

Old Testament had been written by different people and were scattered about in different places. Ezra searched for these books and he copied them; then he put them altogether in one book. This Book of the Law had in it the writings of Moses, then of the judges, then of the kings, and finally of the prophets.

Ezra studied his Book of the Law until he knew it very well. Then he opened up a school where he taught other men to know the Law and to love it. These men were called "scribes," which means "writers," for they made their own copies of the Law from Ezra's books.

When Ezra heard about the poor Jews in Jerusalem, he knew that he could not give any money to help them, but there was something just as important he could give. He could go there and teach them God's Law. If they learned God's Law and obeyed it, God would help them have the other things they needed.

So Ezra and the scribes took the Books of the Law that they had found and copied to Jerusalem. Here Ezra opened his scrolls and read to the people. Many of them had never heard anyone read from the word of God before, and they were thankful to Ezra for bringing it to them. They listened carefully and decided to quit the evil things they were doing and obey God's plan for His people.

After Ezra had read from the Law, he stayed in Jerusalem and taught the people how to live by the things it said. He reminded them that they were God's special people and that they were not to marry anyone from the nations around them. They were only to marry another Jew. He showed them that God meant for them to obey His words just exactly as He had given them.

Ezra was a great help to the people of Jerusalem. Following God's Law as it was written made them feel that God was with them once more.

Questions:

1. What news traveled to the Jews who were living in different parts of the world? 2. What did Ezra feel that he could do to help the Jews in Jerusalem? 3. What kind of school did Ezra teach? 4. What was in the "Book of the Law"? 5. What did the people in Jerusalem do when Ezra read God's law to them? 6. How did this help them?

Jerusalem Made Safe

So built we the wall; and all the wall was joined together unto the half thereof: for the people had a mind to work.
Nehemiah 4:6

WHEN the Jews in other parts of the world heard about the troubles the people who had returned to Jerusalem were having, they wanted to help in some way. Ezra did his part by taking God's word to them and teaching them how to obey it.

Another man who was touched by the stories of the rebuilding of Jerusalem was Nehemiah. Nehemiah lived in Persia and had a very high office in the palace of the Persian king. He was known as the "cup-bearer." This meant that he tested the king's wine before he gave it to the king to make sure that no one had put poison in it. You can see that the king trusted Nehemiah.

One day Nehemiah talked with some people who had come from Judea. "The people in Jerusalem are really in trouble," they told him. "The walls of the city are broken down and the gates have been burned." This news made Nehemiah very sad. He cried and prayed to God for the people in Jerusalem.

At dinner time, when Nehemiah served the king his wine, the king noticed that Nehemiah looked unhappy. "Why do you look so sad?" he asked his servant. "I do not think you are sick. Your heart must be sad."

Building the Walls of Jerusalem

So Nehemiah told the king about the crumbled walls and broken gates in Jerusalem. The king then understood why Nehemiah was worried. "Is there some way I could help you?" he asked.

"If it pleases the king and if I find favor in your sight," Nehemiah replied, "let me go to Judea and build up the walls again."

"How long would it take you?" asked the king. "And when would you come back?"

So he and Nehemiah talked about it and decided upon a time for Nehemiah to return. Then the king gave Nehemiah letters to the rulers of the countries through which he would travel so that he could pass safely. He gave him another letter to the keeper of the king's forest, permitting Nehemiah to take wood to make the gates and walls strong. The king was very good to give Nehemiah everything he needed.

When Nehemiah arrived in Jerusalem, he did not tell the people right away that he intended to build a new wall. First, he wanted to look over the old wall and see how it was. One night Nehemiah and a few friends went out quietly and rode all around the city, inspecting it. He found that heaps of stone and ashes lay where the strong walls had once stood. In some places his horse could not even walk over the rubbish.

The next day Nehemiah went to the rulers and priests of Jerusalem and said, "You can see that you are in trouble with your city open to all who want to come in. Come, let us build a wall around Jerusalem to keep it safe."

The people listened to Nehemiah and admired him because the king of Persia had given him permission to come to their city. They were eager to follow him in building the walls, for they knew what he said was true. Everyone agreed to build some part, whether it was just a small portion in front of his own house or a long section. Even some of the women helped to build.

Now the Samaritans, who had tried to stop Zerubbabel from building the Temple, heard that the Jews were trying to build a wall around their city. These Samaritans did not want to see Jerusalem strong once more. They tried again to make trouble for the Jews. First, they made fun of them.

"What are you trying to do?" a leader called Sanballat asked. "Where are you going to find stones in all that rubbish?"

"Why, a fox could break down that wall," another called Tobiah said.

But Nehemiah answered, "God is going to help us with our work, and surely He will punish you." And the Jews went right on working.

When the Samaritans saw that the wall was really going up, they began to be worried. They and the other nations around planned to go to Jerusalem and fight. But the Jews prayed to God to help them. Nehemiah gave orders for half the men to build and half to stand guard with spears and swords. Some of the men worked with one hand and carried something to fight with in the other.

Surely enough, God stayed with His people. Their enemies never were strong enough to come and fight. The people kept working, and in fifty-two days the city of Jerusalem was surrounded by strong, new walls.

Nehemiah stayed in Jerusalem for awhile and was the governor. During this time Ezra was there, too, reading from the Law of God and reminding the people to obey. Because of these two men, the city of Jerusalem began to grow. Other Jews from foreign lands came back to live and to worship God in the Temple. One more prophet, Malachi, came, but with his words our story of the Old Testament ends. He spoke to the people who were trying to serve God. He told them about a time when the Lord Himself would return to the Temple. We know that he was speaking of God's own Son, Jesus Christ. With him, the next portion of the Bible begins.

Questions:

1. What job did Nehemiah have in Persia? 2. Why did Nehemiah look sad? 3. How did the walls look when Nehemiah got to Jerusalem? 4. Who tried to stop the Jews from building? 5. What did Nehemiah have the people do when they heard that they might have to fight? 6. How long did it take to build the new wall? 7. Why did Jerusalem need a strong wall around it?

A Message from Gabriel

And the angel said unto her, Fear not, Mary: for thou hast found favour with God.
Luke 1:30

THE Jews seemed to obey God as He wanted them to when they first came back to Jerusalem from Babylon. They built the Temple again so that they would have a place to worship. They listened to Ezra read the Law of Moses and they tried to do as it said. But after a time, they forgot about these things; and they began to disobey the commands God had given them. Just as He had done in the past when His people forgot Him, God let the enemies of the Jews come into their land. For many years, the Jews were servants of different nations who were stronger than they.

At the time when Christ came to earth, four hundred years had passed since the Jews had returned from Babylon; and the mighty Romans were ruling the world. The Roman emperor had named a man called Herod to rule the land of Judea for him. Herod lived in a palace in Jerusalem since it was the largest city in Judea. He pretended to believe in God like the Jews who lived there and he even made the Temple more beautiful than ever before, but he was really a mean and cruel man.

The Jews did not like Herod and they hated to serve the Romans. They wanted to have a leader who was one of their own people, but they knew that the Romans would

Mary and the Angel

never let a Jew rule. The Romans did not think that the Jews were as good as they were.

Because of this, the people of Judea thought that their only hope depended on God's sending them the Savior He had promised many, many years before. First, He had made the promise to Eve, when she disobeyed in the Garden of Eden. Eve had brought sin into the world, but God told her that someday He was going to send someone who would bring *goodness* back into the world. This One would "save" the people of the world, so he was called a "Savior." Then when God called Abraham and his children to be His own special people, He promised that the Savior would be born into their family. Later on, the prophets, seeing into the future with God's help, told about the mighty kingdom that the Savior would rule.

The Jews thought that this meant that their own nation would be strong again like it was in King David's and King Solomon's day. They wanted the Savior to come right away so that he could make the Romans leave and be the ruler in Herod's place. But God had a wise plan; and although He was ready to send the One He had promised, he was going to be a different kind of king and savior than the Jews were expecting.

Now for many years, each young Jewish girl had hoped that she would get to be the mother of the new king. The one whom God chose was a pure and lovely girl named Mary. She lived in Nazareth, a small town of Galilee, with her mother and father; but she was engaged to be married to a fine man named Joseph.

One day when Mary was all alone, an angel of God named Gabriel suddenly appeared before her. The angel told Mary that God was going to send her a son and that this child would also be the Son of God. He would be the Savior that God had promised to the Jews—the one who would rule over a mighty kingdom.

Mary was surprised when she heard of this, and she was a little confused. "How can I have a baby," she asked, "when I am not married?"

"Your child will not have an earthly father," the angel explained. "His Father is the most high God in heaven."

How happy Mary was to know that she, of all Jewish women, had been chosen by God to be the mother of the Savior. "Let it happen just as you have told me," she said softly to the angel.

Before he left, Gabriel told Mary that her cousin Elisabeth, who was married to the priest, Zacharias, was going to have a baby, too. Then he disappeared as suddenly as he had come.

Mary's head was whirling when the angel left—she had so much to think about! "To whom could she talk?" she wondered. Then she remembered her cousin Elisabeth, who was also expecting a baby. She gathered her things together and went to visit Elisabeth.

When Mary saw Elisabeth, she ran up and put her arms around her. Then Mary sang a beautiful song that told Elisabeth about the marvelous thing that was going to happen to her. Was that not a wonderful way to tell her the good news?

Elisabeth understood why Mary was so happy and thankful to God. She invited Mary to stay with her and Zacharias for a few months. What wonderful days the two ladies had—making tiny clothes for their new babies and talking about the joy the children were going to bring to them and even to the whole world.

Questions:

1. Why were the Jewish people having to serve other nations? 2. How did they hope to make the Romans leave their land? 3. How did they know God was going to send them a Savior? 4. Who was the first one to know that the time had come for the Savior to be born? 5. Who told her? 6. How did this make Mary feel? 7. Whom did she tell?

"His Name Is John"

And he asked for a writing table, and wrote, saying, His name is John.
Luke 1:63

MARY'S cousin Elisabeth and her husband Zacharias lived down in Judea near Jerusalem, and they were much older than Mary. Zacharias was a priest in the Temple in Jerusalem. For many years these two had had one thing to make their life unhappy—God had never sent them any children.

One day Zacharias was in the Holy Place of the Temple, burning incense on the golden altar, while the people worshiped outside where the great altar stood. Suddenly an angel of the Lord appeared on the right side of the altar of incense. Zacharias stepped back, shaking with fear, when he realized that he stood before an angel; but the angel began to speak kindly to him. His message was a happy one: God was going to send Zacharias and Elisabeth a son whom they were to name John. This son was going to make the old couple very happy; and he was going to please God, also. God's Spirit was going to be with John and make him powerful in leading the people back to God and preparing them to hear God's own Son when he came. He would do the same kind of work the prophets of old had done.

Zacharias could hardly believe the angel. Why, he and Elisabeth were so old that they were not expected to have

Mary and Elisabeth

children any longer. "How can I know that what you have said is true?" he asked the angel.

"I am Gabriel and have come from the very presence of God," the angel replied. "Because you have not believed my words, you will not be able to speak until they have come true."

Now the people worshiping outside had begun to wonder what was keeping Zacharias inside the Holy Place for so long. When he finally came out to them, he had to motion to them with his hand, for he could not talk. They finally understood that he was trying to tell them that he had seen a vision.

Several days later Zacharias finished his work in the Temple and went home to Elisabeth in the hill country. When Elisabeth found that she really was going to have a baby, at last, she was very happy.

A few months later Gabriel was sent from God again, this time to tell Mary that she was to be the mother of the Son of God. We know that after the angel's visit, Mary came to see Elisabeth and to tell her of the good news. How excited the two were to make plans for the babies God was soon going to send! Mary stayed for about three months before she went back to her home in Nazareth.

Mary had not been gone long when Elisabeth's baby was born. When her neighbors and friends heard that Elisabeth had had a little boy, they came to visit her and to see it.

Like all Jewish people did then, Zacharias and Elisabeth planned to name their baby when he was eight days old. On that day, their kinfolk came to see what name they would choose. Many of them had suggested that they call him Zacharias, after his father.

"No," Elisabeth disagreed. "This baby is going to be named John."

"Why are you going to name him John?" her aunts and uncles and cousins asked. "There is no one called John in our family."

Now old Zacharias had not spoken since the day he had seen the angel, but someone noticed that he was trying to tell them something with his hands. Finally, they saw that he wanted a tablet. When one was brought, he simply wrote, "The child's name is John." Once this was done, he was able to talk again. His first words were to praise God; and the crowd in his home joined him, saying, "What a wonderful blessing this child will be!"

John grew to be a fine boy, strong in body and in mind. He loved to be alone to think about God; and while he was still a young man, he went to the desert to live. Here he prayed and got ready to do the great work God had given him—that of preparing the Jews to meet the Savior, or Christ.

Questions:

1. What kind of work did Zacharias do? 2. Why were Zacharias and Elisabeth sad? 3. Where did Zacharias see the angel? 4. What did the angel say? 5. What happened to Zacharias because he did not believe the angel? 6. What did everyone want Elisabeth to name the baby? 7. Why did Zacharias name him John? 8. What happened to Zacharias once the baby was named?

A King Is Born

For unto you is born this day in the city of David a Saviour, which is Christ the Lord.
Luke 2:11

ABOUT the time that Mary's baby was ready to be born, the Roman emperor commanded that a count of everyone in the whole world be made. Already he was taking a lot of money from the people, but he wanted to make sure that he missed no one. Each person in Judea had to go to the town from which his family had come and see that the Roman officers there had his name on their list.

Mary went with her husband Joseph to the little town of Bethlehem, near Jerusalem. Joseph came from David's family and Bethlehem had been David's home. Now Bethlehem was just a small town and it was very crowded with the people who had come there to be listed. When Mary and Joseph arrived after their trip from Nazareth, they could not find a single place to stay. They looked and looked, but Mary was so tired that they finally stopped at a stable, where horses and cows were kept, to spend the night. During that night, Mary's baby came. She wrapped him up warmly and laid him to sleep in the only bed she could find—a manger, or food box, for the animals, which had been filled with soft hay.

Yes, God's own Son, the Savior and King of all the world, had been born that night in a barn, but no one even knew it except Mary and Joseph—that is, no one on earth. In

The Birth of Jesus

heaven, however, angels knew it and were singing praises to the Child King around God's throne. God sent one of them to earth to tell the news to some shepherds who were watching their sheep on the hills around Bethlehem. From out of the starry sky, the angel suddenly appeared, shining with the glory of the Lord. The shepherds were frightened by the angel; but the angel said, "Behold, I bring you tidings of great joy which shall be to all the people: for there is born this day in the city of David, a Savior which is Christ the Lord." The angel also told them that they could find the baby in Bethlehem in a stable. Then a great chorus of angels appeared, singing praises to God.

The shepherds, filled with wonder by this wonderful message from the angels, hurried to Bethlehem to find the baby. Surely enough, they found him in the manger, just as they had been told. When they saw him, they realized that they were looking at the promised Son of God, and they bowed before the little baby. Then they went back to their sheep, praising God and telling everyone they met about the things they had seen and heard.

When the child was eight days old, he was named Jesus, as the angel had said he was to be named before he was born. This name meant "savior."

Then when Jesus was a month old, his parents brought him to the Temple in Jerusalem, as the Law of Moses commanded, and made an offering of two pigeons to show that the child would belong to the Lord. There was an old man named Simeon living in Jerusalem at that time who was filled with God's Spirit. He was so anxious for the promised

Savior to come, that God promised him he would not die until he had seen Jesus. On the day that Mary and Joseph came to the Temple to make their sacrifice, the Spirit of God led Simeon there, also. When he saw the baby, his heart told him that this was the one he had been waiting for. He took Jesus from Mary and held him fondly in his arms while he thanked God. "Now I am ready to die," he said, "for with my own eyes I have seen the one God has sent to be the glory of the Israelites and to save the whole world."

There was also in the Temple an old woman named Anna, who spent most of her time praying. When she heard Simeon, she gave thanks to God with him and told many in Jerusalem of the coming of the Christ child.

Mary and Joseph looked at one another proudly and remembered what Simeon and Anna had said, just as they remembered the praise of the shepherds on the night Christ was born. It was a wonderful thing and yet hard for them to realize that this baby God had sent to them *was* going to save the Jews from their evil and would be able to permit everyone who followed him to live forever with God some day.

Questions:

1. Why did Mary and Joseph go to Bethlehem? 2. Where did they have to spend the night? 3. What happened during the night? 4. How did God tell the shepherds His Son had been born? 5. What did the shepherds do? 6. What was the baby named? 7. Who saw Jesus in the temple?

Wise Men Follow a Star

Where is he that is born King of the Jews? for we have seen his star in the east, and are come to worship him.
Matt. 2:2

FAR away from Jerusalem and Bethlehem, in a country to the east, there lived some wise men who spent their time studying the stars. They had no modern telescopes, like our scientists have, but they had learned a great deal by watching the movement of the stars. They knew the stars so well that it was easy for them to see one night that there was a new star in the sky. In some way God sent a message to the hearts of these men, telling them that this star was in honor of the birth of a new king in the country of Judea, the home of the Jews.

The wise men gathered together precious gifts, suitable for a king, and started on the long journey to Judea. They traveled on camels during the cool of the night when they could follow the star. At last their travels brought them to Jerusalem about the time Jesus was born. They began asking the people they met to show them the way to find the new king. They were dismayed and puzzled when no one seemed to know what they meant.

As you remember, the Romans, who ruled that part of the world, had appointed a man named Herod to be king over Judea. Word came to Herod that some strange men from the East were in Jerusalem looking for a new king that had been born. This news worried Herod because he

The Wise Men

was the king and he did not want anyone to take his place. He did not like this talk of a "new king." Once he had heard that the Jewish people were looking for their God to send them a king of their own people, so he called in their priests and scribes to tell him more about this. Now these men spent their time studying the Law of Moses and the prophets, so when Herod asked them where their king was to be born, they knew to answer, "The prophet Micah told us that he was to come from Bethlehem."

When he found this out, Herod called for the strangers from the East to come to the palace. He questioned them about the strange star they had followed. Then he suggested that they go to Bethlehem and if they did find a child king, they were to come and tell him, for he wanted to go and worship it also. Herod really did not want to worship the child, but he wanted to find out if there really was such a person so that he could destroy him before he had a chance to become king.

On their way to Bethlehem, the wise men again found the bright star shining in the sky; and they followed its moving path until it stopped over the very place where Baby Jesus lay. The men alighted from their camels and entered the house. There they kneeled before the tiny child who they knew would become a great king. From the treasures they had brought, they took out gold and precious perfumes called frankincense and myrrh, used in offering sacrifices.

Then instead of returning to Jerusalem to tell Herod of the baby they had found, the wise men were warned by God in a dream to return home by another road. Herod waited for them to come back, and he was angry when he saw that they had escaped him. He decided to find the child and destroy him another way.

After the wise men had gone, God sent Joseph a dream in which He said, "Take Mary and the baby to Egypt until I give you word that it is safe to return. Herod is looking for Jesus and would like to kill him." Immediately, Joseph got up and awakened Mary, even though it was the middle of the night. He told her to get ready for a journey. Quietly they gathered up their things, wrapped up the baby, and left for the faraway country of Egypt.

By this time Herod was sure that the wise men were never going to return to him, and he thought of a wicked plan he would use to be sure the future king was destroyed. He sent soldiers to Bethlehem who killed every baby boy who was under two years old. This way he just knew that he had gotten rid of the child who might take over his kingdom. But God had taken care of His Son, and Jesus was well and safe with his parents down in Egypt.

Wicked Herod did not live very long after this. When he died, God told Joseph that it was safe to go back to the land of Israel. But before he had reached Judea, Joseph heard that Herod's wicked son was ruling in his place; and he was afraid to settle in Bethlehem, so near to Jerusalem. Instead, he went to the north to a part of the country called Galilee. A more gentle king ruled there. At last the family settled in the little town of Nazareth, where Mary had lived as a girl. There Joseph opened a carpenter's shop and built a home where Jesus lived for many years.

Questions:

1. Why were the wise men excited when they saw a new star? 2. How did they find their way to Jerusalem? 3. Why did Herod want to know if there really was a new king? 4. What did the wise men do when they found Jesus? 5. Why did the wise men not go back to Herod? 6. Why did Joseph take Jesus and Mary to Egypt? 7. What did Herod do to get rid of a future king? 8. Where did Joseph and Mary finally make their home?

Lost in Jerusalem

And he said unto them, How is it that ye sought me?
wist ye not that I must be about my Father's business?
Luke 2:49

WHILE he was a boy, Jesus lived in the little town of Nazareth. His home was probably a very simple, country cottage; and he was taught to work hard and to help Joseph in the carpenter shop. Most Jewish boys of that time went to school at the village house of worship, called a "synagogue." Here they were taught from the Law of Moses and the books of the prophets. Since each book had to be copied by hand in those days, the boys had no books of their own and they had to learn their lessons by heart.

Jesus also went to the synagogue with his family on the Sabbath each week for worship. They did this to obey the law God had given as part of the Ten Commandments: "Remember the Sabbath day." Here the Old Testament was read and explained, just as in school, so it is easy to understand why many Jewish boys knew much of it by memory.

To Jesus' parents, just as to other Jews, the most important time of the year was the Passover, when Jews from everywhere went to Jerusalem to celebrate the sacred feast and remember the time when God brought their people out of slavery in the land of Egypt. When Jesus was twelve years old, his parents let him make the trip to Jerusalem with them for the first time. Together with others from

Jesus in the Temple

Nazareth, they traveled the sixty miles to Jerusalem. Some walked and some rode donkeys in a large caravan. Along the way, others going to worship joined them. For two or three days they traveled—talking, singing, greeting old friends, and making new ones.

Finally they saw Jerusalem spread out before them. What an impression the great city and the splendid Temple on Mount Moriah made on the young boy! Already Jesus' heart was full of love for God, his Father. Seeing the house of worship and the priests and taking part in the solemn feast of the Passover made him want to begin His Father's work. He lingered around the Temple, as though he could not see enough.

The feast of the Passover lasted for seven days, and then Mary and Joseph prepared to go back to Nazareth with their friends. They began the trip and traveled all one day without Jesus, but they were not worried because they felt sure he was walking along with those of his age. When evening came and he had not joined them, they began to look for him among their friends and relatives. No one had seen Jesus all day.

There was nothing for the worried parents to do but go back to Jerusalem and look for their son. For two days they went every place in Jerusalem they thought Jesus might be. On the third day, the tired couple thought of looking in the Temple. There they finally found their boy, sitting with some of the smartest students of the Law, listening to them and asking them questions. These smart men seemed interested in this lad who could ask such thoughtful questions and also give answers that showed a deep understanding.

Mary and Joseph were surprised to find their son talking to the brilliant men. Mary had not forgotten the worry he had caused them for three days; and she could not help saying, "Son, why have you done this to us? Your Father and I have been looking everywhere for you and we have been so worried."

"Why did you look for me?" Jesus asked. "Do you not realize that I have my Father's work to do?"

Jesus realized that he was old enough now to get ready for the great work God had sent him into the world to do. Mary did not quite understand, but she remembered the words he told her, and she thought about them afterward.

This time Jesus went with Mary and Joseph and returned to Nazareth. As years passed by, he grew "in mind and in body, more pleasing to God and to men." He was like other boys around him, but in one way he was different—he never did wrong. He was not boastful or proud about his goodness, but he prayed often to God and God made his mind and thoughts pure so that he always wanted to do the right thing. This made those around him love him, and God saw that His Son was pleasing in every way.

Questions:

1. Where did Jesus live as a boy? 2. Where did he learn about God's Law for His people? 3. Why did Jesus and His parents go to Jerusalem? 4. What did Jesus see in Jerusalem that He liked? 5. Why did Mary and Joseph leave without Jesus? 6. Where did they find Him? 7. What was He doing?

A New Prophet Speaks to Israel

And it came to pass in those days, that Jesus came from Nazareth of Galilee, and was baptized of John in Jordan.
Mark 1:9

UNTIL he was about thirty years old, Jesus lived with his family at their home in Nazareth. He was busy working as a carpenter with Joseph, but he never forgot the greater work that God had planned for him to do.

During this same time, John, the son of Zacharias and Elisabeth, had gone to the wild country in the south to live. Here he was all alone and he had a lot of time to think about God and about the Savior whom God was going to send. John grew used to the rough life he had to live in the desert. He ate locusts and wild honey that he found, and his only clothes were a simple robe of camel's hair tied around his waist with a leather belt.

One day John heard the call of God to leave the desert and go up to the country near the Jordan River. There he was to begin telling people about the kingdom of heaven that was coming and about its mighty king. You see, God meant for John to get the people ready to meet Jesus.

It did not take long for word to travel that a new prophet was preaching beside the Jordan River. For four hundred years God had sent no prophets, and the Jews were excited to see a man who spoke just as God told him. Many

John the Baptist Preaching

traveled from Jerusalem and the cities and villages around to hear what John was saying. They heard him tell each one of them to turn from doing wrong and to be baptized to show that his heart was now clean and pure. By doing this, they would be ready for the kingdom of heaven, which was soon to come.

The people were impressed by these words and they told John: "We want to live better lives and turn away from evil so we can be a part of the kingdom. What should we do?"

"You can share your food and clothes with those who have none," replied John.

Some of the men in the crowd were tax collectors and they wanted to live right before God, also. John told them: "Take no more money from the people than the law allows you to take." To the soldiers he said, "Be gentle to the people and be sure that you are right before you accuse anyone of some wrong. Then, too, you are not to complain about the money you are paid."

When the people accepted the message John taught and promised God that they would try to serve Him better, John baptized them in the Jordan River as a sign that their sins were washed away. Because of this, he became known as "John the Baptizer" or "John the Baptist."

So many people came to John and accepted his preaching that the word began to spread that perhaps he was the coming Savior. When John heard this, he quickly said, "I am not the promised One of God. He is so much greater than I that I would not even be good enough to stoop down and fasten his sandal. I have baptized you only with water, but he will baptize you with the Holy Spirit."

Crowds upon crowds of people were baptized by John, and among the last to come was Jesus of Nazareth. When John saw Jesus, he knew that this was the one greater and holier than he. He was timid about baptizing Jesus, for he said, "You should baptize me, rather than my baptizing you."

Jesus replied kindly that it was God's will for him to do this, as it was for him to do all things that were right. Then Jesus and John walked out into the water, and John baptized him just as he had all the others. When Jesus came out of the water, he was praying. In that moment, the sky opened; and the Holy Spirit flew from heaven in the shape of a dove, alighting on Jesus. Then a voice came out of heaven, saying: "You are my beloved Son, and you have pleased me greatly."

John and those in the crowd could not take their eyes from the man who had come that day to find John beside the Jordan River. They all knew that their search for the coming King was over. He was among them at last.

Questions:

1. Where did Jesus live until he was about thirty years old? 2. Where did his cousin John live? 3. What did John eat and wear? 4. What was the work God wanted John to do? 5. What did the people do to show that they wanted to do better and get ready for the new kingdom? 6. Why did John not want to baptize Jesus? 7. What happened after Jesus was baptized?

Satan's Three Tests

And Jesus answered and said unto him, Get thee behind me, Satan: for it is written, Thou shalt worship the Lord thy God, and him only shalt thou serve.
Luke 4:8

AFTER Jesus was baptized by John, the Spirit of God led him into some deserted country so barren and lonely that only wild animals lived there. While he was there, Jesus prayed and talked with God, trying to understand perfectly the work he had to do on earth. For forty days and nights he stayed, and during all that time he never had anything to eat.

When the forty days had ended, Jesus was so hungry that he was actually starving. He felt weak and knew that he had to find food right away. While he felt like that, the devil came to him, just as he does to us when we are not strong and are not expecting him. The devil knew that Jesus was a man and the son of Mary, but that he was also the Son of God. He wanted to see if he could make Jesus sin just as he had made everyone else sin since he first persuaded Eve to disobey.

Now Satan knew that Jesus was very hungry, so he suggested: "If you are the Son of God, all you have to do is say the words and these stones on the ground would become bread for you to eat."

Jesus knew that indeed he did have the power to turn the stones into bread, but he also knew that his power had

The Temptation of Jesus

not been given to him to use selfishly, but to serve others. He answered the devil by quoting from the Law of Moses he had learned so well, "Man cannot live on bread alone; he needs the Word of God, as well."

But Satan does not give up easily. He tried the weary Savior with something else. This time he took him to Jerusalem, to the highest point on top of the Temple. "Why do you not jump from here and let the angels save you from harm? I, too, know that your own prophets have said that the angels would bear you up before your foot had touched a stone. If you did this, everyone could see that you are the Son of God."

Jesus knew that God had not commanded him to show his power in such a way. He was going to show his power through love and good works. This was only putting God to a test; so he answered the devil, "It is also written that 'you shall not test God's power.' "

Still Satan would not go away. He took Jesus with him to the top of a very high mountain. There, in a moment of time, he showed to Jesus all the kingdoms of the world and their glory. With the memory of all that splendor on his mind, Jesus was told that he could have these kingdoms if he would only bow before the devil and worship him.

But Jesus had no intention of worshiping Satan, not even for all the glory that was in the world. He had come to earth to conquer the devil, not worship him. He said, "Leave me, Satan. The Law of Moses commands, 'You shall worship the one true God, and He is the only one you shall serve.' "

Finally the devil was willing to give up for awhile. He went away to stay until he could find a better chance to attack God's Son.

Jesus was left all alone. He was weary from having faced the devil and starving from having gone without food. But God, in His kindness, had not forgotten His Son. Angels came from His throne to Jesus, bringing the food and the strength that he needed.

Questions:

1. How long did Jesus stay in the desert country alone? 2. Why was he weak afterward? 3. How did Satan want Jesus to get some food? 4. Why did Jesus not do this? 5. How did Satan suggest that Jesus prove that he was the Son of God? 6. What would Satan have given Jesus if Jesus had worshiped him? 7. Why would Jesus not do that? 8. How did Jesus finally get some food?

Five Men Find the Christ

He first findeth his own brother Simon, and saith unto him,
We have found the Messias, which is, being interpreted, the Christ.
John 1:41

ONE day, not too long after the baptism of Jesus, John the Baptist and two of those who believed his message stood talking. When John looked up, he recognized Jesus coming toward them. He turned to the two men with him and said, "Look! Here comes the Son of God now! This is the very one I was speaking of when I said that someone greater than I is coming."

The disciples of John were excited to think that they might get to meet the future King. They left John and ran down the road behind Jesus. When Jesus heard them following him, he turned around and asked, "What do you want?"

"Master, we would like to know where you are staying," the two replied.

"Come with me and see," Jesus told them.

So the men followed Jesus and stayed with him all day, listening to the wonderful words he had to say. By evening, they were sure that he was God's own Son, and that he was the Savior the Jews were waiting for.

One of the men who visited with Jesus that day was named Andrew. The other was John. Now Andrew and John lived north of the place where John the Baptist was

The First Disciples

teaching, up nearer Jesus' home in Nazareth; but perhaps they had come down to hear John and be baptized by him. When Andrew left Jesus, his heart was about to burst with the news that he had found the Christ. The first thing he did was to look for his brother Simon. "We have found the Anointed King, the Christ!" he told Simon.

Together Andrew and Simon went to find Jesus again. Before Andrew even had time to introduce Simon, Jesus said to him, "You are Simon, and your father is Jona. I am going to call you Peter, which means a 'rock.' " From that time on, Peter and Jesus were fast friends.

The next day Jesus began his journey back to Galilee, the country where he lived. On the way, he saw a man named Philip, whose home was the same town in which Peter and Andrew lived. Jesus saw right away that Philip would make a wonderful follower, so he called to him, "Follow me." Philip must have already heard something about the Christ, for with only those words, he gladly came.

Like Andrew, Philip could not keep his new discovery to himself. He went to his friend Nathanael and said, "I have found the very one whom Moses and the prophets talked about. He is Jesus, the son of Joseph, from Nazareth."

Now Nathanael himself lived not far from Nazareth, and he knew it was only a small town. It was hard for him to believe that God's Anointed One had been living there. "Can anyone like this come from Nazareth?" he asked.

"Just come and see," Philip replied.

So the two went to Jesus. As they were walking toward him, Jesus looked up and saw them. "Here comes an Israelite with a truly pure heart," Jesus said, speaking of Nathanael.

Nathanael blinked with surprise. "How did you know about me?" he asked.

"Before Philip ever called you, I saw you standing under a fig tree," Jesus replied.

At this Nathanael believed that Jesus was from God, for he knew more than just a man could know. "Master," he said, "You are the Son of God, the King of Israel."

"Do you believe in me just because I saw you under the fig tree?" Jesus asked. "Truly you are going to see greater things than this that will make you know that I am God's Son."

After this, those who followed Jesus did begin to see greater things. They saw Jesus change water into wine at a wedding feast, they saw him lash out at the money changers who were cheating the people in the Temple, and they watched as he healed a nobleman's son who was very sick. More and more believed when they saw these miracles, and those who followed Jesus were called "disciples."

Questions:

1. Who were the first two men that followed Jesus? 2. Whom did Andrew bring to Christ? 2. What new name did Jesus give Simon? 4. Why was it hard for Nathanael to believe that Jesus was the Christ? 5. How did Jesus surprise Nathanael? 6. What were those who followed Jesus called?

Water into Wine

His mother saith unto the servants, Whatsoever he saith unto you, do it.
John 2:5

ON his way back home from the Jordan River, where he had been baptized by John, Jesus met five new followers—Andrew, John, Peter, Philip, and Nathanael. When the six of them finally reached Jesus' home in Nazareth, they found that Jesus' mother was going to a wedding in the nearby town of Cana.

"Come with me," Mary said to Jesus and his friends. "You will all be welcome."

Now in those days Jews celebrated a wedding by having a great dinner party. Sometimes the guests would stay all night, or even a day or two, eating and drinking and having fun with their friends.

Mary and Jesus and the new disciples were just a small part of the huge crowd that stood around the tables at the feast. The food all looked so good that each person filled his plate and cup again and again.

After a while Mary came and called Jesus off to one side. "They have run out of wine," she said. "The servants do not know what to do."

Somehow Mary knew that Jesus could do something to help. She felt that he was powerful enough to do anything, for she knew that he was God's Son, as well as hers. So she gave him a pleading look and then she turned to the

Jesus' First Miracle

servants. "Do whatever he tells you to do," she told them.

Jesus looked about the room. Near him stood six huge jars, about the size of barrels. The Jews put water in these to use for washing themselves before eating, which was a command of the Law. "Fill these jars with water," Jesus said.

So the servants filled them with clear water to the very brim, even though they thought it seemed rather silly.

"Now," Jesus said, "take some of the water out and let the ruler of the feast taste it."

Into a jar, one of the servants dipped a ladle and brought it out, dripping and full. But it was not full of water! It held a delicious wine!

The ruler of the feast took the ladle and tasted it. "This is wonderful!" he said. "Where did it come from?"

Then he called the bridegroom over. "Taste this," he said; "this is the best wine in the house. Most people serve the good wine at the beginning of a party and save the worst until later, but you have saved the finest until now."

At this, the crowd began to whisper and to look at Jesus. "What kind of man is Mary's son?" they asked each other. Up until then, Jesus had not used the power that God had given him, but now it was time for his work to begin. Now it was time to show them that he was God's Son and that he had come to help them.

Questions:

1. Where did Jesus, his mother, and his friends go? 2. What

was Mary worried about? 3. What did the servants put in the jars? 4. What came out of the jars? 5. What did the ruler of the feast think of the wine? 6. This was Jesus' first "miracle." Why did he do miracles?

A Jew Talks with a Samaritan

How is it that thou, being a Jew, asketh drink of me, which am a woman of Samaria?
John 4:9

AFTER Jesus changed the water into wine at the wedding feast, word began to spread that he was an unusual man. The thing that was unusual about him was that he was God, as well as man. He came to earth to show people what God was really like and how much He loved them.

One way Jesus showed God's love to the world was by traveling around, talking to people and helping them. On his journeys, Jesus and some of his followers passed through the little country of Samaria. You may remember that some of the Samaritans were descendants of the ten tribes of Israel who broke away from the kingdom. They had mixed idol worship with the worship of the true God. Because of this, the people of Judah, or those who had stayed loyal to God, hated them. After the Jews rebuilt Jerusalem and Solomon's Temple, some of the Samaritans wanted to come there and worship, but the Jews would not let them. So the Samaritans built their own temple and worshiped in the way they wanted.

Now Samaria was a hot, dry country; and Jesus and his disciples grew tired and thirsty as they walked along. About noon, they were glad to find that they were coming to a village. At the edge of the village there stood an old well that had been dug by Jacob.

Bouts

Elijah Comforted by an Angel

EECKHOUT

Elisha and the Shunamite Woman

Rosa

Jonah, the Reluctant Prophet

REMBRANDT

Esther and Mordecai

Bloch

The Annunciation

Bloch

The Visit to Elizabeth

MURILLO

The Birth of Jesus

SEEKATZ

The Flight Into Egypt

HOFMANN

The Boy Jesus in the Temple

Bloch

The Sermon on the Mount

BLOCH

The Transfiguration

DEGER

Christ's Entry Into Jerusalem

The Woman at the Well

"I think I will sit here by this well and rest," Jesus told his friends. "You go on into the village and buy food, if you would like."

While Jesus sat alone by the well, one of the women from the town came out to draw water. Now Jesus was thirsty, but he had no way to get water from the well; so he asked the woman for a drink from her bucket.

The Samaritan woman gave Jesus an odd look. "Do you mean that you, a Jew, are asking a Samaritan to give you a drink?" she asked.

"If you knew who I am," Jesus replied, "you would ask me to give you living water."

"What do you mean?" the woman asked. "You have no bucket and the well is deep. Where are you going to get 'living water'?"

"If you drink water from this well," Jesus said, "you will get thirsty again; but the water I am speaking of is different. It refreshes you over and over again."

You see, Jesus was talking about his Spirit of love that he could give her. It would make her soul feel as good as water made her body feel. But the woman did not understand this. "Give me some of that water," she said; "then I will not have to make the trip out to this well again."

In order to show the woman his power in another way, Jesus told her things about her life and family that a stranger could not know. The woman was surprised at this. She began to feel that this Jew was some kind of a man of God.

"Sir," she said, "for a long time I have worried about something, and I think you can give me an answer. My people have always worshiped on this mountain, but you Jews say that Jerusalem is the place where men ought to worship. Which is right?"

"The time is coming when people will not have to worship God at any particular place," Jesus answered. "They will see that God is everywhere, all the time, and that we should worship Him and keep Him in our hearts. Then we will be worshiping in the true way."

"I know that God is going to send a Savior," the woman said. "When he comes, he will teach us the truth."

Jesus looked up at the Samaritan woman. "I am the Christ," he said quietly.

Just at this time, the disciples arrived with food from the village. In the confusion, the woman forgot all about her water and ran back to the city. "Come and see a man who told me everything I ever did," she said to her people. "Do you think he might be the promised One?"

A crowd gathered around the woman and followed her back out to the well. When they saw Jesus and talked to him, they believed what the woman had said. They asked Jesus to stay there in their town, but he could stay for only two days. During that time, many people came to believe that he was the Christ.

"At first we believed because of what you told us," they said to the woman; "but now we have seen for ourselves that he is the Savior of the world."

Questions:

1. Who were the Samaritans? 2. Where did Jesus rest while the disciples went to get food? 3. Why was the Samaritan woman surprised when Jesus asked her for a drink? 4. What was the "living water" Jesus was talking about? 5. What did Jesus tell the woman that surprised her? 6. Where did he tell her was the right place to worship? 7. What did the Samaritans of that village decide about Jesus?

Even the Winds and Waves Obey

But the men marvelled, saying, What manner of man is this, that even the winds and the sea obey him!
Matt. 8:27

BECAUSE of his miracles of healing, more and more people began following Jesus. They would come to see him make people well, and then he would have a chance to talk with them about the new kingdom over which he was going to rule. He told them that they would have to make their hearts pure before they could become members of his kingdom. He taught them that he was going to ask more of them than simply following the Law of Moses; his new law was that they love everyone, both friends and enemies.

Many thought that Jesus' teachings were true and they would invite him to speak in their synagogues on the Sabbath day when people of the village came to worship. He would read from the Law of Moses and show them how he was making the words of the prophets come true. Only in his home in Nazareth did the people get angry at this. Those in Nazareth could remember that he had grown up there as a poor boy and could still see the simple home where he had lived. They could not believe that he was going to be a king. When he spoke in the synagogue there, they drove him out and would have killed him if he had not slipped away.

Jesus and the Storm

After this Jesus spent most of his time in the other cities in Galilee where people wanted to hear him. In the middle of the country is the beautiful Sea of Galilee, and Jesus taught many lessons right there by its shore. Day after day he stood in the middle of a crowd, healing those who came or were brought, speaking always of his Father in heaven and the life the Father wanted those on earth to live.

One time, after he had spent several days teaching constantly, Jesus began to be very tired; but the people would not go away. Wherever he went, they followed close behind, begging for his healing touch or his words of life.

When he saw that there was no other way to rest, Jesus said to his closest disciples, "Let us get in a boat and row to the other side of the lake."

Soon a boat was found and they began rowing across the Sea of Galilee. Exhausted, Jesus went to the front of the boat to rest on a cushion. Within a few moments, he had fallen fast asleep, not noticing the dark clouds that were swiftly covering the sky.

The disciples began to worry when they saw the darkening sky. Then the wind began to blow and the boat to rock. Still they would not wake Jesus because they knew how tired he was and how much he needed the rest. But the wind blew stronger and stronger, and the waves got higher. They beat against the boat, lifting it high. Some broke over its side and filled the floor with water.

No longer were the disciples only worried; now they were terribly frightened. They grabbed Jesus and shook him to wake him. "Master, we are about to be drowned!" they cried. "Help us, save us!"

Jesus sat up and looked about at the raging storm. All he had to say was, "Peace, be still." At once, the winds ceased and the water grew calm. The dark clouds passed by, and the little boat rocked gently once again on a calm sea.

"Why were you so afraid?" Jesus asked the disciples. "Why did you get so worried when I was here all along? Do you not believe in my power?"

The disciples looked in amazement at the still water, then at Jesus, and finally at one another. They shook their heads as if they could not believe what they had seen. What kind of man was this who could control even the wind and the water? How could anyone fail to believe that he was the Son of God?

Questions:

1. What did Jesus try to teach the people who came to him? 2. What happened when Jesus went back to his old home in Nazareth? 3. Where did Jesus go to try to get away from the crowds? 4. Why did Jesus not know that a storm had come up? 5. What did he do when the disciples woke him? 6. What did the disciples think of this?

She Was Only Sleeping

He said unto them, Give place: for the maid is not dead, but sleepeth.
Matt. 9:24

IN a city near the Sea of Galilee, many people were waiting for Jesus' return. When he had been there before, he had made the sick of the village well. He had also told stories to the people and talked to them about the way they should act. Those who did as he said had found that their lives were much happier. They wanted Jesus to come back and tell them more.

Finally word came that Jesus was sailing across the sea toward their city. Everyone was so excited to hear it that they left whatever they were doing and came to stand by the water and wait for him to arrive.

But there was one man in the city who did not come and wait for Jesus that day. He was Jairus, a ruler of the synagogue, which was the Jewish house of worship in that town. Jairus was at home with his daughter, who was very sick. Jairus and his wife had done everything they could to make the little girl feel better. They had had doctors come and try to make her get well. But the girl grew sicker and sicker until finally Jairus knew that there was nothing else anyone could do for her.

About that time, Jairus heard the noise of the crowd meeting Jesus as he came ashore. Now Jairus had heard some strange things about this man from Nazareth. "I

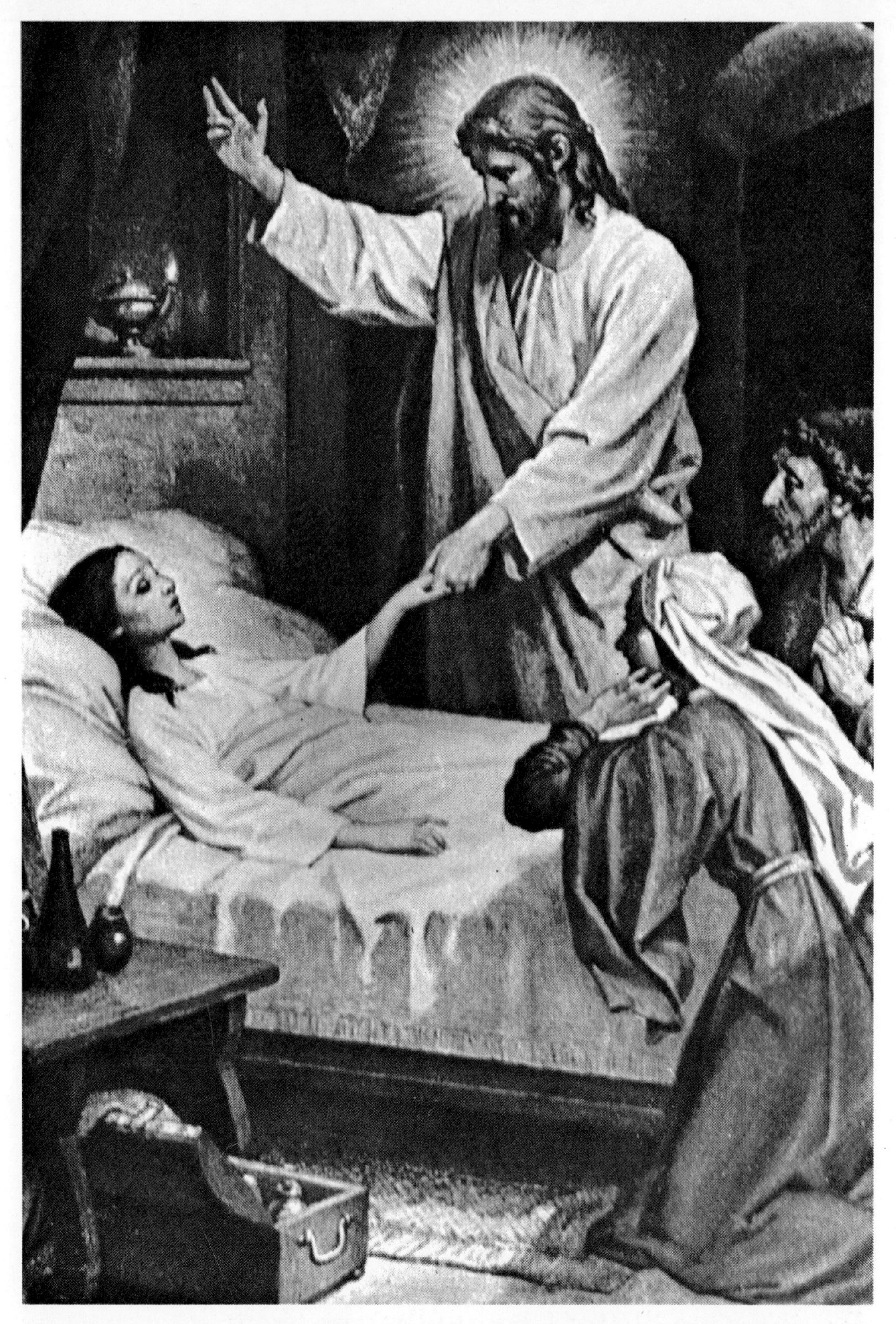

Raising Jairus' Daughter

wonder if they are true?" he thought. Then he looked over at his daughter, lying still and quiet with her eyes closed. "I will go to Jesus now," Jairus decided. "Something must be done quickly."

When Jairus reached the seaside, the crowds were thick around Jesus; but when they saw Jairus, they stepped aside and gave him room. You see, as ruler of the synagogue, Jairus was one of the most important men in that town. Finally, Jairus came face to face with Jesus. As he looked into Jesus' kind eyes, he knew that here was someone who could help him. Jairus fell on his knees right in front of Jesus and said, "My little girl is just about to die. You must come—just lay your hands on her—and I know she will get well."

Jesus smiled at Jairus. "I will come with you. Lead me to your house." So the two started toward Jairus' home, but the whole crowd came right along. There were so many people trying to walk down the narrow streets with Jesus that he could not move very fast.

In the crowd there was a woman who had been sick for twelve years. She had been to one doctor after another and had given them all her money, but she got no better.

No one in the crowd moved aside for this poor woman as they had for Jairus. She tried and tried, but she could not get close enough to get Jesus' attention. "If I could only touch the bottom of his coat," she thought, "that would be enough to make me well."

At last the woman made her way near to Jesus. She reached out her hand and timidly touched the hem of his robe. Immediately, she felt better and knew that she was well.

Suddenly Jesus turned around and asked, "Who touched me?"

"What do you mean?" someone replied with a little laugh. "Why, with this crowd there are people pressing against you and touching you on every side."

But Jesus had felt a special touch and knew that his power had gone out to help someone.

The woman still stood back in the crowd, afraid that she had done something wrong. At last she came forward, shaking and frightened. She fell down on the ground before Jesus and told him what she had done. But Jesus looked down at the woman and smiled. "Daughter," he said, "you have been made well because you believed that I could do it. Now, go in peace."

While Jesus had been taking time out to talk with this woman, Jairus had been standing beside him, waiting anxiously. He knew that they had to hurry on to his house if they got there in time to save his daughter. But about that time, a messenger arrived from there. "You need not trouble the Master any further," he said to Jairus. "Your daughter is already dead."

Jairus hung his head at these words, but Jesus turned to him quickly. "Do not be afraid," he said; "just believe in me and your daughter will be made well." Then they hurried as fast as the crowd would let them until they reached Jairus' home.

Already the house was full of aunts and uncles and cousins who had come to comfort Jairus and his wife. They were crying loudly, for they had loved the sweet little girl.

"Do not cry," Jesus said when he saw them. "She is not dead—just sleeping." But the kinfolk did not believe Jesus. They had seen the girl and they knew she was dead.

Jesus cleared the crowd out of the way until just Jairus and his wife and three of Jesus' disciples were left. Not until then did he go to the room where the little girl lay. He bent over the child and took one of her cold hands in his. "Little girl, get up!" he said simply.

As he spoke, the girl opened her eyes. She sat up and threw her legs over the side of the bed. Then she stood up and walked to her mother and father.

The parents stood there and looked at their daughter. They were so stunned and amazed they did not know what to do. "Give her something to eat," Jesus said. Then as the mother hurried to find food for her daughter, Jesus and his three disciples walked out of the house and back to the crowd that was waiting for them.

Questions:

1. Who was sick at Jairus' house? 2. Why could Jesus not go to Jairus' house very quickly? 3. Why did so many want to see Jesus? 4. What did the sick woman do in order to be healed? 5. Could Jesus tell she had touched his robe? 6. Why were Jairus' kinfolk at his house crying? 7. What did Jesus do to the little girl? 8. What did she do?

Five Loaves and Two Fishes

There is a lad here, which hath five barley loaves, and two small fishes: but what are they among so many?
John 6:9

THERE were so many people trying to hear Jesus and wanting to be healed by him, that he could not see them all nor visit all the places where he was wanted. Because of this, Jesus called to him his twelve closest disciples, whom he had named to be "apostles," and gave them the power to heal all kinds of sickness. Then he sent them out in pairs to the different towns where he could not go. They were to preach to the Jews about the coming kingdom, just as John had done. In every village where good people believed their message, the apostles would stay for a while, talking of Jesus and making sick people well. Some of the apostles have names we already know—Peter, Andrew, James, John, Philip, and Nathanael or Bartholomew. The other six were Thomas, Matthew, another James who was the son of Alphaeus, Thaddaeus, Simon the Canaanite, and Judas Iscariot.

After a while the apostles returned to Jesus and told him about their trips to the villages. All of the time they were talking with Jesus, crowds of people pressed closer and closer, trying to be near the healer from Nazareth. The apostles were already tired from their travels, and now they found that they could not even get past the crowd in order

Feeding the Five Thousand

to eat. Jesus saw how weary his friends were and that they had to get away and rest. So he climbed into a nearby boat with them and began rowing to a quiet spot across the Sea of Galilee.

The people, however, saw what Jesus and his apostles planned to do, and they went around the lake on foot. When the boat landed, the crowds were already there, waiting for Jesus. When Jesus saw them, his heart was touched. He could not leave them when he saw how badly they wanted and needed him, so he stayed and talked to them all afternoon.

As evening came on and the sun was disappearing, the apostles grew worried. They called Jesus to one side and made a suggestion. "Lord," they said, "it is getting late and there is nothing here for the people to eat. In their hurry to follow you, they forgot to bring food. Send them away now, so they will have time to reach a town and buy something to eat before dark."

Jesus knew that the people were tired and hungry. He said to the apostles, "There is no need to send them away. You can feed them."

Now the apostles had had a tiring day themselves, and they were growing a little impatient. Philip answered for them. "It would take a great deal of money to buy enough bread for all these people," he said; "and we have no money at all." It was still hard for them to understand that Jesus could do all things.

Jesus had patience with his closest friends. He saw that they needed the lesson he was about to teach as much as the crowd did. He asked them, "Is there anyone here with any food at all?"

Andrew had searched among the people and he answered, "There is a little boy who has brought himself a supper of five loaves of bread and two fishes. He is willing to share his small bit."

"That will be plenty," was Jesus' puzzling answer. "Ask the people to sit down in groups of hundreds and fifties upon the grass."

Some of the people were already getting ready to leave; but the apostles walked through the crowd asking everyone to stay. Soon all were seated in orderly groups, waiting to see what Jesus was about to do.

When the crowd grew quiet, Jesus held the loaves and fishes before him and gave thanks to God. Then he broke the food in pieces, dividing it among the apostles so they could pass it to the people in baskets. At Jesus' touch, the food seemed to multiply. The more he broke it, the more there was. Finally the apostles reported that everyone present—about five thousand—had been fed, and each had eaten enough.

When the meal was finished, the apostles passed again through the crowds with their baskets and picked up all the food that was left over. Even the scraps filled twelve baskets!

The people suddenly began talking among themselves when they realized what a wonderful miracle they had just seen. They stood and began begging for Jesus to be their

King. They wanted to crown him like David and Solomon and let him rule in Jerusalem.

You see, Jesus was their King, but he was not going to be that kind of king. Instead, he was going to rule over the kingdom of heaven, made up of all those everywhere who loved and believed in him. He was trying to teach this to the people, but he saw that they did not yet understand. He quietly ordered the apostles to sail without him, and he slipped away into the mountains to pray after the crowd had gone.

Questions:

1. Who were the "apostles"? 2. What power had Jesus given to them? 3. How did Jesus and the apostles escape from the crowd? 4. How did the crowd fool them? 5. Why did the apostles want Jesus to send the people home? 6. With how much food did Jesus feed the people? 7. How many people were fed?

Walking on the Water

And in the fourth watch of the night Jesus went unto them, walking on the sea.
Matt. 14:25

AFTER feeding the five thousand people, Jesus had ordered the apostles to sail across the Sea of Galilee without him. He went up into the mountains alone to pray, and he planned to meet them later.

The apostles had rowed their boat out a good distance from the shore when the night grew very dark and a stormy wind began to blow. From the mountain, Jesus could see far across the water, and he saw the men fighting the waves in their little boat. In the middle of the night he came down to the seashore and began walking toward his friends on the water, walking just as if it were dry ground under his feet.

Through the darkness the apostles saw the strange figure coming toward them on the water. Already frightened by the rocking boat, they began screaming with fear. "It is a ghost!" they cried out. Actually, there are no such things as ghosts, but they did not know how else to explain the weird sight.

Then they heard a familiar voice from across the water. "Do not be so afraid," it said. "It is I." They knew it was their Lord.

Peter called out to him, "Lord, if it really is you, let me come to you on the water."

Jesus Rescues Peter

"All right, Peter," Jesus answered. "Come."

Peter climbed over the side of the boat and tried to take a few steps. Surely enough, the water was firm under his feet. With his eyes on Jesus, he began walking toward him.

But the sound of the wind rushed past Peter's ears, reminding him of the storm. He took his eyes from Jesus and looked at the leaping waves. In that moment, when he forgot Jesus and began to be afraid, Peter started sinking. He called out, "Master, save me!"

Jesus immediately stretched out his hand and caught Peter's. He pulled him up and helped him to his feet again. Then he said, "Peter, you have so little belief in me. Why did you become afraid when you knew that I was with you?"

Peter had no answer to give. He hung his head in shame.

Once Peter and Jesus reached the boat, the stormy wind stopped as suddenly as it had come. Everyone there realized again the power of this man whom they were following. They bowed before him and said, "Truly you are the Son of God."

Questions:

1. Where did Jesus go after he had fed the five thousand people? 2. What did he look out and see from the mountain where he stood? 3. How did he come to the apostles to help them? 4. What did Peter want to do? 5. What happened when he tried? 5. Why did Peter start sinking? 6. What did the apostles think about Jesus?

A Glimpse of Glory on the Mountain

And was transfigured before them: and his face did shine
as the sun, and his raiment was white as the light.
Matt. 17:2

ONE day when Jesus and his disciples were traveling to some towns north of the Sea of Galilee, Jesus gave them a question to answer.

"Who do people say that I am?" he asked.

"Some say that you are John the Baptist; others say that you are Elijah or Jeremiah or one of the prophets come to life again," they answered.

Then Jesus said, "Who do *you* say that I am?"

"You are the Christ, the Son of God," Peter spoke up.

"Peter, you will be blessed for saying that," Jesus replied. "My Father has given you the faith to believe in me."

Then Jesus told his disciples about some sad things that were going to happen to him. You see, he had asked these questions to test them and see if they were ready to understand what he had to say. He told them that the Jews were going to turn against him and kill him, but that he would rise from the dead in three days.

The apostles did not like to hear Jesus talk this way. They still wanted him to be a great king on earth. They did not understand that Jesus had to be punished for men's sins so that we would not have to be punished ourselves. Then he

Jesus on the Mountaintop

could be king over his heavenly kingdom and those he had saved could be members of his kingdom.

About a week after Jesus had had this talk with his disciples, he took three of them with him upon a mountain to pray. The three were Peter, James, and John. These men seemed to be closer to Jesus than all his other followers. They were the three whom he had taken with him when he healed Jairus' daughter.

While Jesus was praying on the mountain that day, his face began to shine like the sun and his clothes became a dazzling white. A heavenly glory seemed to beam from him. Then two men appeared and talked with Jesus—they were Moses and Elijah.

Peter, James, and John stared at the wonderful sight before them. Here was their Lord, the great leader Moses, and the mighty prophet Elijah, glowing with a heavenly light. "Lord," Peter said, "it is so good for us to be here. Let us set up three places of worship—one for you, one for Moses, and one for Elijah."

But Peter did not really know what he was saying. He was so confused that he spoke before he had time to think. Just as he said this, a cloud from heaven came down and covered all of them there on the mountain. Then a voice came out of the cloud, saying, "This is my beloved Son; listen to him."

The glorious vision, the cloud, and the voice made the three apostles fall to their knees and hide their faces. They hardly knew what to think. Then they felt a tender touch. "Get up," Jesus said; "do not be afraid."

Timidly, the men raised their eyes. There was Jesus, all alone. His glory could not be seen any more, but these three would never forget how Jesus had looked. To them, more than ever before, he was their Savior and King.

Questions:

1. Who did people think that Jesus was? 2. Who did Peter say that he was? 3. Which was right? 4. Who went up on the mountain with Jesus? 5. What happened to Jesus? 6. Who came and talked with him? 7. What did the voice in the cloud say? 8. Why did God let Peter, James, and John see Jesus in his heavenly glory?

“Who Is My Neighbor?”

Which now of these three, thinkest thou, was neighbour unto him that
fell among the thieves? And he said, He that shewed mercy on him.
Luke 10:36-37

AFTER Jesus had been teaching and healing for about two years, he went down to Jerusalem in the fall of the year to celebrate a Jewish feast day. Afterward he stayed in the country around Jerusalem and taught the people there. Now most of the Jewish scholars, men who studied the Law of Moses, lived in Jerusalem. Word came to them of the teacher from Nazareth who claimed to be the Savior and King of the Jews. These men did not want to believe in Jesus and tried to find something wrong with him. You see, they thought they understood God and His Law better than anyone else, and they did not think that Jesus was the kind of king God was going to send.

In order to trap Jesus, these experts of the Law would try to think of questions that Jesus could not answer. They wanted to make him look foolish, while they appeared to be very smart.

In his teaching, Jesus had told the people that the members of his kingdom were going to have eternal life. This meant that when they died and were buried, they would come to heaven and continue living on and on with him and God, his Father. This idea was a hard one to under-

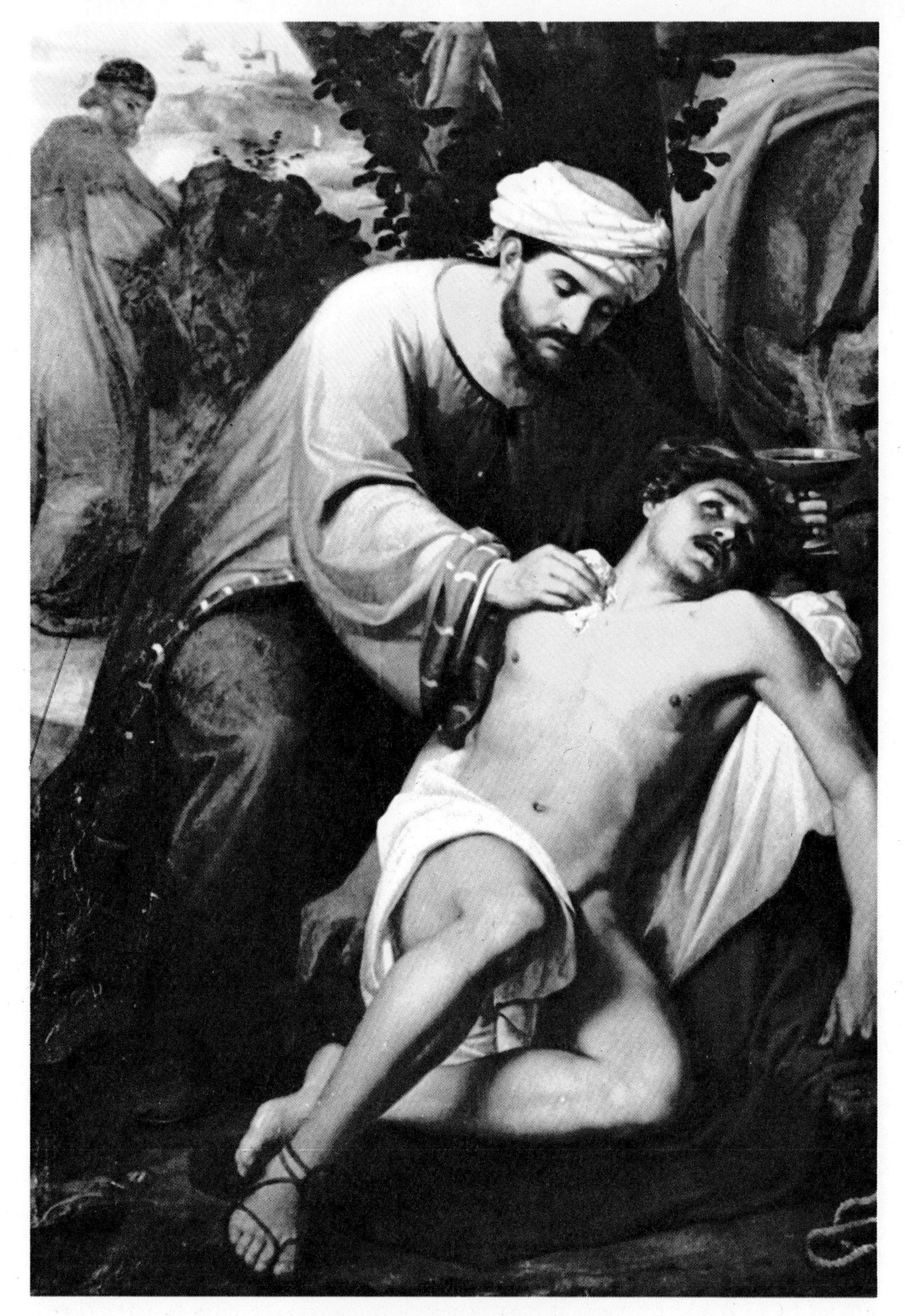

The Good Samaritan

stand. Even the lawyers wondered what it meant; and they came to Jesus, hoping to catch him in a mistake.

"Master," one of them asked, "what can I do to have this eternal life that you speak of?"

"You know God's Law," replied Jesus. "What does it tell you to do?"

The scholar was surprised at Jesus' question. He answered, "The Law says that I am to love God with all my heart, all my soul, all my strength, and all my mind. And I am to love my neighbor as myself."

"What you have said is right," Jesus said. "If you do that, you will be able to live forever."

This did not satisfy the man. He tried to trap Jesus again by asking, "The Law says I am to love my neighbor—just who is my neighbor?"

The best way Jesus knew to explain was to tell a story. This was what he told:

One day a man was taking a trip from Jerusalem to Jericho. The road between these two cities is a dangerous one. There are great rocks along the way where robbers and thieves hide. As this man was traveling alone, he was overtaken by a band of robbers. They beat him, stripped off his clothes, took his money, and left him there beside the road, barely alive.

Now that day a priest, one who served in the Temple, was making a trip along the very same road. This priest, who was supposed to give his life to serve God, saw the beaten man; but he did not stop to help. He went as far as he could to the other side of the road and passed by.

Later on, a Levite, a member of the Jewish tribe who led in the worship, came by. He, too, merely glanced at the suffering man and continued on his journey as though nothing were unusual.

Finally, a Samaritan came along. Now the Samaritans were hated by the Jews because some of their ancestors had been in the ten Jewish tribes who turned from God to idols. The Jews thought that they were much better than the Samaritans and would not even come near to one. Remember how surprised the Samaritan woman was when Jesus talked to her by the well?

When this Samaritan saw that the sick man was a Jew, he could have hurried on his journey; but his heart was touched by anyone who was in trouble. He took some oil that he had and cleaned off the cuts the man had gotten in the terrible beating. Then he bandaged them up. Finally he lifted him to his own horse and led it until they came to a place to stay. All night he sat with the sick man, taking care of him.

The next day he saw that his patient was going to get well. He went to the keeper of the house and gave him some money. "Use this to care for the man I brought here. If you have to spend any more, I will repay you when I come back by."

When the story was finished, Jesus turned to the lawyer and asked, "Now which of these three—the priest, the Levite, or the Samaritan—was a neighbor to the man who was robbed?"

"The one who helped him, of course," the lawyer answered.

"Then you go, and help in the same way," Jesus told him. He wanted the lawyer to know that he was to help anyone who needed it, no matter who he was. He was never to think that he was too important to be kind to someone.

Questions:

1. Why did the experts of the Law of Moses not want to believe Jesus? 2. How did they try to make him look foolish? 3. Who passed by the sick man on the side of the road? 4. Who *should* have helped him? 5. Who did help him? 6. What had been the lawyer's question? 7. Did this story answer his question? 8. What was the answer?

A Runaway Son Comes Home

For this my son was dead, and is alive again; he was lost and is found.
Luke 15:24

THE people who came to Jesus loved to hear him tell stories like the one about the good Samaritan. They showed how Jesus wanted them to act and what his kingdom was like in a way they could understand. These stories of Jesus that teach great lessons are often called "parables."

Among the crowds of people who loved to hear Jesus were some who had been living sinful lives. His words made them feel sorry for their sins, and they would decide to change and try to be as good and kind as he was. Because they did not like to leave Jesus even for a little while, they would persuade him to come home and eat with them at mealtime. This way, Jesus could go right on talking to them.

Now the most particular Jews, some of them scribes and some from a party called the Pharisees, were shocked to see Jesus being friendly with those they knew to be bad people. They thought that a King of God's nation should not pay attention to folk like that. They thought that he ought to notice only important people, those like themselves.

Jesus saw that these Jews needed to hear one of his parables, too; so he told them about the adventures of a runaway son. This is the way the story went:

A Runaway Son Comes Home

Once there lived a man who had two sons. Now this man had worked hard to make a lot of money that he could leave for his boys when he died. One day his younger son came to him and said, "Father, I am no longer happy here with you. I want my share of your money now so I can spend it as I please." Sadly the father divided up all that he had and gave the son his portion.

Happy with his new riches, the son gathered up his things and left home. He traveled to a country far away, sure that his money was going to make him very happy.

When he arrived in the strange country, the young man found many things to spend his money on. Wicked people taught him to gamble and took many dollars from him. Others pretended to be his good friends and talked him into buying things for them. Every time he turned around he was paying for their rich food and a lot of wine for them to drink.

Before long, the young man found that all his money was gone. Those who had acted as if they were his friends paid no attention to him. He saw that he was going to have to find a job in order to have something to eat.

Then a famine came upon that country, and food became very scarce. There were no crops to tend, and the man could not find a job. Finally, he found a farmer who agreed to let him feed his pigs. By this time he was so hungry that he would have eaten some of the husks that were fed to the pigs, but no one gave him any.

Among the smelling, grunting pigs, the young man could not help thinking of the clean home he had left. He thought of the servants who worked for his father and how much better off they were than he was. He made up his mind right then: "Why, I will go back to my father. I will tell him how wrong I have been and that I know I do not deserve to be his son any longer. Maybe he will let me live at home just as a hired servant. That would be enough."

Immediately he set out on the long journey toward home. For many days he traveled. Finally he saw his father's house in the distance. And someone stood there waiting for him—it was his father! The two began running toward each other and fell into each other's arms.

"Father," began the son, "I am not good enough to be your son."

But the father could not stand to hear his boy speak that way. He turned to a servant and said, "Bring a fine robe for my son, and put a ring on his hand and shoes on his feet. Then we will kill a fat calf and prepare a great dinner. It is time for a celebration!"

Now the older brother had stayed at home all this time, helping his father. He had not asked for his part of the father's fortune and wasted it. He did not think that his brother deserved to be treated kindly by their father, and he would not come to the dinner. The father came outside and found him sulking. He put his arm around his boy and said, "Son, this does not mean that I love you any less. You have been so good to stay with me. But now we should be glad that your brother has come back to us. He that was lost has been found!"

With this story, Jesus showed the important Jews that sinners could become God's children also. The bad people whom Jesus helped were like the runaway son who came back. The important Jews were like the sulking older brother. God, of course, is like the father in the story—he is always ready to welcome those who turn to Him.

Questions:

1. Why did the people like for Jesus to tell stories? 2. What are his stories often called? 3. What did the runaway son do with his father's money? 4. What was the only job he could find? 5. What did he finally decide to do? 6. Was his father glad to see him? 7. Was his older brother glad that he had decided to do right? 8. Tell what Jesus was trying to show to the Jews who thought they were so important.

"Bring the Children to Me"

Suffer the little children to come unto me, and forbid them not: for of such is the kingdom of God.
Mark 10:14

ALL around the countries of Judea, Samaria, and Galilee, the people had come to love Jesus, the Christ. When news came that he was coming to a particular village, everyone in that town would leave whatever he was doing and run to meet him. Some would help sick friends reach his side so they could be healed. Others would come to listen to his stories and learn the great lessons that helped them become better men and women. The little children loved just to sit around on the ground, as close to his feet as they could get. They could not understand everything he said, but they loved just to hear his kind voice and look into his loving eyes.

Now Jesus talked a great deal about the kingdom over which he was going to rule. His apostles wondered what kind of kingdom it was going to be. As his closest friends, they wondered what kind of jobs they would get to hold in the new kingdom. Perhaps one thought he might be a governor over an important country, or maybe another wanted to be prime minister, second under Christ. Anyway, they soon got into quite an argument over which one would be the greatest.

Jesus and the Little Children

Jesus looked sadly at the bickering apostles. It was so hard for him to show them that his kingdom was not going to be like they thought it was. He needed some way to teach them a great lesson. Then he saw his chance:

From the group standing near, he called to a little child, "Come here." Immediately the child ran to his arms. Jesus gave him a squeeze, and then still holding him, he turned to the apostles and said, "This is what my kingdom will be like. Unless you become like this little child, you cannot be a part of it."

"Doing good for a little child is just like doing good for me," he continued. "But a terrible punishment should go to anyone who teaches a child to do wrong. Why, these little children have angels before God's throne who watch over them."

Later on, the mothers began bringing their children to the one who loved them so. They wanted to be able to tell their little boy or girl that he had been held and blessed by Jesus, the Savior.

The disciples thought that Jesus was too busy to see so many little children. They said to the mothers, "Our Lord is busy. He cannot possibly see all of you."

But Jesus said, "Do not turn the little children away. Let them come to me. Remember that the kingdom of heaven belongs to them and those like them."

Then he touched each little child and said a kind word to them.

The apostles thought and thought about Jesus and the children. It took a long time for them to realize that he meant that their hearts would have to be as pure as a child's in order to be in his kingdom. He wanted them to learn to be as loving, as trusting, and as gentle as the very young. And as children do, he wanted them to put their trust in God as their Father and know that He would care for them.

Questions:

1. Why did the children like to come to Jesus? 2. What were the apostles arguing about? 3. Whom did Jesus use to show them what the members of his kingdom would be like? 4. In what way should a grown person be like a little child? 5. What did Jesus do to the children to show he loved them?

From Death to Life

And when he thus had spoken, he cried with a loud voice, Lazarus, come forth.
John 11:43

WHILE he traveled about from place to place, Jesus really had no home of his own. Instead, he ate in the homes of his followers and slept there, too, when he was invited. Some of these people he would visit again and again as he came back to their village.

About two miles from Jerusalem, there stood a little town called Bethany. Whenever Jesus came to Bethany, he always stayed with the same family. In this family there was a man, Lazarus, and his two sisters, Mary and Martha. These three became very good friends of Jesus.

One day when Jesus was far away across the Jordan River, a message came from Mary and Martha. "Come quickly, Lord," it said; "Lazarus, whom you love, is sick."

But Jesus did not seem worried by this news. "This sickness will not lead to death," he told his disciples, "but to the glory of God and His Son." Then Jesus stayed for two more days in that same place.

Finally, on the third day, Jesus said to his disciples, "Let us go back to Bethany."

But they answered, "You know you should not go so near to Jerusalem, Master. Why, the last time you were in Jerusalem, the important Jews there tried to kill you."

Jesus Raises Lazarus

"Our friend Lazarus has fallen asleep," Jesus replied. "I am going to awaken him."

"Well, if he is just asleep," they said, "he will get well."

Then Jesus spoke to them plainly: "Lazarus is dead."

The disciples looked from one to another, not knowing what to think. How did Jesus know that Lazarus was dead? Why had he not gone in time to heal him? Why was he risking his life to go back now that nothing could be done for his friend? They could not answer these questions, but they did know that they believed in their Lord.

"Come, let us go with him," Thomas said to the others. "If they kill him, we will be there to die with him."

So they went to Bethany. The trip took two or three days, and when they arrived, they found that Lazarus had already been buried for four days. The house was full of friends from Jerusalem who had come to try to comfort Mary and Martha.

When word came that Jesus was coming at last, Martha ran out to meet him at the edge of town. Her eyes were full of tears. "Lord," she said, "if you had just been here, my brother would not have died."

Jesus answered her: "Your brother will rise again."

"I know he will rise again at the resurrection, at the last day," Martha said.

Then Jesus looked straight into her eyes. "I am the resurrection and the life," he said. "He who believes on me will live even if he dies. Do you believe this?"

"Yes, Lord," Martha replied; "I believe that you are the Christ, the Son of God, who was promised to come into the world."

Then Martha went back to tell her sister that Jesus had arrived. Mary jumped up quickly to go to Jesus when she heard the news. Her friends, thinking that she was going to Lazarus' grave, came with her. When Mary saw Jesus, she fell down in front of him and cried, "Lord, if you had been here, my brother would not have died."

Jesus was troubled to see Mary and all of her friends crying. "Where have you buried him?" he asked.

"Come and see," they said.

Then Jesus wept with them. When the Jews from Jerusalem saw this, they said, "Look how much he loved Lazarus." But some of them said, "He has healed others. Could he not have kept Lazarus from dying?"

About this time, the sad group came to the cave where Lazarus lay buried. A huge stone covered the entrance.

"Take away the stone," Jesus said.

Martha looked up, surprised. "Lord, he has been dead four days!" she said.

"Did I not tell you that if you believed in me, you would see the glory of God?" he asked.

So the stone was rolled away. When it lay at one side, Jesus looked up toward heaven and prayed. "Father," he said, "thank You for hearing me. I know that You hear me always, but I say it now so that everyone here will believe that You sent me."

Then Jesus shouted into the grave, "Lazarus, come forth!"

And out walked Lazarus. After having been dead for four days and still wrapped in his burial clothes, Jesus' friend stepped forward into the fresh air.

"Take off those wrappings, and let him go," Jesus said.

Eagerly the sisters tore away the clothes that bound Lazarus' hands and feet. They threw their arms about their brother and then backed away from him to look again. Yes, it was he! Lazarus was alive!

Questions:

1. Whom did Jesus always visit with when he came to Bethany? 2. Where was Jesus when he received the message from Mary and Martha? 3. How long was it before he came to Bethany? 4. What had happened to Lazarus? 5. Why did Jesus pray in front of the tomb? 6. What did Jesus shout into the grave? 7. What happened when he did?

Mary's Gift

For the poor always ye have with you; but me ye have not always.
John 12:8

WHEN Jesus raised Lazarus from the dead, you will remember that there were some people from Jerusalem there. Naturally, they went back to the city and told their friends of the wonderful thing they had seen, and more people than ever believed that he was the promised Savior. The Jewish priests and members of the Pharisee party, however, hated Jesus even more when they heard of it.

"He is turning our people away from us with these miracles of his," they said. "What are we going to do with him?"

"It is better that he die than our whole nation be led astray," Caiaphas, the high priest, decided.

So from that time on, they planned how they might capture Jesus and kill him.

Jesus was not afraid of these important Jews. He knew that his time on earth was nearly gone. He was more concerned that his disciples understand about the kingdom that was coming and the work they would have to do after he left them. For hours every day he talked to them and explained these things.

When the time for the Passover feast came, Jesus set out for Jerusalem to celebrate it, just as the other Jews did. It

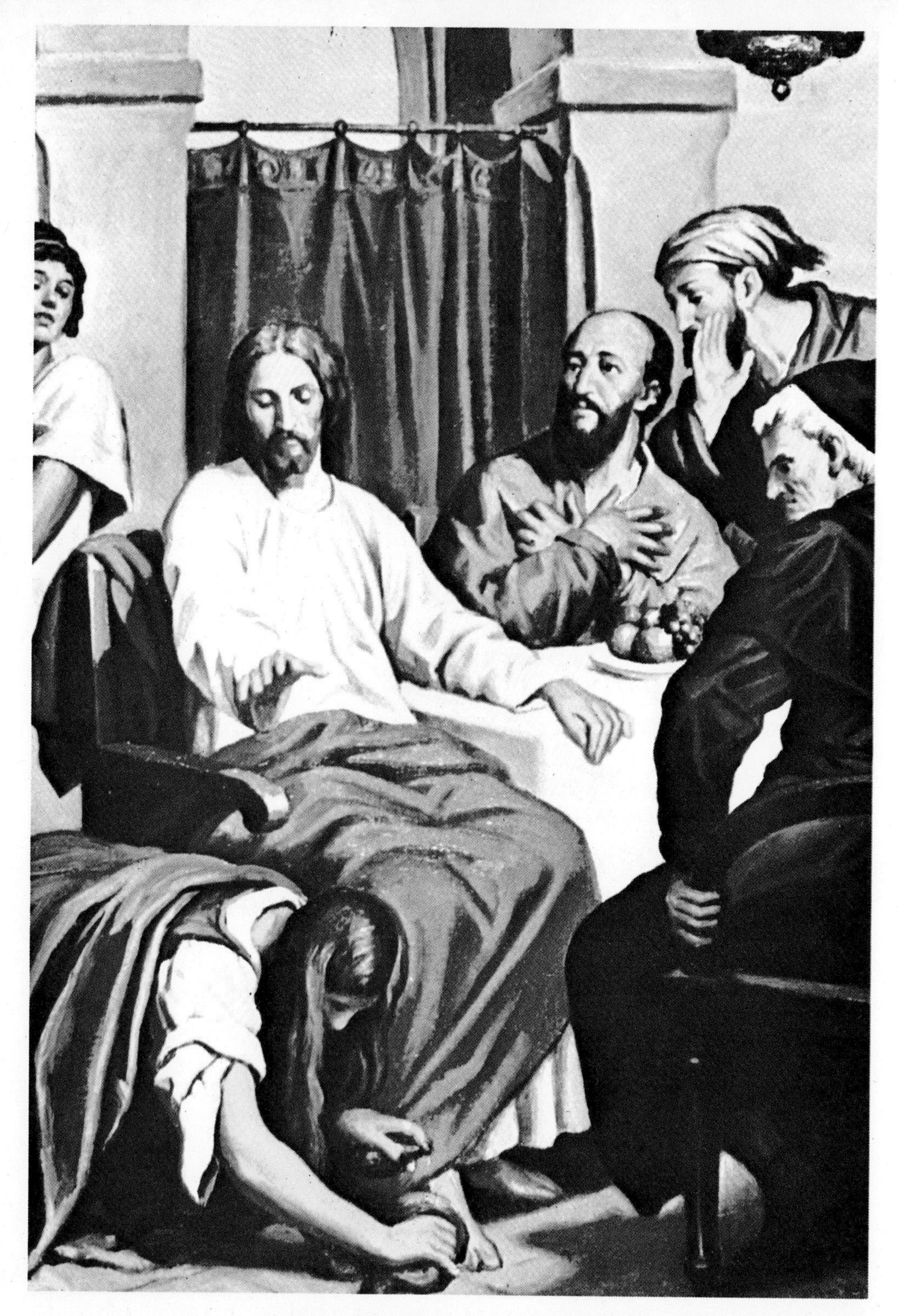

Mary Washing Jesus' Feet

did not matter to him that the priests were looking for him to try to kill him. He knew what was about to happen, and he was ready to face it.

At the edge of Jerusalem, Jesus stopped for the last time in Bethany to visit with Mary and Martha and Lazarus. You can imagine how glad this family was to see Jesus! If it were not for him, the two sisters would be all alone without a kind, strong brother to help them.

While Jesus was in Bethany, he and his friends went to a dinner at the house of a man named Simon. Simon wanted to honor Jesus because Jesus had once cured him of a terrible disease called leprosy. Lazarus and Jesus had important seats at the dinner party, and Martha helped to serve the food.

During the party, Mary, the other sister, tiptoed shyly into the room and came and stood beside Jesus. Now Mary loved Jesus very much and she had always listened carefully to the things he said. She was also very thankful to him for bringing her brother back to life. Somehow she had wanted to tell Jesus all these things that were in her heart, so she had bought a very expensive box of sweet perfume. As she stood near her Lord, she let some of the perfume fall on his head. Then she poured some onto his feet and wiped them with her beautiful, long hair.

As the smell of the perfume filled the room, the others at the dinner stopped talking and looked at Mary with surprise. "Now, why did she do that?" Judas, one of the apostles, asked. "That perfume was very expensive. It could have been sold and the money given to the poor." Actually,

Judas did not feel sorry for the poor. He kept the money that belonged to the apostles, and sometimes he stole from it. He wanted this money to spend on himself.

"Let her alone," Jesus told Judas. "Why are you bothering her? She has done a good thing. There are always going to be poor people for you to help, but I am not going to be with you much longer. I am going to have to die, and she has prepared my body for burial with this perfume. I tell you the truth, when people preach about me all over the world, they will tell of what Mary has just done, in memory of her."

Judas was stung by these words. He let Satan come into his heart and rule it instead of Christ. From that time on he planned on a way that he could give Jesus over to his enemies.

Questions:

1. What did the people think about Jesus' raising Lazarus from the dead? 2. Was Jesus afraid to come to Jerusalem and face the men who hated him? 3. Where did he stop to visit right outside Jerusalem? 4. Who gave a dinner for Jesus? 5. Why did Mary want to do something for Jesus? 6. What did she do for him at the dinner? 7. What did Judas think about this? 8. Did Jesus agree with him?

"Here Comes the King!"

Hosanna: Blessed is the King of Israel that cometh in the name of the Lord.
John 12:13

NOW the time had come for the Passover feast, and Jews from all over the world traveled to Jerusalem to celebrate the solemn occasion. Many of them from far away hoped to catch a glimpse of the teacher from Nazareth while they were there. Jesus himself had not gone into the city yet, as the feast was still nearly a week away. He was staying in a little town named Bethany, a few miles away. Here he visited with Mary, Martha, and their brother Lazarus. They went to a dinner together and Mary poured some expensive perfume on Jesus as a gift.

Word spread in Jerusalem that Jesus was in Bethany with Lazarus. Many men, women, and children decided to walk the two miles to Bethany and meet him there. They also wanted to see the man who had been dead and buried and was now alive.

Jesus decided at the same moment that the time had come for him to go into Jerusalem, even though the Jewish priests were so angry with him and his teaching that they were trying to kill him. He sent two of his disciples to a nearby village and said, "When you get into the town, you will see a colt tied near its mother. Unfasten the colt and bring him to me. If anyone asks why you are taking him,

Jesus Enters Jerusalem

just say that the Lord needs him. They will let you have him."

In the village, the disciples found things just as Jesus had said they would. As they were untying the colt, the owner came up and asked, "Why are you taking my donkey?"

"Our Lord needs him," they replied. The owner asked no more questions, but let them lead it away.

When the disciples reached Jesus with the colt, they spread some coats of their own across his back for Jesus to sit upon. Jesus mounted the young animal and began his short trip. As he came near the city he met the crowd that was coming out to see him. When they saw him riding upon a colt as a king might, they grew wild with joy. They thought that he was coming to set up his kingdom in Jerusalem.

Many of the people took off their coats and spread them in the road to make a carpet for Jesus to ride on. Others cut branches from palm trees and spread them on the ground. Then they walked before him and shouted, "Bless this son of David! Bless this One who comes from God! Bless his great kingdom! God bless our King!"

When the shouting crowd reached the city, people heard the commotion and came out to ask, "Who is coming?"

"It is Jesus from Nazareth," came the answer.

The priests and leading Pharisees tried to get the crowd to quit shouting after Jesus, but Jesus turned to them and said, "You cannot change anything by making the people quiet. If they were still, even the stones would cry out that I am God's Son."

The Pharisees could only step back and let the parade pass on. But they were not ready to give up. If they could not turn the people away from Jesus by just talking, they were determined to do it another way.

Questions:

1. Why was Jesus going to Jerusalem? 2. How did Jesus get a colt to ride into the city? 3. What did the people think when they saw Jesus on the colt? 4. What did the people use their coats and palm branches for? 5. What did the priests think of the parade? 6. Were they able to stop it?

An Old Feast and a New Supper

For as often as ye eat this bread, and drink this cup, ye do shew the Lord's death till he come.
I Cor. 11:26

DURING the three years that Jesus spent teaching in the villages and cities, twelve men stayed close to his side. These were the ones he had chosen to be his apostles. Some of the things he told them about his kingdom were hard for them to understand, but they tried their best to learn everything Jesus taught. They loved him more than anything else in the world, and they believed that he was truly the Son of God. Of course, none of these men were perfect, but each one tried to let Jesus rule his life. Only one let Satan enter his heart. This was Judas Iscariot.

Now Judas had wanted to serve Jesus well at first. He was happy when he was given the responsibility of taking care of the money with which the apostles bought food. Gradually, this money became more important to him than the words Jesus was saying. Sometimes he would take some of it without telling any of the others and buy something that he wanted very badly. He grew selfish and was displeased when he saw Lazarus' sister give Jesus some expensive perfume instead of putting the money for it in his bag.

The Last Supper

Now the rulers of the Jews had decided that they had to get rid of this Jesus of Nazareth. They felt that their explanation of God's Law and prophecy was right, and that this poor teacher and healer could not possibly be the Savior for whom they were looking. But they could not persuade the people to turn away from him Killing him was the only way they felt that they could gain control of the people once more.

After Jesus spoke sharply to Judas about Mary's gift, Judas became very angry. He wanted to do something to hurt Jesus. Then a wicked plan came to his mind. He would sell Jesus to the priests and Pharisees who wanted him killed. Secretly he went to the chief priests and asked, "What will you give me for turning Jesus over to you?" The priests agreed upon thirty pieces of silver, and Judas was satisfied. "I will let you know when the time is best for you to take him," Judas told them; and he returned to the other apostles. None of them guessed what he had done; but Jesus, of course, knew.

A few days later, on a Thursday evening, Jesus and all of the twelve ate the Passover feast together in an upper room in Jerusalem. Like all other Jews for many centuries, they did it to remember the time the death angel passed over the Israelites in Egypt. During the meal a sadness seemed to hover over the group, something no one could explain. After eating the roast lamb of the Passover, Jesus kneeled and washed the feet of each one there, including Judas. He did this to show them that the one who served others the best would be the greatest in his kingdom.

Later, as they sat about, Jesus looked around at the men and made a startling statement: "One of you here with me is going to betray me and give me up to be killed."

A hush fell over the group. Each one turned to him, hurt at the idea that one of them might harm him. "Is it I?" they asked, one after another. No one noticed that Judas said nothing.

"It is one of you eating from this same dish with me," Jesus replied. "I feel sorry for the one who betrays me," he added as a warning. "It would have been better if he had never been born."

Finally Judas was able to whisper the words, "Is it I, Lord?" Jesus dipped some bread into the dish of sauce and handed it to Judas, meeting his gaze. "You have said it, Judas. What you must do, do it quickly."

Immediately Judas left the room and went out into the night. The other apostles hardly realized what had happened. They might have thought that Judas was simply going on some errand.

After this, Jesus served the apostles the bread and the wine that we call the "Lord's Supper." He told them that he wanted them to eat this when they were members of his kingdom; and when they did, they were to remember him.

Then the Lord gave his apostles their last lesson. "Do not be worried," he said. "You believe in God; believe also in me. I am going to my Father now, where I will prepare a place for you. When it is ready, I will come again and take you there with me.

"Now I am going to give a new commandment to you: love one another as much as I have loved you."

Jesus said many other things to his apostles and he prayed for them. Then they all sang a Passover hymn and went out into the night.

Questions:

1. Was Judas a good disciple to select to keep the money? Why? 2. What did Judas decide to do to hurt Jesus? 3. How much did the priests pay Judas for leading them to Christ? 4. Did Judas tell anyone about this? 5. Where did Jesus and the apostles eat the Passover feast? 6. Was Judas there? Did he stay? 7. What new supper did Jesus give his apostles? 8. When were they supposed to eat it? Why?

A Kiss from Judas

But Jesus said unto him, Judas, betrayest thou the Son of man with a kiss?
Luke 22:48

AFTER Jesus and his apostles had eaten the Passover supper in the upper room, they walked through the dark to the Mount of Olives. Here at the base of the mountain, there was a garden called Gethsemane. It was a quiet, shady place where they often came to rest or pray.

By the time they reached the garden, Jesus' heart was very troubled by the suffering he knew he was facing. He felt that he needed to talk with his Father. "Wait here while I go and pray," he said to the disciples. Then he took Peter, James, and John and went a little further into the garden.

"My heart is almost breaking," Jesus confided to these three, who were his closest friends. "Stay here and watch with me." Then he went off a short distance by himself and fell to the ground. Here, alone with God, he could admit that the death before him was almost more than he could bear. But he promised that he would go through any suffering if it were God's will.

After praying so earnestly, Jesus came back to his friends. He found all three of them asleep. "Why are you sleeping?" Jesus asked Peter. "Could you not watch with me just one hour?"

Judas Betrays Jesus

Then a second time Jesus went away and prayed to his Father for help. When he came back to his friends, they had drifted off to sleep again. They were ashamed of themselves, but they could not manage to stay awake and help Jesus when he needed it so badly. The third time that Jesus went away to pray alone, God sent an angel to wipe his sweating forehead and to comfort him with words from his Father.

Jesus was now ready to meet his enemies if they came. Once more he came and stood by the drowsy apostles. "Go ahead and sleep now," he said as he looked sadly at them; "the time has already come when I am going to be given over to wicked men."

At that, torches lit the garden. The loud shouts of an angry mob broke the silence of the night. Into sight came Judas, leading a band of armed soldiers.

When he had left the Passover feast, Judas had gone to the chief priests of the Jews. "Now is the time to capture Jesus," he said. "His followers are in their homes eating the Passover feast, and they will not find out about it until we have caught him. He and his disciples have already eaten the supper, and they will probably go to the Mount of Olives. We can meet them there."

So the priests gave Judas a group of soldiers to take with him to capture Jesus. As they reached the garden, Judas whispered to the officers, "Stay behind until I show you which one Jesus is. He will be the one that I kiss."

Then he stepped forward and came face to face with Jesus. "Master," he said, as though he were glad to see him. He leaned forward and kissed Jesus.

The Lord gave Judas a long look of pity and said, "Judas, do you mean that you would betray me with a kiss?" Then he turned to the officers and asked, "Who are you looking for?"

"Jesus of Nazareth," they replied.

"I am he," Jesus said; "you will not need to use your swords to take me."

Now Peter had been watching all of this and could not stand by any longer. He drew out his sword and cut off the ear of the high priest's servant. Jesus turned to Peter and said, "Put your sword away. Do you not realize that my Father could send angels to save me if I asked Him? But this must be done in order to fulfill God's will." Then he healed the servant's ear.

Finally, he turned to the soldiers and said, "Why did you come to get me with your swords as though I were a criminal? I have not tried to hide, but I have been teaching openly in the Temple." Then he gave himself up to them and allowed them to lead him away.

The disciples were confused and terrified. When they saw that Jesus was not going to let them fight for him, they ran away in fright, leaving him to face his betrayers alone.

Questions:

1. Why did Judas think that Jesus and the apostles might go to the garden of Gethsemane? 2. What did Jesus want to do in the garden? 3. How many times did Jesus go off alone and pray? 4. What did he pray for? 5. Did the apostles pray with him? 6. How did Judas show the soldiers which one Jesus was? 7. What did Peter do to fight back?

The Jewish Court Says "Guilty!"

What think ye? They answered and said, He is guilty of death.
Matt. 26:66

FROM the Garden of Gethsemane, Judas and the guards led Jesus to the house of Annas, who was once a high priest and was still a very important man among the Jews. Annas was expecting Jesus when he was thrust into the room by the soldiers. He was glad to have a chance, at last, to see this man who was causing such a stir. He asked Jesus about his followers and about his teaching.

"Why do you ask me about my teaching?" Jesus replied. "I have never tried to hide, but I have always spoken openly in the Temple and synagogues. Ask those who heard me; they know what I said."

When Jesus said this, one of the officers holding him struck him with his hand. "How dare you speak this way to a high priest?" he growled.

Outside, Peter and John were waiting with a crowd in the courtyard to see what was going to happen to Jesus. While Peter was standing, warming his hands by a fire, one of the maids came up and asked him if he was a friend of Jesus. "I do not know the man," Peter claimed, ducking his head and trying to move away from her.

Jesus Before the High Priest

Later on, another maid saw him and said the same thing: "This man was with Jesus!"

"I do not know what you are talking about," Peter hotly denied.

When the third person paired him with Jesus, Peter got very angry. He began to swear, declaring that he did not know what they meant. When he did, he heard a rooster crow, for morning was breaking. He remembered that Jesus had told him, "Before the rooster crows, you will deny me three times." And just a few hours before, Peter had promised that he would go to prison or die before he would deny that Jesus was his Lord. Peter could not stay in the courtyard another minute. He ran outside and fell down, crying as though his heart would break.

By this time, Annas had all the information from Jesus he cared to hear. He dismissed him and sent him, carefully guarded by the soldiers, to the house of Caiaphas, the high priest. Inside with Caiaphas, the respected elders and lawyers who made up the Jewish court were waiting. It was very unusual for them to be called to meet in the middle of the night, but they were anxious to find some reason to declare Jesus guilty now that they had him in their power.

One by one witnesses spoke against Jesus while the court tried to find some excuse for putting him to death, but no two of them even agreed. Through it all, Jesus never said a word. Finally the high priest himself stood and faced Jesus. "Are you the Christ, the Son of God?" he asked.

"I am," Jesus said, finally breaking the silence, "and one day you will see me sitting on God's own throne and coming in clouds of glory."

Caiaphas turned pale with anger. He turned to the rest of the court. "Have you heard what this man said? We need no more witnesses; he has placed the blame on himself! Do you agree?"

"He is guilty of blasphemy!" came the answer. "Surely this man from Nazareth blasphemes when he claims to be the Son of God. He should be killed!"

The servants holding Jesus turned to him and began spitting on him. Some of them blindfolded him and hit him. Then they asked him to prophesy and tell who it was that had touched him.

Now Judas had been watching all the things that had been happening to Jesus since he had been brought from the garden. When he heard the high priest accuse Jesus and realized that he would be killed, Judas saw what a terrible thing he had done. He went to the priests and elders and begged them to take their money back. "I have betrayed a man who has done no wrong," he said.

But the leaders did not want to have any more to do with Judas. "That is your business now. You take care of it," they replied, refusing to take the money.

There was nothing Judas could do now. He threw the thirty pieces of silver on the floor, and went out and hanged himself from a tree. Later the priests took the money and bought a field in which to bury strangers. It came to be known as the "Field of Blood."

Questions:

1. To whom did Judas and the soldiers first take Jesus? 2. Where did Peter wait while Annas was questioning Jesus? 3. How many times did Peter claim not to know Jesus? 4. What made him remember what Jesus had said? 5. Who was Caiaphas? 6. What did the court decide that Jesus was guilty of? 7. What is blasphemy? 8. What did Judas try to do with the money when he realized what he had done?

"What Shall I Do with Jesus?"

And Pilate answered and said again unto them, What will ye then that I shall do unto him whom ye call the King of the Jews? And they cried out again, Crucify him.
Mark 15:12-13

AFTER the Jewish court decided that Jesus was guilty, Friday morning had begun to dawn. Before they could go ahead and kill Jesus, they still had to get permission from the Roman officials. The Roman governor of Judea to whom they went that morning was a man named Pontius Pilate. They told Pilate that Jesus was teaching against the Roman government, teaching that he was the king instead of Caesar.

When Pilate heard this, he took Jesus away privately to question him; but he could not find anything wrong with him. He went back out and reported this to the Jews. But the Jews were so excited by this time that they were determined to find some way to kill Jesus. "He has stirred up the people in Galilee," they reminded Pilate.

"Well, then," Pilate said, "I should not even be judging him. Herod, governor of Galilee, is in Jerusalem. Take him to Herod."

But Herod kept Jesus only a short time. Then he sent him back to Pilate, saying that he could find no reason for Jesus' death.

By this time, Pilate was very worried about the decision the Jews were asking him to make. He was convinced that

Jesus Before Pilate

Jesus had done nothing worthy of death; Herod had decided the same thing. Then, too, Pilate's wife had sent a message to him. "Let this Jesus go free," it read; "there is something very strange about him. This very night I suffered in a dream that had to do with him."

Desperate now, Pilate thought of one more chance to save Jesus. He came out and said to the Jews, "It is the custom for us to release one prisoner at your festival time. Let me release Jesus of Nazareth this year."

"No," shouted the people, "let us have Barabbas!" Barabbas was a wicked prisoner being held at that time, and the priests had suggested to the people that they call for him.

"Then what shall I do with Jesus, who is called the Christ?" asked Pilate.

"Crucify him! Crucify him!" chanted the mob.

Pilate was afraid to stand up against them any longer. "Go ahead and crucify him," he told the Jews. "But I want no part in it. I wash my hands of the whole matter."

"We will take the blame," shouted the angry crowd.

So Jesus was led away to be beaten and crucified, and the murderer Barabbas was released in his place.

Questions:

1. Why did the Jews have to take Jesus to the Roman governor? 2. What did they tell Pilate that Jesus had done? 3. Could Pilate find anything wrong with Jesus? 4. Why did he send him to Herod? 5. Why was Pilate's wife worried? 6. How did Pilate think he might let Jesus go free? 7. Whom did the crowd want instead?

God's Greatest Gift

For God so loved the world, that he gave his only begotten Son, that whosoever believeth in him should not perish, but have everlasting life.
John 3:16

THE enemies of Jesus had finally gotten Pilate, the Roman governor, to agree to Jesus' death. For nearly three years, these Jewish leaders had listened to the carpenter from Nazareth claim to be their promised Savior. From the beginning, they had refused to believe him; but recently he had been causing such a stir and arousing so many of the people, that they decided they had to kill him in order to keep the control of the Jewish nation.

The order for crucifixion was given by Pilate early on a Friday morning after the night of the Passover supper. Afterward, soldiers took Jesus away and beat him. Then they dressed him up like a king, with a scarlet robe and a crown of thorns. In his hand they placed a reed to serve as his scepter. What fun they made of him! "Hail, O King," they mocked, and then they spit on him.

Without a word Jesus stood, calm and composed in the middle of a howling, angry crowd. But the beating had left him exhausted. When they gave him his heavy cross to carry all the way to the place of crucifixion, he stumbled under its weight. Down the winding little streets of Jerusalem he dragged it, prodded along by the guards on either side of him. Finally, he dropped to the ground. A guard grabbed a man named Simon from the crowd. Simon was

Jesus on the Cross

not even from Jerusalem—he had merely come into town from the country—but something about the stranger bowing under the weight of his own cross made Simon willing to help. Out of the city and up a hill called Calvary, the "Place of the Skull," Simon and Jesus marched. Behind them came two criminals who were also being crucified, some Roman soldiers, the Jewish leaders, and a crowd of curious onlookers.

By this time, the day's activities were beginning throughout the city, and word was spreading that the Jewish leaders had captured Jesus during the night. Now many of the people in Jerusalem loved Jesus and believed his message. When they heard that he was about to be crucified, they, too, hurried to Calvary. How horrified they were to see three crosses already lying on the ground and soldiers digging the holes to set them in. The disciples looked helplessly from Jesus to one another.

When the holes were dug, the Roman soldiers stretched Jesus out upon his cross and nailed him to the wooden beams, driving heavy spikes into his hands and feet. Across the top they fastened a sign that read, "Jesus of Nazareth, the King of the Jews." Then they stood the cross upright and dropped it into the hole they had prepared. There Jesus hung, dying just like the thieves on either side of him. With the blood pouring from the wounds the nails had made, Jesus looked down and said, "Father, forgive them, for they do not realize what they are doing."

Yes, Jesus could still pray for those who had nailed him to the cross. And all the while, the Roman soldiers stood unconcerned right beneath him, dividing his clothes among themselves. But the disciples who had gathered clung to each other and wept. Among them was Jesus' own mother, Mary, and John, an apostle whom Jesus dearly loved. When Jesus looked down into their sad faces, he said, "John, take care of my mother for me." And to Mary he said, "John will be like a son to you in my place."

Some in the crowd curled their lips in disgust when they saw the sorrowful disciples. These were the Jewish scribes and priests who had paid Judas to bring Jesus to them and voted that he was deserving to die. They were glad to see that he would soon be out of the way. They looked up at him and mocked, "You saved others. Why don't you save yourself?"

One of the thieves hanging beside him joined in, "Yes, why don't you save yourself and us, if you are really God's Son?"

But the other thief said to him, "How can you speak this way, knowing that you are about to die? You and I deserve to be here, but this man has done no wrong."

Then he turned to Jesus and said, "Lord, remember me when you come into your kingdom."

With the great love that he still possessed, Jesus answered, "This very day you will be with me in Paradise."

At noon, the sun disappeared from sight and God caused an awful darkness to cover the earth for about three hours. During this time Jesus' pain became more and more dreadful. Although he had done only good all his life, he was having to bear the pain because man was sinful, and God wanted man to be saved. This was the only way it could be done—for God's perfect Son to die for man's sins.

Christ, as God, had always known that he had to suffer this death, but he was a man, too. As a man, it was almost more than he could bear. At last he could not help sobbing, "My God, my God, why have you forsaken me?"

A little later Jesus took a little drink of vinegar from a sponge that was held up to him. Then about three o'clock in the afternoon he saw that his work on earth was nearly over. He whispered his last words, "It is finished. Father, into Your hands I give my spirit." After that, he died.

At that moment, the curtain of the Temple that separated the Holy Place from the Holy of Holies was torn from top to bottom. The ground shook and trembled as during an earthquake. The Roman captain in charge of Jesus' death looked at his noble prisoner and kneeled before the cross. "Truly this *was* the Son of God," he said.

Questions:

1. How did the soldiers dress Jesus for his crucifixion? 2. Who helped Jesus carry the cross? 3. What sign was nailed on Jesus' cross? 4. Who was crucified next to Jesus? 5. Did Jesus hate the people who killed him? 6. Whom did Jesus ask to take care of his mother? 7. What happened when Jesus died? 8. Why did Jesus have to die?

An Empty Tomb

Ye seek Jesus of Nazareth, which was crucified: he is risen;
he is not here: behold the place where they laid him.
Mark 16:6

ON the same afternoon that Jesus died, one of the Jewish rulers who had believed on him went to Pilate and asked for Jesus' body so that he might bury it. Pilate checked with the captain in charge of the crucifixion; and when he found that Jesus was already dead, he gave this man, whose name was Joseph, permission to take the body away. Joseph wrapped the body with fine linen and with it laid the spices another disciple had given. Then he and the few faithful followers who had stayed at the cross took the body to a tomb that Joseph had bought for himself. It was a tomb common in those days, one carved like a cave out of a ledge of rock. Here they gently laid Jesus to rest and then rolled a stone over the opening of the grave.

The next day was Saturday, the Jewish Sabbath, and the Jewish priests and Pharisees met to celebrate the death of Jesus. One of them said, "I remember Jesus' saying something about rising from the dead in three days. Perhaps we had better seal his tomb carefully or one of his disciples will come and steal the body and say that he has risen." So they went to Pilate, who gave them permission to seal the tomb and also to keep soldiers there on constant guard.

The Morning of the Resurrection

The apostles and the women who had followed Jesus returned to the upper room where Jesus had eaten the Passover and spent a very sad day. For three years they had given their lives to a man whom they loved above everything else. Now there was nothing left except a body in Joseph's tomb. Gone was their future King before he had ever gotten to reign. Gone was his glorious kingdom of which they were to be members. Jesus was dead.

Early the next morning, Mary Magdalene, a woman whom Jesus had healed, and some other women went to the tomb to take more spices to lay with Jesus' body. On the way, they wondered how they would move the stone that covered the entrance to the grave. But when they came within sight of the tomb, they saw that the stone was already rolled away. You see, earlier that morning the Lord had sent an earthquake and an angel had come down from heaven and rolled away the stone. When the soldiers on guard saw the dazzling angel, they fell to the ground as if they were dead. Later, when they got up, they ran into the city and told the priests what they had seen. The priests were worried when they heard of it—not because they thought they had done wrong in killing Jesus, but because they did not want the people to know of it. They paid the soldiers to spread the story that the apostles had stolen the body while they were asleep.

When the women reached the tomb, they looked inside. In the place where Jesus' body had lain, two angels in shining white clothes stood. "Do not be afraid," said the angels. "You are looking for Jesus of Nazareth, who was crucified.

He is no longer here; he has risen. Go and tell this to the disciples. Tell them that Jesus has gone to Galilee and will meet them there."

The women ran quickly to tell the disciples what they had seen and heard. When Peter and John heard it, they set out running for the tomb. John was younger and could run faster, so he reached it first. He went into the tomb itself and found only the linen cloth in which Jesus' body had been wrapped. When Peter arrived, he went inside even farther and found the cloth that had been wrapped around Jesus' face. They left, believing that the women had told them the truth.

By this time, Mary Magdalene had returned to the garden alone, this time to look once again for a body that might have been stolen or hidden. She stood by the empty tomb crying when Jesus himself stood suddenly beside her. "Mary," he said softly. When she looked and saw that it was he, she could hardly believe it was true. "Master!" she said, and her tears turned to ones of joy rather than sadness, as she ran into the city to tell the disciples that she had seen their Lord alive.

Questions:

1. Who buried Jesus' body? Where? 2. Why did the priests want guards at the tomb? 3. Why were the women going to the tomb on that Sunday morning? 4. What had the guards been paid to say had happened to Jesus' body? 5. What did the angels tell the women? 6. What did Peter and John find in place of Jesus' body? 7. Who was the first to see Jesus alive?

the Mount of Olives and the Garden of Gethsemane. The time had come for Jesus to return to his Father.

"You are to stay here in Jerusalem until the Spirit of God comes upon you," Jesus told his disciples on that day. "When you receive this Spirit, you will have the power to tell about me here in Jerusalem, and in Judea, in Samaria, and even to the far corners of the world."

Then, as they stood there on the mountain, Jesus raised his hand to bless his disciples and began rising into heaven —rising higher and higher until at last a bright cloud hid him from their sight.

While the disciples were still looking into the sky, two angels appeared beside them. "Why are you looking into the heavens?" the angels asked. "This same Jesus who has just gone to heaven is going to come again to earth in just the way that you saw him leave."

The disciples fell to their knees and worshiped God after the wonderful sight had gone. Then they walked back to Jerusalem to wait for God's Spirit to come. You might think that they were sad that Jesus had left them, but they were not. Instead, they were very happy. They knew now that they had believed in the true Son of God. They knew that they could still talk with him in prayer. And they knew that some day he would come again and take them to heaven to live with him always.

Indeed Jesus will come again. When he does, he will receive not only those first disciples, but all whose life was changed by the story of the risen Lord.

Questions:

1. How could the disciples tell that this was the same Jesus who had been killed? 2. Did many people get to see Jesus after he rose from the dead? 3. How long did he stay on earth? 4. What work was Jesus leaving for the disciples to do? 5. Why were they supposed to wait in Jerusalem? 6. How did Jesus leave the earth? 7. Will he ever come back?

The Holy Spirit Comes

And suddenly there came a sound from heaven as of a rushing mighty wind, and it filled all the house where they were sitting.
Acts 2:2

AFTER Jesus went back to heaven to be with God, his Father, the disciples waited in Jerusalem, just as he had told them to do. They prayed together and worshiped God in the Temple. They also chose a man named Matthias to take Judas' place as an apostle.

On a morning ten days after Jesus had left them, about one hundred and twenty disciples had met together to worship. Suddenly, there came the sound of a great, rushing wind; and then something looking like a little flame of fire settled above the head of each one. The Holy Spirit came upon them, and they felt a new power they had never felt before. They began praising God for His wonderful works.

Now people all over the city had heard the sound of the great wind, and they rushed to see what had happened. In the crowd were Jews from all over the world who had come to Jerusalem for the Passover. As they gathered around the disciples, they were surprised to find that each one could hear what was being spoken in his own language.

"What is happening?" some of the foreigners asked. "Are not these men from Galilee? How is it that we can all understand what they are saying?"

Then Peter stood up, no longer afraid to admit that he was a follower as he had done on the night of Jesus' trial.

Peter Preaches at Pentecost

He spoke boldly this time: "Listen to me, all of you. What you are seeing is the Spirit of God being given to us. One of your prophets named Joel told of this day long ago. It is today that you will see the salvation of God.

"You all remember Jesus of Nazareth, the one who did many wonderful miracles by God's power. You put him to death on a cross, but God raised him from the dead. All of us know this is true, for we have seen him. Now he is with God in heaven, for this same Jesus whom you crucified is God's own Son, our Lord and Christ."

When the crowd heard Peter's brave words, they began to see how wrong they had been in killing Jesus. They cried out to Peter and the other apostles, "Men and brethren, what can we do?"

"You can turn from your evil and be baptized, believing that Jesus will forgive you of all that you have done that was wrong. When you do, God will give you His Holy Spirit, also."

That day, about three thousand people told the apostles that they believed in Jesus and wanted their sins to be forgiven. They were all baptized, and with great joy they became part of the band of disciples there in Jerusalem. Those who were saved from their sins became members of Christ's church, the kingdom over which he rules. All the members of the new kingdom were like one family; they loved one another with a love like Christ's. When others saw this wonderful love, they came to believe on the same Savior.

Questions:

1. How long did the disciples have to wait before God's Spirit came? 2. What did they do while they waited? 3. What happened when the Spirit came? 4. Who was in the crowd that came to see what had happened? 5. What did Peter tell them? 6. How did this make them feel? 7. What did they do to become members of this first church?

A Beggar at the Beautiful Gate

Then Peter said, Silver and gold have I none; but such as I have give
I thee: In the name of Jesus Christ of Nazareth rise up and walk.
Acts 3:6

THREE thousand people had become members of Christ's church on the day of Pentecost when Peter preached his first sermon, and the number continued to grow day after day. Some had believed in Christ while he was on earth and they wanted to become members of his kingdom. Others had not believed on Him and had put Him to death, but now they saw that they had been wrong and they wanted to be forgiven. These new Christians loved one another and wanted to be together. Every day they met at the Temple, for it was God's house and they had no church building.

One day Peter and John went to the Temple for the hour of prayer that was held at three o'clock in the afternoon. As they arrived at the gate known as the Beautiful Gate, some people came forward carrying a man who could not walk. This man had been crippled all his life and he had never been able to hold a job. His friends would carry him to this gate every day, and he would lie and beg for money from those who came to worship.

When the poor man saw Peter and John, he asked them to give him something. Now even though the apostles had no money, they did not pass by the beggar. They stopped

Peter, John and the Beggar

and looked down kindly at him. "Look here," Peter said to the man; and he did, thinking that Peter was going to give him some money. Then Peter said: "I have no silver or gold, but what I do have, I will certainly give to you. In the name of Jesus Christ of Nazareth, get up and walk!"

At this, Peter stretched out his hand and grabbed the one that the beggar held out to him. The man's legs began to feel strong, and he let Peter pull him to his feet. He took a few timid steps and saw that indeed he could walk. He stepped through the gate of the Temple with Peter and John and was so happy that he started leaping and running about, praising God. Naturally all the worshipers turned to see who was shouting, and when they did, they recognized the familiar figure from beside the Beautiful Gate. They could not believe their eyes! Here was the same crippled man, running and jumping on strong, healthy legs!

They rushed over to the man, who was still with Peter and John. "What happened?" they asked. "How did you get well?"

When Peter saw the crowd, he spoke out in a loud voice, "Why are you so surprised at this? And why do you look at us as though we did it with some power of our own? It is God who healed this man, and He did it to glorify His Son Jesus. This Jesus is the same man whom you betrayed and disowned even when Pilate wanted to let him go. You asked for a murderer, instead. But God raised His Son back to life, and it is through His name that we have cured this beggar."

While Peter was talking this way, the captain of the Temple guard and some of the Jewish rulers came forward. They were angry to hear Peter telling these people that Jesus had risen from the dead. Remember, they had told the guards at Jesus' tomb to say that someone had stolen His body. The Jews motioned for the guards to arrest Peter and John. They put them in prison and kept them there all night.

The next morning, Peter and John were brought before Annas and Caiaphas and others of the priests, the same ones who had condemned Jesus to die. "By what power did you heal this man?" the priests asked.

God's Spirit came upon Peter and made him answer bravely, "It was done by the power of Jesus Christ of Nazareth—the One whom you killed and whom God raised from the dead!"

When the priests heard this, they were astonished. They knew that Peter and John were not well educated, and yet they spoke boldly. Here were some disciples of Jesus, whom they hated; but there on the other hand was a man who had been healed of his lameness by them. What could they do?

Finally the priests sent Peter and John out of the room while they talked things over. Then they called them back in and told them not to speak or teach in the name of Jesus again. After threatening them a little more, they let them go.

As soon as Peter and John were released, they rushed back to the other believers and told them what had happened. They all prayed to God and He sent His Spirit upon them. From that time on, they preached with more courage than ever.

Questions:

1. Why did the first Christians meet at the Jewish Temple? 2. Why did the lame man's friends bring him to the gate? 3. What did Peter and John have to give other than money? 4. Why did a crowd gather? 5. Why were Peter and John arrested? 6. Why could the priests not punish them? 7. Did Peter and John plan to do as the priests told them?

An African Hears About Jesus

Then Philip opened his mouth, and began at the same scripture, and preached unto him Jesus.
Acts 8:35

AS the high priests saw more people becoming members of Christ's church, they became very alarmed. They tried to put the apostles in prison, as they had once before, but an angel came and opened the prison doors for them to escape. Another time they arrested the apostles and beat them, but it did not stop them from teaching of Jesus, at all. Instead, it only made the Christians glad that they could suffer for their Lord.

When the angry Jews saw that none of their orders were being obeyed and that more and more were coming to believe in Jesus, they began searching in homes for anyone who spoke of Jesus or prayed to him. When they found a Christian, they put him in prison. Soon Jerusalem became a dangerous place for followers of Christ. Although some stayed and faced the anger of the important Jews, many others left the city. Those who did leave made new homes for themselves in other towns of Judea and Samaria. Wherever they went, they told the people there about Christ and his church. This way, the gospel was spread to other places besides Jerusalem.

One of the leaders in the church in Jerusalem, a man named Philip, went to Samaria to live and taught the people there. You will remember that Jesus once talked with a

Philip Explains the Scriptures

Samaritan woman near a well, and many Samaritans came to believe on him then. Now these and many more listened to Philip's preaching and were baptized. When those in Jerusalem heard of Philip's good work, they sent Peter and John to help him for a while.

After Peter and John had gone all over Samaria with Philip, preaching the gospel, they went back to the church in Jerusalem. But Philip did not go with them, for an angel of the Lord appeared to him. The angel said, "Go south to the road that runs from Jerusalem to Gaza, the one that goes through the desert."

Now Philip had no idea why God wanted him to go to that place, but simply because the Lord asked him, he was willing to do it. Once he reached the deserted country, he walked along the road, wondering what was about to happen. Then in the distance he saw the dust of an approaching carriage. Did this have anything to do with the angel's message? As the carriage came closer, Philip saw that it was a very fine one, drawn by handsome horses. In it was a man from a faraway country in Africa—Ethiopia. He was an officer in the court of the Ethiopian queen, the one in charge of her money and her treasure. Somehow, in his home so far away he had heard about the one true God whom the Jews worshiped, and he had gone to Jerusalem to worship there himself. The trip had made the Ethiopian want to find out more about the religion of the Jews, and as he rode along, he read from the writings of their prophets.

Just then, the Spirit of God said to Philip, "Go near to the carriage." As he ran toward it, he heard the Ethiopian reading some words the prophet Isaiah had written about Christ: "He was led as a sheep to the slaughter, and as a lamb before his shearer is dumb, so he opened not his mouth."

"Do you understand what you are reading?" Philip asked the officer.

"How can I," he replied, "unless someone explains it to me? Tell me, is the prophet speaking about himself or some other man?"

So at the Ethiopian's invitation, Philip climbed into the chariot. He explained that Isaiah had been speaking about the coming Savior; then he told him that the Savior had already come, and that he was Jesus. He told him all about Jesus' death and about his new kingdom.

As Philip spoke of these things, the carriage passed near some water. The man turned to Philip and said, "Look! Here is some water. Why could I not be baptized right now?"

Then he called for his driver to stop the horses, and he and Philip stepped down from the carriage. They walked out into the water, and Philip baptized him.

As soon as this happened, the Spirit of God took Philip away suddenly and the Ethiopian officer never saw him again. But we know that he was very happy that Philip had come to him and taught him of Jesus. He now rode toward his home with a joyful heart because of the good news he had to tell to his friends there.

Questions:

1. Why did many disciples have to leave Jerusalem? 2. Where did Philip go when he left? 3. To what strange place did an angel tell Philip to go? 4. What was the man in the carriage doing? 5. What did Philip talk to the man about? 6. Why did the officer want to stop when he saw some water? 7. Why was he more anxious than ever now to go back home? 8. Where was his home?

Da Vinci

The Last Supper

Van Dyck

The Capture of Jesus

Matania

Jesus' Trial

Bloch

The Denial by Peter

RAPHAEL

The Road to Calvary

HOFMANN

The Crucifixion

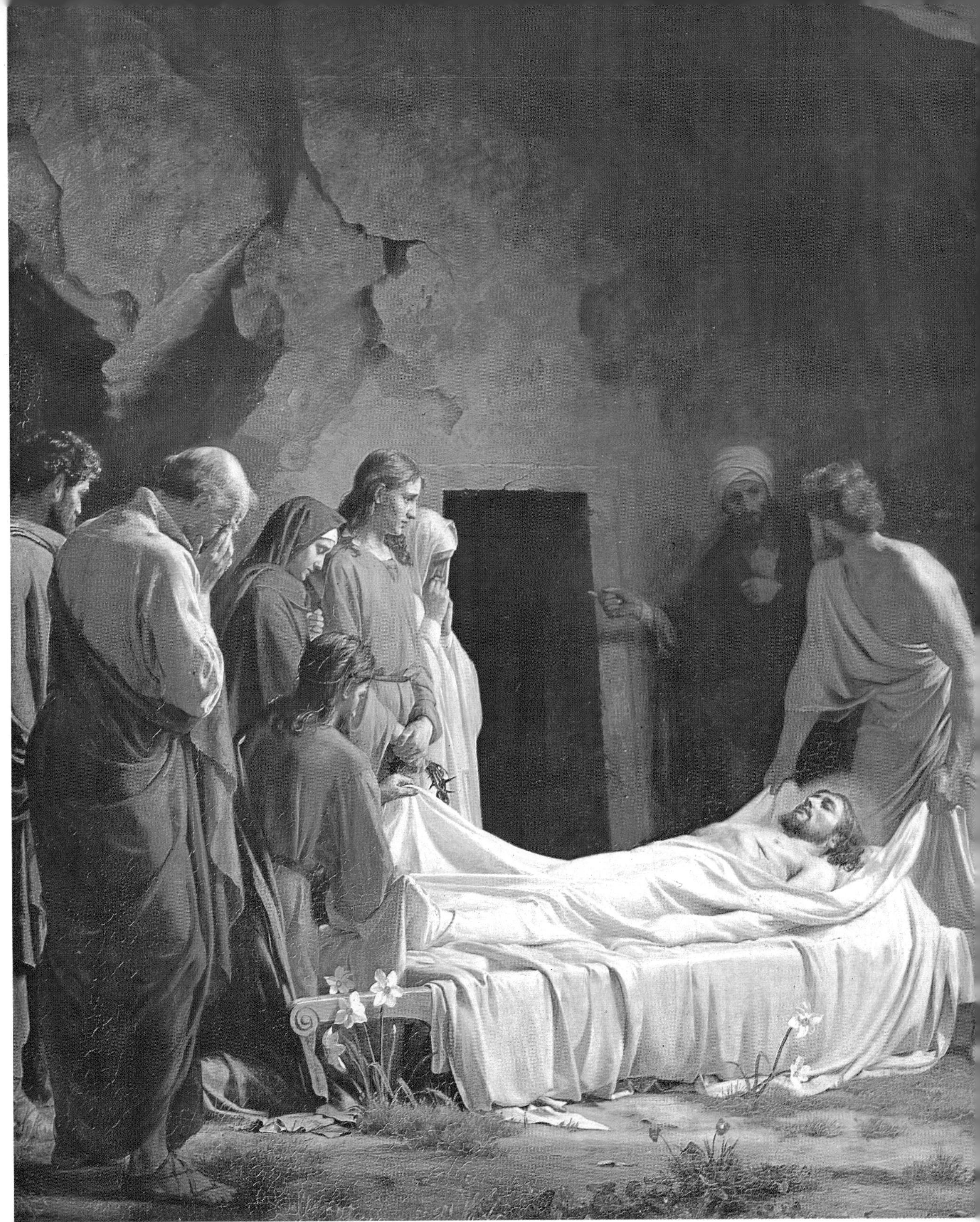

BLOCH

The Burial of Christ

OTTO

The Ascension

Saul Changes His Mind

And he said, Who art thou, Lord? And the Lord said, I am Jesus whom thou persecutest.
Acts 9:5

AMONG the Jews who hated Jesus' followers, there was a man named Saul. Saul had grown up in a faraway city named Tarsus, but his parents were very good Jews and sent him to Jerusalem to study under a Jewish teacher. Saul's teacher was Gamaliel, one of the greatest students of the Law of Moses. While he studied in Gamaliel's school, Saul learned the Law well, and he tried to keep it very strictly. He felt that the followers of Jesus were disobeying the Law and that he should do all that he could to keep them from spreading the gospel.

Every time he had a chance, Saul tried to break up churches by arresting the disciples and having them thrown in prison. And he was not content just to trouble the church in Jerusalem. No; when he heard that churches were meeting in other places, he decided to go there and do what he could to destroy them.

One city where disciples had fled for safety was Damascus. Knowing this, Saul went to the high priest and got permission to go to Damascus and look for followers of Christ. He was told that he could arrest any that he found and bring them back to Jerusalem.

Just about noon a few days later, Saul saw Damascus ahead at the end of the road. Suddenly a light from heaven,

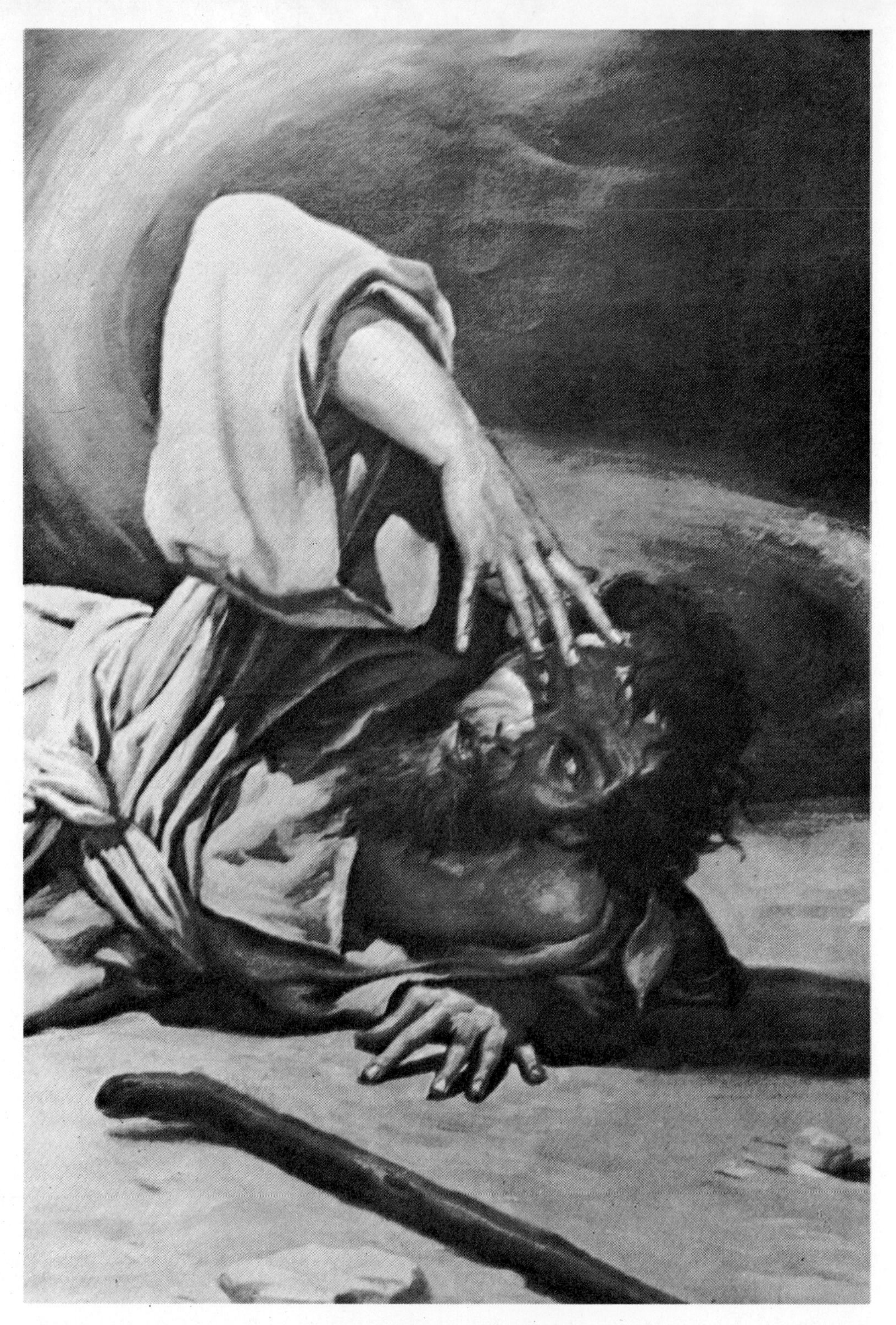

Saul Sees a Vision

brighter than the sun, flashed about him. It was so blinding that Saul fell to the ground, unable to see. Then he heard a voice calling, "Saul, Saul, why do you work against me?"

"Who is speaking?" Saul asked.

"I am Jesus of Nazareth, the one you are fighting," came the answer.

What a surprise this was to Saul! He had thought that Jesus was a false teacher who was dead. But now he knew that he was not dead, for he was speaking to Saul from heaven. He really was God's Son, as he had claimed.

"What do you want me to do, Lord?" Saul asked humbly.

"Go into the city and there you will be told what to do," Jesus answered.

Then the light faded and the vision disappeared, but Saul was still blind. Now the men who had been with him had seen the light and heard the voice, but they had not understood who Jesus was or what he had said. Since they could still see, they led Saul into the city.

For three days Saul stayed in Damascus at the home of a man named Judas. During this time, he neither ate nor drank. Instead, he sat praying to God, worried about the great harm he had done to Christ's church. On the third day, the Lord told a faithful Christian named Ananias to go to Saul. When Ananias first heard this, he was afraid to go. "Lord," he said, "we all know of this Saul. He has done much evil to your followers in Jerusalem, and he has come to Damascus to arrest us."

"Go to him, Ananias," the Lord said. "You have no need to be afraid of him any longer. I have chosen him to take my name to the Jews, the Gentiles, and even kings. He is going to suffer much for my sake."

So Ananias went to Saul. He came to the blind man and spoke gently, telling Saul that the Lord had sent him. Then he put his hands on Saul's eyes and Saul could see once more. "Now," Ananias said, "why are you waiting? Rise and be baptized in Jesus' name so that your sins may be forgiven."

These were the words Saul had been waiting to hear. How happy he was to know that there was some way for him to be forgiven by God for the terrible mistakes he had made. Immediately he was baptized, and he became a member of the very group that he had come to arrest.

Questions:

1. Why did Saul's parents send him to Jerusalem? 2. Why did Saul try to hurt Christians? 3. Why did Saul want to go to Damascus? 4. Who appeared to Saul on the road? 5. How did this change Saul? 6. What did Ananias do for Saul?

God Teaches Peter a Lesson

Then Peter opened his mouth, and said, Of a truth
I perceive that God is no respecter of persons.
Acts 10:34

THE country of Judea had several important cities besides Jerusalem. One of these was a seaport called Caesarea. Here the Romans had stationed a band of one hundred soldiers and left a man named Cornelius to be their captain. Now Cornelius was not a Jew, but he knew about the true God. He worshiped Him and prayed to Him every day, and he taught his family and servants to do the same. He was also kind and helpful to the poor.

About three o'clock one afternoon, while Cornelius was praying, he saw in a dream an angel of the Lord, coming into his room. "Cornelius!" the angel said.

The soldier stared at the angel, terrified. "What is it, Lord?" he finally said.

The angel replied, "Your prayers and good deeds have been seen by God. He wants you to send to Joppa for a man called Peter, who is staying with a man named Simon in a house beside the sea."

Then the angel disappeared. Immediately Cornelius called for two of his servants and a soldier who stayed with him. He told them all that had happened and sent them to Joppa to fetch Peter.

Joppa was another seaport town about thirty miles from Caesarea. Peter had been staying there with Simon while

he helped the church and tried to lead people to Christ.
The day after Cornelius had seen the angel, Peter went up on the rooftop of Simon's house to pray. It was noontime and he became very hungry waiting for dinner to be ready. While he prayed, he fell into a trance in which the sky seemed to open up. From out of the sky dropped something like a great sheet, held up by its four corners. In it were all kinds of animals and birds. Then a voice spoke: "Get up, Peter; kill something and eat it!"

Peter looked with distaste at the animals in the sheet. Long ago, in the Law of Moses, God had told the Israelites which animals were clean and good for food. He had forbidden them to eat any others, and Peter still tried to obey this command. "Never, Lord!" he answered. "I have never eaten anything unclean."

The voice replied, "What God has cleaned, you are not to call unclean."

This same thing happened three times, and then the sheet was taken back up into the heavens.

Peter sat and shook his head. He could not figure out what this vision had meant. What was God trying to tell him?

While he was wondering, there came a knock at the door. Simon answered it and then called up to Peter: "Three men from Joppa are here! They are looking for you!"

The Holy Spirit said to Peter, "Go with these men without any question, for I have sent them."

So Peter went down and met Cornelius' servants. "What can I do for you?" he asked.

"Cornelius the captain, a man who loves God and who is respected by the Jews, was told to send here for you and to listen to your message," they answered.

Peter invited the servants in to eat and rest. The next morning they and some of the Christians from Joppa set out for Caesarea.

When they arrived at Cornelius' house, the captain was waiting for them. He had invited all his kinfolk and friends over to hear what Peter had to say. As Peter entered the house, Cornelius fell down on his knees to worship him. But Peter pulled him to his feet. "Stand up," he said. "I am just a man like you!"

Then Peter spoke to Cornelius, "You know that as a Jew I am forbidden to associate with, or visit, a man of any other nation. But God has just shown me that I should not call any man unclean when He has made him clean. That is why I came here without question. Now, why did you send for me?"

Cornelius told him the story of the angel's visit. "We are ready to listen to the words of God that you bring to us," he said.

So Peter began to speak to them. "I see now," he said, "that God does not love just the Jews, but that He loves those of every nation who obey Him and try to serve Him." Then he went on to tell them about Jesus.

While Peter spoke, Cornelius and his friends and family listened to every word. The Holy Spirit came to them just as it had to the apostles on the day of Pentecost. When the Jewish Christians who had come with Peter saw this, they were amazed. They knew that God wanted these people to be part of the kingdom, also. So Cornelius and his friends, believing Peter's story about Christ, were baptized and became members of the church.

Even though Peter had been with Christ and listened to his teachings many times, he was just beginning to learn what Christ had meant. Now, more clearly than ever before, he knew what his Lord had been saying when he told them to take the good news of his life and death to "all nations."

Questions:

1. What job did Cornelius have? 2. Cornelius worshiped the true God of the Jews. Was he a Jew? 3. How did Cornelius know to send for Peter? 4. What strange vision did Peter have? 5. What lesson did this teach Peter? 6. What did God send upon Cornelius and those in his house? 7. What did the Jewish Christians think about this? 8. Did Christ mean for only the Jews to be saved?

An Angel Rescues Peter

And when Peter was come to himself, he said, Now I know of a surety, that the Lord hath sent his angel, and hath delivered me out of the hand of Herod.
Acts 12:11

WHEN the Jews in the Jerusalem church heard that Peter had baptized Cornelius and his family, they did not like the idea. "Why did you have anything to do with those Gentiles?" they asked Peter. "The Law forbids it, you know." "Gentiles" is the name used for all those who are not Jews. So Peter explained about his vision of the animals and about the Holy Spirit coming on Cornelius, and then they saw that it was the will of God. They praised God for giving the Gentiles a way to be saved.

After this, the unbelieving Jews began attacking the Christians in Jerusalem again. To please these Jews, the Herod who was ruling arrested James, the brother of John and one of the apostles. Later he had him killed. When he saw how much this delighted the Jews, he sent soldiers to capture Peter and put him in prison, also. It was during the time of the Passover feast, and Herod intended to hold him until the feast days were over and then probably kill him, too.

Once before, Peter and John had escaped from prison; and Herod wanted to make sure that this did not happen again. He appointed four different changes of the guard to keep watch on Peter at every moment. At night Peter had to sleep chained to a soldier on either side.

Peter and the Angel

As the feast days came to an end and the time came for Herod to give Peter over to the Jews, the Christians in Jerusalem were very sad. It was already hard for them to get along without James. What would they do if Peter were killed, too? They prayed to God over and over again to save the beloved apostle. They even had meetings and prayed all together for his safety.

On the night before Herod was to come for him, Peter lay sleeping between the two guards, while other soldiers watched at the doorway of the prison. Suddenly a bright light shone all through the cell, and an angel of the Lord appeared. He tapped Peter very gently and woke him. "Get up quickly," the angel said. Peter looked from side to side at the soldiers chained to him, but they slept soundly. Then the chains slipped from his hands and he stood.

"Dress yourself," the angel said. Peter moved as though he were in a dream, but he did as the angel had commanded. "Now put your coat on and follow me," he was told.

Peter still thought that he was having a vision, but he followed the angel out. They walked right through the prison, past the guards, to the great wall that surrounded the jail. When they reached the wall, one of its heavy locked gates swung open all by itself, and Peter and the angel stepped out into the street.

They walked down the dark street a short distance and then suddenly the angel disappeared. Peter looked all around. Where was he? Was he asleep or awake? Then he took a deep breath of the cool night air. Why, it was real! The Lord had sent an angel to rescue him!

Peter began to hurry through the streets until he came to the house of Mary and her son Mark, both Christians. Although it was very late, a light was burning. Inside, a group of Christians were still praying for Peter.

Peter stood at the gate and knocked. You see, Christians had to be very careful in those times, and they kept their gates tightly locked. Finally, a young girl named Rhoda came out. "Who is there?" she called; but she would not open the door.

"It is Peter," came the answer. "Let me in."

Rhoda was so surprised that she did not even stop to open the gate. She burst in upon the prayer meeting. "Peter is at the door!" she cried.

"You must be crazy," everyone replied. "Peter is in prison."

"It is true! It is Peter!" Rhoda insisted.

"It must be just his angel," someone decided.

Now all this time, Peter stood at the door, still knocking. At last someone came to see who was really there. How surprised he was to see that it *was* Peter! Everyone clustered about him and began asking questions all at once.

Peter held up his hands for them to be quiet. Then he explained how the Lord had sent an angel to lead him out of prison.

It felt wonderful for Peter to be back in a comfortable home with his Christian friends, but he knew that he had better not stay. When Herod found that he was gone, he would come looking for him. So he said, "Go and tell my other Christian brothers what has happened." Then he went to another place to hide.

Questions:

1. Why did the Jerusalem Christians wonder about Peter's baptizing Cornelius? 2. What did Herod do to James? 3. How did Herod make sure that Peter would not escape this time? 4. What did Herod plan to do with Peter when the Passover was over? 5. How did Peter get out of the prison? 6. Who first came to the gate when Peter knocked? 7. Did the people believe Rhoda? 8. Why did Peter not stay with his friends?

Preaching by the River and in Jail

And at midnight Paul and Silas prayed, and sang praises unto God: and the prisoners heard them.
Acts 16:25

ONCE Saul became a believer in Christ, he wanted to teach others about the Lord just as much as he had once wanted to kill those who taught. He was so enthusiastic and courageous that he caused a stir everywhere he went. At first, other disciples were suspicious of him, not knowing whether he had really changed; but they came to love him when they saw how sincere he was.

When Saul returned to Jerusalem and his old friends among the Jewish rulers heard that he had become a Christian, they tried to kill him. He had to leave and go far away to continue his teaching.

Finally Saul came to a city called Antioch and worked with a good man named Barnabas for the growing church there. Then, after a message was received from the Holy Spirit, they left Antioch to travel about and preach the gospel to the Gentiles.

Now the Gentiles were all those who were not Jews. At first the apostles had only tried to teach other Jews, but God had showed Peter that He wanted everyone to have an opportunity to be saved. Many of the Gentile people had

Paul Preaching by the River

never had anything to worship but idols, and Saul found them anxious to hear about the one true God and the loving Savior. Everywhere Saul and Barnabas went they found people whom they taught to believe in Christ; and when they left a town, they would leave a little church behind.

Paul, as Saul was called after this, and Barnabas had a wonderful trip. There were times when the Jews made them suffer for their belief in Christ, but they realized that they were doing a wonderful work, taking the story of the gospel to places where it had never been heard before.

Finally they returned to Antioch and told the church there about their journey. They stayed a while, and then Paul became anxious to leave and visit again with the little churches that he and Barnabas had started.

This time Paul took a man named Silas with him. Their travels carried them far away to a country in Greece named Macedonia. They came to a Macedonian city named Philippi. Philippi was so far from Judea, the home of the Jews, that there were few, if any, Jews there. At least, there were not enough to build a synagogue, so Paul had no place to preach. Finally he found a spot down by the river where people came to pray. A few women were gathered there, and Paul and Silas talked with them about Jesus.

One of the ladies by the riverside was a business woman named Lydia. When Lydia heard about Christ, her heart was opened to him and she believed in him. Although she lived in another town, she came to Philippi often to sell her purple dyes, and she had a home there. She invited the preachers to stay with her.

One day, while still in Philippi, Paul and Silas healed a poor little fortuneteller of an evil spirit. When the spirit left her, she would no longer work for her cruel masters; and they became angry because they made all their money from her fortunetelling. They stirred up a mob against Paul and Silas and had the missionaries beaten and thrown in prison. In the jail, they were locked in wooden stocks which held their arms and legs so tight that they could not move.

You might have expected Paul and Silas to complain about all of this; but there in the darkness of the prison, they sang hymns and praised God that they were able to suffer for His sake. The other prisoners grew quiet, listening to them.

Suddenly, the ground began to rock with a great earthquake. The foundations of the prison shook, and all the cell doors flew open. Even the stocks fell apart, setting Paul and Silas free.

When the jailkeeper saw that his prisoners all had a chance to escape, he grabbed a knife to kill himself, for he knew that he was responsible for them. But Paul cried out, "Do not kill yourself! No one has escaped—we are all here."

Then the jailer called for a light and rushed to Paul and Silas. He knew that they must be men of God. He begged them, "What must I do to be saved?"

So Paul and Silas told the jailer about Jesus Christ, the one who had died for every man's sins. When the jailer heard, he believed on the Savior and he was baptized then, in the middle of the night.

Afterward, he brought Paul and Silas to his home, washed their sore places, and fed them. He and his whole family could not thank the missionaries enough for bringing them the gospel, or good news, of Christ.

Questions:

1. What happened to Saul when he went back to Jerusalem as a new Christian? 2. Where did Saul and Barnabus preach for a while? 3. What did they do on their trip together? 4. Where did Lydia and the ladies hold their prayer meetings? 5. Why were the men mad at Paul for healing the poor fortuneteller? 6. Did Paul and Silas complain about being in jail? 7. How were they set free? 8. What did the jailer do that night?

"Great Is Diana of the Ephesians!"

This Paul hath persuaded and turned away much people, saying that they be no gods, which are made with hands.
Acts 19:26

AFTER Paul had baptized the jailer at Philippi, the rulers of the city asked him and Silas to leave before they caused any more trouble. So they visited some other cities in Macedonia. In most of the places they found only a few Jews who wanted to believe in Jesus, but the Gentiles were always willing to listen to them.

Next, Paul went to Athens, the most important city in that part of the world. There he made a wonderful speech about the one true God to the educated men of the city. Then he went on to Corinth, another large city, where he stayed for more than a year. Later on, Paul sent two letters back to the Christians he had been with in Corinth. We have these letters in our Bible—First and Second Corinthians.

From Corinth Paul sailed across to Ephesus, a city in Asia, taking Priscilla and Aquila, some Christian friends, with him. But it had now been a long time since Paul had been in Jerusalem, and he wanted to go back. He promised those in Ephesus that he would return; and leaving Priscilla and Aquila there, he went to Jerusalem.

While Paul was gone, Priscilla and Aquila found a man in Ephesus named Apollos, one who had learned of Jesus through the preaching of John the Baptist. But Apollos had not learned of Jesus' death and resurrection nor about the coming of the Holy Spirit on the day of Pentecost. He was happy for Priscilla and Aquila to tell him of these things. Afterward, he left Ephesus and went about teaching the way of the Lord more perfectly, always helping the churches where he went, for he was a wonderful speaker.

At last, Paul kept his promise and came back to Ephesus. For a while he preached in the synagogue of the Jews; but when some began to stir up trouble, he moved to a lecture hall. Here his friends came to him and he taught classes for them for two years.

Now for years the people of Ephesus had been idol worshipers. In their city there was a great temple to the moon goddess, Diana. Within the temple stood a huge statue of Diana, which the people worshiped. The silver craftsmen of the city made little images of this great statue and sold them to visitors who came to the temple.

While Paul was in Ephesus, however, the church grew so strong that fewer and fewer people went to Diana's temple to worship. Instead, they met with the Christians and worshiped the true God.

Demetrius, one of the silversmiths, was angry at Paul's success. He knew that if Paul kept telling the people about the foolishness of idol gods, he would not be able to sell any images. He called the other silver craftsmen together. "Men," he said, "you know that we make our living by selling these little statues. If this man Paul continues to tell the people that images are not gods at all, our business will be ruined. Furthermore, the people will begin to neglect the great temple and the mighty goddess Diana."

When the men heard this, they became furious and began shouting, "Great is Diana of the Ephesians!" They made such a noise that the whole city was turned into an uproar. They went and found two of Paul's friends and dragged them into the theater. Paul himself wanted to go and try to talk to the crowd, but the disciples were afraid he might be hurt.

The mob in the theater was so confused that they all shouted different things. Most of them did not even know why they had come there at all. When a man named Alexander came forward to make an explanation and they saw that he was a Jew, they shouted so loudly that he could not be heard above them. For two hours they kept on shouting and screaming, "Great is Diana of the Ephesians! Great is Diana of the Ephesians!"

When they had finally yelled themselves hoarse, the town clerk came out and quieted them down. "Men of Ephesus," he said, "everyone knows that our city guards the great temple of Diana and the statue of her that came to us from the gods. There is no need for you to become upset and do something you might regret later. You have been blaming men who have actually done no harm. If Demetrius himself has something against them, he should take it to court and handle it in a sensible way. Otherwise, you had better be careful or you will be put in prison for causing a riot." And with this, he sent them home.

Afterward, Paul felt that it was time for him to leave Ephesus. He called the disciples together and said goodbye to them. Then he set out once more on his exciting journeys for Christ—this time to Macedonia.

Questions:

1. Name some important cities Paul visited. 2. Whom did Paul leave at Ephesus? 3. Who was Apollos? 4. How was Paul ruining Demetrius' business? 5. What did the silversmiths start shouting? 6. How long did they keep this up? 7. How did the town clerk quiet them down?

Paul in Trouble

Then the chief captain came, and said unto him, Tell me, art thou a Roman? He said, Yea.
Acts 22:27

WHEN Cornelius and the first Gentiles were baptized, most of the Jews were glad that God had made it possible for them to be saved. But some of them did not like to think that the Gentiles were just as good as they were. They wanted to make the Gentiles become Jews as well as Christians.

When Paul preached mainly to the Gentiles on his missionary trips, these jealous Jews became angry. They tried to find something wrong with Paul so they could stir up the people against him. When they saw Paul in Jerusalem with some of his Gentile friends, they began to spread the story that he had taken these Gentiles into the Temple with him and made the holy place impure. They managed to make a whole crowd of people believe this; then they led the mob to Paul and were about to kill him before he could even explain that none of the story was true.

While Paul was trying to save himself from the angry crowd, someone went and told the Roman colonel that all of Jerusalem was in a riot. As soon as he heard it, the officer took some soldiers and ran to the place where people had gathered around Paul.

When the Jews saw the Roman officer coming, they stepped away from Paul and stopped beating him. The colonel hurried up, took Paul from them, and bound him with chains. "What was this man doing?" he demanded of the mob. But the answers were too confused for him to make any sense out of them. He tried letting Paul talk to the people himself, but this only made them more angry. "Kill him!" they shouted to the soldiers. "He is not fit to live!"

This was too much for the colonel. He carried Paul back to the barracks with him. There he ordered that Paul be beaten until he admitted what he had done that was wrong. While they were strapping him down for the beating, Paul turned toward a soldier near him and asked, "Is it lawful for you to beat a Roman citizen without giving him a trial?"

The soldier's eyes grew large with surprise. He ran to the colonel. "Do you know what we were about to do?" he stammered. "This man is a Roman citizen!"

Now this was real news for the colonel. In those days, while Rome ruled the world, Roman citizens had many privileges that no one else had. When someone accused a Roman of doing wrong, he had to come before him and repeat the accusation in court. Then the person who was accused had a chance to defend himself.

"Are you really a Roman citizen?" the colonel asked Paul.

"Yes," he replied.

"I had to pay a lot of money to become a citizen," the colonel admitted.

"But I was born one," Paul answered.

At this, the colonel unstrapped Paul and gave him a place to spend the night.

The next day the commanding officer called the Jewish court together and then took Paul over to their meeting. But the Jewish priests began arguing among themselves over Paul and the colonel could not tell what was wrong any better than he had the day before. When he saw that the men had become angry again and were about to tear Paul to pieces, he ordered his soldiers to take him back to the barracks for safety once more.

Poor Paul! What was going to happen to him? His old Jewish friends hated him for becoming a Christian. The Jewish Christians suspected him for preaching to the Gentiles. Of course, the Gentiles whom he had taught loved him; but they were scattered all over the world in the cities where he had been, and they could not help him now.

Someone was with Paul, however. In fact, this Someone had never left Paul. This was God. That night in the barracks God appeared to Paul. "Take courage!" the Lord said, as He stood by His faithful servant. "You are not going to be killed here in Jerusalem. I am going to send you to Rome to tell the people there about Jesus."

To Rome! The capital of all the world! Paul had always wanted to go to Rome and he had written the people there that he was coming, but he had never guessed that it would be . . . as a prisoner!

Questions:

1. Why were some of the Jewish Christians angry at Paul?

2. What was wrong with Paul's preaching to the Gentiles? 3. What did Paul's enemies tell about him that made all the people angry? 4. How was Paul saved from the angry Jews? 5. Why did the colonel not beat Paul? 6. What did it mean to be a Roman citizen? 7. What did God come and tell Paul?

Shipwreck!

And now I exhort you to be of good cheer: for there shall be no loss of any man's life among you, but of the ship.
Acts 27:22

AFTER the Jews in Jerusalem confused the colonel who held Paul in his barracks, he sent Paul to Felix, the governor, to let him decide the prisoner's strange case. But even when the Jews came to Caesarea and spoke to Felix against Paul, Felix could not find anything wrong with him. But he held Paul in prison for two years, anyway. Then another governor named Festus took office.

Now Festus wanted to send Paul back to Jerusalem to have a trial, but Paul knew what would happen to him if he went back there. Already there had been plots to kill him that he had barely escaped. He did not want to take another chance. There was only one way out: to use his privilege as a Roman citizen and ask to be tried before the highest court in the land—Caesar himself! So Paul said to Festus, "I have done nothing to harm those Jews. If I were a criminal, I would deserve to die; but none of the things they say against me are true. Therefore, I appeal to Caesar."

"You have appealed to Caesar—then to Caesar you shall go!" announced the governor.

Of course, Caesar's palace was in Rome, which was a long way from Judea. In order to go there, one had to make

Saved from the Sea

a long trip by boat. And in those days, the only boats were powered either by rowing or by sails. If the weather was bad or the wind was blowing in the wrong direction, even a short trip could take a long time.

When Paul began his journey to Rome, he was turned over to a centurion named Julius, who was to see that the prisoner arrived safely. They made part of the trip on one boat, and then they changed to a large seagoing ship to cross the widest part of the Great Sea.

The ship traveled from the mainland to a large island named Crete, but then it began to have trouble. The winds were against it, and it had a hard time making the trip down the island coast. At last, the ship reached a port called Fair Havens. From there it was to set sail across the wide part of the sea to Greece. But so much time had been lost because of the bad winds that winter was coming on and the sailing season was nearly over. Paul went to the centurion and warned him: "If we try to go ahead and make this voyage now, we are likely to have considerable losses—not only to our ship, but even to our lives."

But Julius paid more attention to the owner of the ship, who wanted to go on. Besides this, Fair Havens was not a very good harbor in which to spend the winter; and he wanted to move to another place up the island coast, if no farther.

So when a good breeze sprang up, the ship sailed out of Fair Havens, bound for a port up the coast of Crete. But while at sea, a great wind came up out of the north. The wind blew so hard that the captain had no control over the ship at all. He just had to let it drift with the storm.

For many days, the sky remained black with the storm; and the winds continued to blow. All the passengers on the ship gave up any hope of being saved. Having already thrown all the cargo and ship's tackle overboard, there was nothing else they could do to make the ship any safer or stronger. It was just a matter of time until one of the great waves swept them all under the ocean.

Then Paul stood up and spoke, "Men, you should have listened to me and never have left Crete. But we cannot change that now. However, you can take courage in this: no one's life is going to be lost, even though we shall lose our ship. I know this because an angel of the God I serve told me this in a vision. We shall be saved, but our ship will run ashore on some island."

After the storm had roared for fourteen days, the sailors tested the depth of the water and found that they were nearing land. Afraid that the ship might run into rocks near the coast, these sailors wanted to leave it in a lifeboat. But Paul said to the centurion, "Unless these men stay, you will lose your life." So the men cut the rope holding the lifeboat, and let it drift away without them.

While they waited for day to break so that they could see what the coast ahead was like, Paul urged everyone to eat. "For two weeks we have all been too worried to eat," he said. "Now we are all going to need some food to give us strength for what is ahead." With this, Paul gave thanks to God and took some food. Everyone began to eat, and soon all of the two hundred seventy-six aboard felt better.

When daylight came, no one recognized the coast before them. But they saw a sandy shore where they thought they might land the ship. So they cut the anchors and began making their way toward shore. Then the ship struck a shoal and ran aground. The bow stuck fast in the sand and the back part of the ship was about to break under the force of the waves.

The soldiers on board advised the centurion to kill the prisoners so that they would not try to swim ashore and escape, but the centurion would not hear of it. He knew that Paul was innocent, so he gave orders. "Jump overboard and swim to shore if you can," he said. "All the rest of you hang on to planks and make your way the best you can."

So it came true that every single one reached shore safely. During the storm, the ship had traveled nearly to the coast of Italy; so once winter was over, they easily finished their trip to Rome.

Here the story of Paul that we find in our Bible ends. We know that Paul stayed in Rome as a prisoner until he was finally killed. Even while he was in prison there, however, he continued to do what he could for Christ's church by writing letters to the churches where he had taught. Many of the books in the New Testament are these very letters that Paul wrote while in the Roman prison. From Jerusalem to Rome was a long way for Paul to go to carry the gospel, but he did it because he knew that Christ had died for everyone in the whole world and he wanted to do what he could to let the whole world know of it.

Questions:

1. Why did Paul want Caesar to judge his case? 2. Why did Paul's ship have trouble sailing? 3. What did Paul advise them to do? 4. For how long did the storm blow? 5. What message did an angel give Saul? 6. Why did the ship not make it to the coast? 7. How did the passengers get ashore? 8. Were any lost?